Frank Wadleigh Chandler

Romances of Roguery

An Episode in the History of the Novel. Part 1

Frank Wadleigh Chandler

Romances of Roguery
An Episode in the History of the Novel. Part 1

ISBN/EAN: 9783744776233

Printed in Europe, USA, Canada, Australia, Japan

Cover: Foto ©Thomas Meinert / pixelio.de

More available books at **www.hansebooks.com**

ROMANCES OF ROGUERY

AN EPISODE IN THE HISTORY OF THE NOVEL

BY

FRANK WADLEIGH CHANDLER

IN TWO PARTS

PART I

THE PICARESQUE NOVEL IN SPAIN

New York

PUBLISHED FOR THE COLUMBIA UNIVERSITY PRESS BY

THE MACMILLAN COMPANY

LONDON: MACMILLAN & CO., LTD.

1899

PREFACE

THIS essay was submitted in partial fulfilment of the requirements for the degree of Doctor of Philosophy at Columbia University. The subject falls naturally into two parts, the first dealing with the origin, rise, and decay in Spain of the romance of roguery, commonly called the picaresque novel; the second dealing with Spanish influence and native development beyond the Peninsula, in France, Germany, Holland, and England. The second part will be presented in a future publication, the research for which is already accomplished; but the first part, now issued, besides treating Spanish picaresque fiction in full, together with the social and literary causes leading to its ascendency, is concerned outside of Spain with translations of these novels and their direct incorporation in other literatures.

Hitherto, while no consideration of Castilian letters has failed to notice the picaresque novel, and its descendants abroad have met with frequent recognition, still a detailed or comprehensive view of the growth of the type and an indication of its historical place in the development of modern fiction have been lacking. This the author has endeavored to supply. No pains have been spared in research. In all cases original editions, where available, have been consulted. The Library of the British Museum, the Bodleian, the Bibliothèque Nationale and the Bibliothèque de l'Arsenal at Paris, and the Ticknor Collection of Spanish books in the Boston Public Library have furnished most of the materials, and it is hoped that the appended Bibliography, as prepared *in extenso* from these sources rather than from bibliographers' manuals, may possess intrinsic value. In addition, there is given a brief list of those authorities chiefly consulted beyond the obvious general histories of literature.

For kind suggestions and generous assistance I am indebted to my friends and associates,

Mr. John Garrett Underhill and Mr. Joel Elias Spingarn of Columbia University. I also desire to acknowledge the uniform courtesy and the privileges extended to a stranger in the libraries whose facilities I have enjoyed. But to Professor George Edward Woodberry, under whose immediate direction this study has been prosecuted and without whose unfailing sympathy and aid it could have been of little worth, I owe the deepest obligation. My gratitude to him can find no adequate expression here.

F. W. C.

Columbia University,
June, 1899.

CONTENTS

ROMANCES OF ROGUERY

CHAPTER I

THE ROMANCE OF ROGUERY: ITS ORIGINS AND EARLY ENVIRONMENT

The romances of roguery which flourished through Europe in the wake of the Renaissance found their first and most characteristic development in Spain in the fiction of the *gusto picaresco*. But after a career of vagabondage at home, the Spanish rogue who took his birth in the bed of the river Tormes was naturalized abroad, in France, in Germany, in Holland, and in England. Wherever he came, his exploits and the tales devoted to them were modified, more or less, by the genius of the nation as well as by the talent of transcribers. The fine French mind, bringing to bear its energies upon the cultivation of this type, produced, after a century of careful tending, the most perfect, if a blended specimen, in *Gil Blas*. The Germans, who had experienced in the Thirty Years' War something of the same disorders which in the Peninsula had earlier called men to observing the pageant of life, found in Grimmelshausen one with sufficient skill to graft the Spanish branch upon the Teuton trunk. The Dutch, on French example and through political contact, brought forth a Nicolaas Heinsius, Junior; and the Italians, least original here of all, were content with transplanting into their language the primitive Spanish itself. But while the Continent remained true to the main type, England, after a few inconsequential efforts, developed a species of her own, the result of native conditions, as the Spanish type had been. It was neither so amusing nor so influential as the latter, but it is identified with the beginnings of the third and final stage in the evolution of fiction — the novel of character. The gulf between the old story for the story's sake and the new story of the ethical life is bridged by these romances of roguery, reaching from Spain to England; wherever they appeared, they marked a sure progression toward the modern novel. Thus there is to be discovered in them, not merely the sleights and shifts of vagabonds and adventurers, not merely the earliest and most vivid picturing of manners and times, but the organic growth of modern fiction.

Although the picaresque[1] tale was indigenous to Spain, its elements had existed earlier and elsewhere in literature. The Greek novels had employed pirates and robbers with unfailing regularity. In them leaders of land and water thieves were prominent figures, although these as rogues could claim no merit or especial character; for in the Greek novel, which was fitted to live again only in the heroic genre of Gomberville, Calprenède, and Scudéry, even the rogues were heroes, not anti-heroes. The Plautine comedy had offered a nearer approach to the ideal of Spanish roguery in the *Epidicus*, *Mostellaria*, or *Persa*, for the intriguing slave and the parasite of the classic stage bore some resemblance to the picaro living by his wits. Encolpius in the *Satyricon* of Petronius Arbiter has been hailed as the forerunner of

[1] *Picaresque*, pertaining to or dealing with rogues or picaroons, from the Spanish *picar*, to peck or nibble at; *pícaro*, rogue, rascal, knave.

Spanish rogues,[1] and the facts that most of the Peninsular picaresque authors were classicists, and that Petronius in the sixteenth and seventeenth centuries had a special vogue, have been adduced as proving a probable bond between the *Satyricon* and the romances of roguery. But the low-life adventures of the decadent voluptuary or the excesses of the feast of Trimalchio have little in common with the shifts of the unfortunate rascal in service. The *Ass* of Apuleius in his changes of masters bore a closer analogy to the picaro and his vicissitudes than any other classic type; yet Lucius, the man beneath the ass's hide, was no rogue, but rather the victim of unhappy chance and his own curiosity. Allowing, however, for the absence of roguery in the hero, the *Golden Ass* may be deemed an important model of the picaresque novel. Beyond the fact that many of its incidents were taken bodily into the Spanish and subsequent fictions, this fable undoubtedly furnished to the first romances of roguery

[1] Jan Ten Brink, *Eene studie over den Hollandschen schelmenroman der zeventiende eeuw*, Rotterdam, 1885: "*Encolpius . . . schijnt de eerste der vroolijke picaros te zijn, wegbereider van Lazarillo, Guzman, Pablo, Gil Blas, Estevanillo en Mirandor.*"

the essential idea of describing society through the narrative of one in servitude whose passage from master to master should afford opportunities for observation and satire. The method of Petronius is faithfully copied even to the insertion of anecdote and extraneous incident, and the resemblance throughout remains too strong to have been purely fortuitous. In the course of most of the Spanish novels, too, the *Ass* receives honorable mention, and the *Pícara Justina* expressly proposes it among others as a pattern.

But if Apuleius supplied the idea of the form of the romance of roguery, the content was a slow and independent growth of the Middle Ages. Below the level of fiction, these centuries had produced certain catalogues and classifications of peoples and events, examples of which may be found in the *Dit sur les états du monde* or the *Dance of Death*, where the classes of society defile in the order of the social hierarchy. Here opportunity was given for a description of the ranks and conditions of the world, Death dancing with the Pope, the Emperor, the King, and through the whole series in succession down to the meanest thrall. The new fiction of observation availed itself of such scholastic schemes, reviewing distinctions of caste and remarking the traits of each profession from the point of view of the servitor to each. The *Roman de Renart* also, with its masquerade and bold parody, and its rogue hero, the fox, went a long way toward preparing for the advent of the picaro. Those animals, Renart, Ysengrin, Tibert, and the rest, were individualized characters, operated by human motives, and holding up the glass to human folly; nor was Renart the only rogue among them, but rather the most astute. Fraud and deceit were glorified ironically; no class in society was exempted from attack, and the spirit of chivalry already found a foe. Inexhaustible in gayety and indiscriminating in satire, the *Roman de Renart*, which would spare the *villain* no more than the *chatelain*, was marked by its sympathy with the anti-hero, and from it to the picaresque novel descended perhaps the latter's best inheritance in its example of consistent roguery.

In the early stages of the rogue romance attention was bound to be focussed less upon the doer than upon the thing done; the deeds proper to a rogue therefore filled the foreground. Such deeds are cheats, tricks, and frauds; and from time immemorial lists of these had existed as a part of the stock of popular story. Specific examples were presented in great numbers by *fabliaux* and Italian *novelle*, in which a particular style of anecdote dealt exclusively with the tricks played by one person upon another. The *fabliau* of the *Three Thieves* of Jean de Boves, or that of the *Blind Men of Compeigne* by Courte-Barbe, were episodes ready made and to hand for appropriation by the novel of the anti-hero, as were many of the *Gesta Romanorum* and some of the *Cento novelle antiche.* Massuccio, Straparola, Sacchetti, and Cinthio furnished sharping incidents later incorporated in the romances of roguery, and the series of cheats suffered by Calandrino at the hands of his brother artists, Nello, Bruno, and Buffalmacco, in the eighth and ninth days of the *Decameron*, were essentially picaresque in kind. Moreover, aside from mere tricks, the *novelle* gave to the Spanish novel and its successors a host of gallant ruses and of tragic situations.

Before the birth of the romance of roguery, however, separate accounts of wit employed at the expense of others began to be strung as anecdotal beads along the thread of a single name. Correlated cheats had suggested, as the connecting link between them, the cheater himself. His name was that of one who perhaps had really lived and won a reputation for cleverness in dissimulation, although presently the fact of actual existence was disregarded and a fictitious name substituted. Here, then, from the deeds that he did the doer gradually emerged; and this correlation of tricks reached its best and earliest development in Germany, although the same process was at work elsewhere. In the *Pfaffe Amis* of Der Stricker and the *Til Eulenspiegel* of Thomas Murner, the rogue of fiction began to draw breath, even if for a long time yet he could not venture to dispute an equal share of attention with that bestowed upon his actions, much less think to make them subservient to an interest in him for his own sake. The *Schwänke* and *Volksbücher* were picaresque stories in embryo. They celebrated the court fools of German princes in books of roguery like Gregor von Hayden's *Salomon und Markolph* or Von der Hazen's *Narrenbuch.* They showed the devil plotting mischief under a friar's frock in *Bruder Rausch*, and they made even Æsop the subject of a rogue biography by Heinrich Steinhöwel. At the opening of the sixteenth century, then, there was flourishing in Germany a popular fiction strongly allied, so far as mere roguery was concerned, to the later tales of the Spaniards. But the heroes of the *Schwänke* for the most part existed only as the sum total of their tricks; and while satire on the frauds of the world and enmity to the Church were in evidence, observation of life was merely incidental and not, as in the Peninsula, uppermost. *Til Eulenspiegel*, the best specimen of its class, the first printed edition of which is of 1519, borrowed from predecessors with both hands and without scruple; but the only arrangement it made of appropriated facetiæ consisted in grouping those applicable to Til's youth, and those concerning his sickness and death, and between these two extremes recounting in order his tricks before sovereigns and his stratagems against ecclesiastics, artisans, peasants, and innkeepers. There was no connection between one event and another, and no attempted study of manners; yet, all in all, this little work may be regarded as the closest approach to the picaresque novel antedating the appearance of the *Lazarillo de Tormes.* Between the one and the other there was indeed a wide disparity, for the Spanish anti-hero had finally emerged from his acts as a distinct character in a real and interesting environment, while the Teutonic anti-hero was only a name, the souvenir of a traditional rogue dead by the middle of the fourteenth century, but to whom arbitrarily had come to be attributed ingenious cheats gathered here, there, and everywhere.

An analogous but tardier development produced in England the famous Scoggin, licensed as *The Geystes of Skoggon* in 1565–1566, and attributed to Andrew Borde; while in its train followed the versified *XII Mery Jests of the Wyddow Edyth* of 1573, by Walter Smith, and the *Merrie Conceited Jests of George Peele,* printed in 1607, its actual knave-hero having died in 1598. These all outran the ordinary English books of mirth in centring their tricks about a single rogue, with the separate exploits sufficiently detailed to serve as parts of a picaresque sketch, yet failing still to tell the story of the rascal's life. The cheats of John Miller in the *Merie Tales newly imprinted and made by Master Skelton poet laureat*, licensed in 1566–1567, were recommended in 1578 by Gabriel Harvey as surpassing those of Scoggin, Eulenspiegel, and Lazarillo; but the collection in which they were contained, like most in England, sought no unity. In Italy the Solomon and Marcolphus legend from the East, which had played a part in France, in England, and in Germany, and early tried a Latin dress, found its leading rôle at the end of the sixteenth century, in Julio Cesare Croce's *Vita di Bertoldo*, but only after the *Lazarillo* had won fame in Spain, and then in quite a different field of roguery. The jests and wisdom of Bertoldo and his rise from peasant to privy councilor made him rather a hero of the people, like the English Jack of Newbury, than an anti-hero, like the picaro. In France, by the thirteenth century, a bold rogue, Eustache le Moine, had become the centre of a versified *Roman*, which set forth his life and deeds as thief and pirate; and Rabelais, the arch-mocker, gave the *fabliaux* a new lease of life. His Gargantua, whose youth was spent in tricks and learning *baliverneries*, proved even something of a picaro.

In addition, moreover, to collections of facetiæ on the one hand, and to accounts of historic Robin Hoods of land or sea on the other, and distinct from them, the Books of Beggars occupy an important place, marking the influx into letters of actual and minute observation of rogues. These curious catalogues of the orders of rascals and their cheats, preceding or contemporary with the appearance of picaresque fiction, were its invaluable adjuncts, and the collectors for it of raw material. The *Liber vagatorum* in Germany, probably of 1510, versified in 1517, and reëdited in prose by Martin Luther at Wittemberg in 1528, was the earliest volume of the kind. England followed with John Audley's *Fraternity of Vacabondes* in 1561, and Thomas Harman's *Caveat for Common Cursetors* in 1567. The latter was the basis for the conny catching pamphlets of Greene and Dekker, which in turn were to be revived in the next century by the *English Rogue* and similar fictions. In England, as in Germany, a consideration of thieves' slang and a vocabulary were prominent features; as also in the series of Beggar Books in France which began with *La vie genereuse des mercelots, gueuz, et boesmiens* of 1596. The canting dialect was even more exclusively the theme in *Le jargon ou le langage de l'argot reformé* and in the *Responce et complaincte au grand coesre sur le jargon de l'argot reformé.* In the Italian production of this class, however, Giacinto Nobili's *Il vagabondo* of Venice, 1627, only the thirty-seven orders of rogues were treated, their functions being illustrated by anecdotes. The Italian and German Beggar Books were mere amplified lists, while the French and English frequently advanced well within the bounds of fiction. The English did this more generally, perhaps, yet without attaining so definite a form as the French in *La vie genereuse*, where the story, if it arrived nowhere, was autobiographical and entirely picaresque in character. In Spain, Juan Hidalgo in 1609 published his *Romances de germanía* with the *Vocabulario por la orden del a. b. c.*, celebrating thieves' slang, and *Guzman de Alfarache* in 1599 included passages that were of a piece with those in the *Liber vagatorum* and its successors. Still more explicit as to organized roguery was the *Des-*

ordenada codicia de los bienes agenos of 1619. The latter, indeed, like Hidalgo's little work may be considered a kind of Spanish Beggar Book, although it embraced a distinct story and a long laudation of thieving and thieves besides.

But though the picaresque novel unfolded from other types and individual works,— the *Ass* of Apuleius and the mediæval reviews of estates contributing the plan, the *Roman de Renart* and tales of outlaws adumbrating the idea of abstract roguery, and compilations of tricks in facetiæ and of observed cheats in the Beggar Books affording objective instances of fraud,—the romance of roguery, in fact, rather evolved negatively from the notion of the anti-hero. As in the drama the mask with its solemn ceremony gave rise to the comic anti-mask, so in fiction the story of the hero produced the story of the rogue. Into the gap created by the recoil from the hero of fiction stepped the anti-hero of society, —the Spanish picaro. He was the parody incarnate of the elder hero, the central figure of an opera-bouffe. But because observation and a return to nature were concerned in his very being, the picaro transcended other anti-heroes.

They might contrast one fantasy with another; he must contrast the obviously real with the fantastic. A study of actual life was thus his aim, observation the method, and the most striking things of everyday experience the subject, as those of imaginary experience had been the matter of antecedent types. Blatant sounds, pungent odors, what was crude to the touch and strong to the sight, appealed to him. No refinements could be expected from his story, nothing but a scrutiny through eager senses of what best would give them immediate satisfaction. The picaresque novel was thus grossly real and usual; more than that, it emphasized and made prominent in all ways the lower elements of reality. From the matchless knight or noble who was all perfection, it passed to the sharper, destitute of grace. The palace dissolved before the gutter, the tilting field before the *hampa* of Seville, and as the courage of the paladin was replaced by the clever cowardice of the pickpocket, so the war against monsters and enchantments succumbed to the common conflict against hunger and thirst. Instead of portraying the whole of life, this reactionary fiction of the anti-hero was confined to a world of its own, from which the better part of reality even was excluded.

In form, the romance of roguery was a retrogression and a rebeginning. The story for the story's sake had already reached a highly organized form from centuries of cultivation; but the new fiction disregarded the tradition of its predecessors, and proved the lowest type of book-organism. Its unity was an inferior unity, not that of time or place or action, but merely of the identity of the hero. It might run on indefinitely; it could and did accommodate endless continuations. It unrolled itself usually from the hero's own narration, as the easiest and most natural method of exposition, and since he could never tell of his death, he thus secured, by accident, a convenient pledge to immortality. The only check his garrulity could receive was the unwillingness of his auditors to listen further. Formlessness and lack of restraint were accentuated by the undue attention paid to detail, and even in the best specimens of the picaresque novel are to be discerned faults attributable to this want of symmetry and unity in the plan.

The spirit of the story of the anti-hero was

necessarily satirical and corrective. The world of actualities, although a fresh interest in it had been discovered, was depicted in order to be attacked. Nor, on the other hand, could extravagant ideals hope to remain unscathed. Whatever their merit, the novels of chivalry and of shepherds had taken themselves seriously. Humor had been inimical to them. Incongruities existed, but their business had been to shut their eyes to the incongruous. Like the lovely edifices of enchantment, at a peal of laughter within they would have come tumbling down, as Cervantes later proved. Already they were in danger from the laughter without; for the fiction of the anti-hero was bound to be matter of fact and comic where they had been serious and inflated; the influence of satire to which it was subject, and that of mediæval jest and farce, confirmed its comic drift, and if at first it failed to attack its rivals directly, the antipathy was always there by inference.

Of the three competitors of the picaresque novel already in the field at its advent, it was prepared to oppose both the romance of chivalry and the pastoral; the *novella* it came to reënforce. In the former two an imaginary free world had been contrasted with that actually about; but the *novella*, observing life in its simplest realities, abandoned the old expedients of the symbolic and supernatural. The matter of everyday experience, so long deemed unworthy the artist's consideration, had attained a value at the Renaissance compelling its recognition, yet the Italian *novella* shows but the beginning of this process, and it left no direct inheritance to later fiction. Pointing the line of development that should succeed, it might not itself follow along that way because of mediæval limitations. Instead, it supplied the European drama with a thousand plots, and through that medium, and in the shape of incident, reëntered the stream of story transformed. But the *roman de mœurs*, and in consequence the novel of to-day, harks back to Spain and her rogue romance. In the Spanish Peninsula natural originality was only quickened and not regulated by the Renaissance. The rediscovered joy of life found voice not in scholarship as in Italy, but preëminently in art. With the stir of great events and the mingling and contrasting of all classes of society in reawakened activity, the routine of actual life furnished there the substance for a fiction of immediate realities, and forced attention to itself. More important still, social conditions in the Peninsula provided just the soil adapted to the cultivation of the anti-hero as a literary type.

For Spain in the sixteenth century was the nursery of the adventurer. A romantic war for faith waged at home against the Moor had ceased with the fall of Granada in 1492, but the adventurous momentum gathered then was only to be accelerated, not checked, by subsequent events. The menace of the Turk in the Mediterranean and the East had inspired bold hearts to rove the Atlantic to the south and west on a restless quest of discovery. The infidel enemy who barred the ancient highway to the Indies, and might not be overcome, must be evaded, and with such a lure a new world richer than the Indies was chanced upon. In the two Americas and Europe the age of the *conquistador* had come. United Spain was reaching out her arms to France, the Netherlands, to Germany and Italy. With Charles Fifth, the last and perhaps the greatest of the paladins, immense activities had been launched out, and from Africa to the North Sea, from Naples to the Pacific, Spanish dominion spread victorious. Accompanying this expansion marched an unquestioning faith in the Spanish destiny that was shared from the highest to the lowest. Patriotic enthusiasm drove into the ranks of soldiers and sailors those who might not have entered there from any greed of gain; and every tendency combined to exalt militarism and discourage industry.

Feudalism, surviving in Spain after its extinction elsewhere, crumbled now beneath the stress of new influences. In the transition from a mediæval to a modern state, the nobles, the people, and the towns, losing old prerogatives and limitations, gained others. No class was certain of its new functions, and confusion ensued. But as the nobility was deprived of power, the monarch and the people acquired it. Natural allies one of the other, the emancipated third estate sought service with the king; and the clergy, gradually detaching itself from Rome, ranged round the monarch also. Royal employment in one form or another was alone worth having. Thus the only gateways open to advancement were the Church, the civil administration, and the army. Men of culture and distinguished talents welcomed service as common soldiers in the wars, but even the ignorant and the boors disdained to stoop to the patient business of life. Moreover, the exile of the Jews and the increasing rigorous persecution of the *Moriscos*, which was to end in their expulsion by Philip Third in 1609, had dealt an irremediable blow to productive labor; for the Jews and *Moriscos* were the only classes who had not succumbed already to the common contempt for toil.

So long as military projects were all-absorbing and successful, the lamentable consequence of such conditions was not apparent. There was indeed a scarcity in comforts, a costliness in necessities, but the whirlwind itself was not to be reaped until the turn of conquest. And yet, before the retirement of Charles to Yuste, the vision of glory had begun to pale. Thriftlessness at home had come to balance fortunate gains abroad. Great as had been the demand for men in the armies, not all had been able to secure a footing there. The general panic to serve the king to the sound of the drum had induced a movement which more than sufficed to replenish every gap that might occur. In America death in conflict was all on the side of the defenceless aborigines. In Europe, however sanguinary might prove the combat, there were those willing and waiting to step into the places of the fallen, eager to stand the risks of winning fame and riches. The military aspirants constituted a dangerous class in society; those who had failed in attaining their desired field for endeavor refused any other. They were idlers; and at Seville and San Lucar thousands who could not be accommodated in the fleets that weighed for the Indies, disappointed in dreams of discovery, joined their ranks. The plough and the shop in the provinces had been deserted by those who presently found nothing whatever to do. This nucleus of the vainly proud and discontented received continual accessions from such as had fought in the wars but returned at the summons of peace, their occupation gone. Laden with spoil, and arrogant as conquerors, they still held force their highest law. In an excess of zeal for some decades, Spain had bent every energy to the prosecution of schemes of conquest; but, her acquisitions made, she was at a loss to proceed. The ways of peace had been forgotten, the arts of peace had been abandoned, the healthy and prosperous life of the nation had been sapped by the fever of insane ambition. And at just this moment, from Mexico and Peru, surged back the counter-current of returned adventurers. They had garnered a golden harvest for the asking, laying hands in a moment on what centuries alone could have accumulated. They despised any but the royal road to wealth, and they had come too easily by what they had to value or to guard it.

Now the adventurer defeated saw in the adventurer successful a ready victim. The stay-at-home, if he would not work or starve, must pluck the elated wanderer. And he soothed his conscience with the comfortable pretext that it was but fair the booty should be shared between them. The methods he employed were deception and flattery. His wit supplied the place of hands. He studied trickery with a care which, better directed, might have rendered him respectable. And by a paradox the very antipathy he had felt to the low and mean in life, to the humdrum and the commonplace, reduced him to a sordidness more miserable than any he had sought to avoid. Spain had never been free from the official parasite, the unscrupulous office-seeker haunting the ministries, and dogging the footsteps of the great. In the *catariberas* of the satirist are set forth these scraping knaves, momentarily content with the sop thrown them, but insatiable in their demand for more. Such superficially polished rogues reflected promptly the frauds practised by the more courageous non-producers. From the court to the kennel truth was subordinate to policy, intrigue and sharping were the rule, people lived from hand to mouth and for to-day, and the spirit of chivalry eloquent in the old romances and incarnate in Charles Fifth, remaining without employment under Philip Second, turned to roguery. The rim of the horizon had begun to contract, and the field of adventurous exploit was more than proportionately diminished. Where Charles had been magnetic, Philip was sombre and cold. He dipped the pen where

Charles had wielded the sword, and the bulwarks behind which he sought security were files of official paper. The father had been a military leader, an inspirer of men; the son was a bureaucrat. But omniscient as was his bureaucracy, the country already drained of its best men and resources was left to languish in exhaustion. Not only that; for it was further so crippled by foolish legislation as almost to inhibit the natural recruiting of its energies.

Those peasants who had stood true to their vocation against the temptations of visionary wealth, instead of receiving a reward, met with nothing save oppression. Extortionate taxes were levied not so much upon the careless adventurer as upon the frugal husbandman. His crops were disposed of standing to answer the King's demands upon him, and he was forbidden to go beyond a certain distance to sell what little he had left. Hampered by fatal restrictions, forced to stare starvation in the face, disregarded and despised, what wonder is it that the honest farmer, the manufacturer, and the merchant gave up the battle as unequal? Some there were who struggled on, but the abandonment of farms was widespread, the wilderness encroached on lands that had been tilled, and although the Peninsula had become the envy of her neighbors for her bullion, she was the poorest of them all in the crying needs of common life. Lack of bread was the nation's nightmare. Hunger, "the evil of Spain," is a theme recurrent in the picaresque novels; and the character of the people, never gentle, grew steel-hard under the repeated blows of positive suffering.

With Ferdinand and Isabella, the ideal of government had been political unity founded upon a unity in religion. The Inquisition had been instituted to secure the former by enforcing the latter. The Infidel who had borne the first assaults of this terrible engine might have felt some satisfaction of revenge when it was later loosed upon the Spanish people themselves. It destroyed those whom it had been raised up to protect. It bred a sense of distrust, ferocity, and treachery where docility and simple faith might yet have continued. Its methods were essentially those to unsettle a belief in open justice, to inspire subterfuge, and to disrupt the family and society. Philip Second, the monarch who saw all but was never seen, employed in the political government of his state the same procedure that the Inquisition had adopted to insure religious domination. Surveillance and secrecy, an elaborate system of espionage, were everywhere in force. The individualism in offence, which the foot-soldier had developed when the introduction of firearms made the infantry private as effective as the mounted noble, became an individualism in defence when the common citizen for preservation must guard his word and person as rigorously as the hidalgo. It was each for himself, and the devil take the hindmost. And this compulsory individualism of selfishness yoked with the fatalism that had descended from centuries of Moorish contact fostered a cruelty and an indifference to pain in others that became a trait of Spanish life and letters.

Pity disappeared, although the shadow of it lingered in the popular treatment of beggars. These could outvie their better-known Italian brethren. Their name was legion. As in Italy, they congregated before the church doors and the monasteries. They thronged the highways and plied from town to town, chanting their prayers. Somehow they lived, and while thieving never came amiss to them, they were chiefly recipients of charity. Something of pity must have excited such almsgiving, but in the main it was the result of a peculiar system. As the martial power had been shrinking, the ecclesiastical power had expanded. Across the Peninsula, near ten thousand religious houses swung each day their bells to matins and to vespers, and thousands on thousands of men and women passed their lives in devotion there, dependent upon their private fortunes or more often pious bounties for support. They, too, were non-producers, and a bond of sympathy linked them with the beggars, earlier strengthened by the institution of orders of mendicant friars, and always supported by the prospect of rewards promised to those who should assist the needy. "The poor ye have with you always," was the dictum they accepted; there was a certain satisfaction of caste in the fact. They — the monks and nuns — were the chosen seekers after a heavenly salvation, one of the conditions of which was charity. It was the business of the poor, in their very necessity, to furnish the opportunity for fulfilling that condition. Indeed, it was regarded almost as a providential provision that there should be any poor at all, else how could the religious achieve everlasting bliss? The monasteries, therefore, did dispense charity. The beggar and the vagabond need never faint by the way, although the hidalgo or the rogue in his pride might. The infirmities of the unfortunate were regarded as visitations from above and punishments for sin, precisely as Job's counsellors had regarded his troubles. There was consequently more condemnation than pity for the outcast himself; but the assistance lent him was intended less as a temporal benefit to him than as an eternal benefit to the lender. In spite of royal edicts forbidding general almsgiving, the example and the motives of the monasteries prevailed with large masses of the people, and more especially with those who were themselves reduced in circumstances. Such were already uncomfortable enough to have their thoughts diverted in hope of relief to a future life, and were willing to purchase it at the price even of some further deprivation in this. Moreover, they had nothing to fear from disobedience to the King's embargo. But the fortunate and rich found the present sufficiently attractive to neglect serious thoughts of a problematic future. To conform to the royal decree for them was easy, and they bestowed their gifts upon the rogues who flattered, in preference to the rogues who begged. But for the latter, as for the former, there was always a broad field of practical encouragement. In Spain everything favored beggary and vagabondage, from the advantages to be derived from this self-seeking scheme of charity to the climate itself adapted to an outdoor life. While the percentage of illegitimacy was always large, infanticide in Spain was uncommon, abandonment taking its place. And these neglected children, joining in bands for juvenile depredation, were feeders for companies of elder rogues. So great a scandal had they become, indeed, that in 1552 the Cortes was brought to consider them in a petition requesting the appointment of special officers to have charge of collecting and providing with work the little rascals, who were running wild.

The gypsies, also, who had entered Europe at the beginning of the fifteenth century, had carried their vagabond invasion westward with wonderful celerity. From Bohemia they had overrun Germany, Switzerland, and France, appearing at Paris as early as 1427. The opposition they encountered in France, however, as well as their own restless spirit, kept them moving, and while some retraced their steps to Bohemia, more passed south to sunny Spain. Here they found a sky, a country, and a people peculiarly suited to their tastes. They as well were non-producers. They never harnessed Nature. They took her as they found her, reaping where others sowed, disdaining to sow themselves. One art they practised; for, sinister children of Vulcan, they were universal smiths. The glare of their forges at night lit up the solitary places. But for the rest they were horse-traders, cheiromancers, and cheats. The Inquisition made them no trouble. They were not worth it. They had neither lands nor riches; and the Inquisition had ever an eye to confiscation. If the Jews and Moors had been bitterly attacked, it was through avarice and envy, for they were the Spaniards' superiors in culture and in wealth; but the *gitanos* could offer no such recommendation to the notice of defenders of the faith. Accordingly through the portals of the Pyrenees they poured unhindered, and although many were left by the way in Valencia and Murcia, La Mancha and New Castile, by far the greater number reached their haven of errancy in Andalusia. For the Spaniard they were mere Egyptians; for the thrifty Moor they were *charami*, robbers.

Not until 1499 did the government direct its attention to the pest which then had fastened itself ineradicably upon the Peninsula. In an enactment of that year at Medina del Campo, the Catholic Sovereigns commanded the *gitanos* to forsake their nomadic life and seek out masters or leave the kingdom within sixty days. In 1539 at Toledo, Charles Fifth added a penalty of six years in the galleys for disobedience to the previous enactment; and Philip Second from Madrid in 1586, confirming what had gone before, required that their commercial transactions be registered together with their names. But such hostile measures produced little or no effect upon the gypsies. They were quicksilver, and not to be subject to the finger of legislation. The seventeenth century in its provisions regarding them exhibited a progressive severity which only proves the inefficacy of each preceding effort. In 1619 Philip Third banished them all within six months under pain of death; providing, however, for the reception in large towns of such as wished to remain and would abandon language, name, and dress. In 1633, Philip Fourth forbade any intercourse among them, instituting a heavy fine for dancing, and commanding an observance of the Christian religion. In 1692, Charles Second prohibited their congregation in a single quarter, their selling of beasts except with a notary's seal, and the pursuit of any business save tilling the earth. Finally, in 1695, the same monarch, along the same lines, punishing strolling with the galleys, laid his ban upon their blacksmithing, or even their having horses. Well intentioned although futile legislation continued throughout the eighteenth century, but the old complaint of Dr. Sancho de Moncada, who had urged Philip Third to drive forth this people as he had the Moors, was never outgrown: "In all parts they are accounted famous thieves, concerning whom wonderful things are written." If, however, among the wonderful things written of the gypsies the testimony of the romances of roguery be accepted, the conclusion must be that their relation to the army of picaros was one of juxtaposition rather than of interaction. Their methods were often the same. Fraudulent gain was their aim, and trickery their weapon. But the gypsies possessed no individual courage, no chivalry gone astray, such as lurked often beneath the rags or livery of the lowest Spanish rogue. They were of a different race, a meaner extraction, and incapable of broad conceptions even in roguery. In life they herded together, affiliating with the picaro no more than with the rest of the world, and in the Spanish romances of roguery wherever they appear it is as his enemies or unworthy rivals. But the *gitano* played into the hands of the picaro, whether wittingly or not, by contributing to the prevailing disorder. Bands of gypsies, mustering a bravado through numbers, scoured the country from time to time, requiring the intervention of troops for their quelling. They were accused of poisoning cattle and water, thus inducing a plague in towns to be sacked when resistance was reduced to a minimum.[1] It was common to lay to their charge as well as to that of the *Moriscos* the kidnapping of children to be sent for slaves to Barbary. Whatever truth there was in popular opinion regarding them, it is certain they were among the most unprofitable elements of an unprofitable society.

Philip Second, whose nominal success in internal administration was neutralized by his signal failures abroad, had raised by religious intolerance a storm of protest in the Netherlands that swept away completely the prestige of the Spanish army. Later, in his project against England he had despatched the Armada to destruction, and in the accession of Henry Fourth he had seen the death of his hopes regarding France. So when the reign of Philip Third opened, Spain had lost faith in herself by land and by sea. The consummation of the country's industrial ruin followed shortly when with three days' warning the Moors were hounded out. Other errors, retentions of mediæval economic policy, produced

[1] *e.g.* Logroño; see Francisco de Cordova, *Didascalia*, Lugduni, 1615, Cap. 50, p. 405.

their effect. The specie concentration was out of all proportion to the natural wealth. Prices were fabulously high. What exports there were must be raw materials, since, for manufactured goods, Spain was wholly dependent upon importation. Heavy taxes, levies, and loans were more and more necessary. Already in 1573 and 1574 Philip Second was owing Genoese and Spanish merchants thirty-seven millions borrowed at twenty-two per cent, the interest on which he afterward refused to pay, it being conveniently represented to him that the contract on the part of the merchants was made "against charity and the law of God, and that but for some remedy, within a year he would not have a *real* for food." Sir John Smythe, sent by Queen Elizabeth to examine into the condition of the Peninsula, after compiling an elaborate report, casting up the debit and credit of the entire realm, concluded that "little can be left over at the end of the year for so great a prince as the King of Spain since his expenses are immense and his kingdoms so dispersed."[1] Philip's monetary needs may be

[1] Sir John Smythe MS., Lambeth Palace, 1577. The controversy with the Genoese is reviewed there too at length.

further divined by his confiscation for five consecutive years of all the gold brought from the Indies.

The decadence was thus well inaugurated. The Spaniard, proud and idle before, became confirmed in his aversion to work. Cardinal Navagiero, on a mission from the Pope and making the tour of Spain in 1524, had declared of the people, "They are not industrious or frugal nor do they willingly till the earth. But they are given to other things, rather going to the wars or to the Indies to make their fortunes."[1] But the Indies and the wars were no longer the sure resort they once had been, and Seville, which, through the outpouring of adventurers, the Cardinal had remarked as deserted by its inhabitants and almost in the hands of women,[2] was repopulated, in part at least, with the choicest scoundrels of the kingdom. The *valientes*, or bullies, formed a distinct class. It had become the fashion for gentlemen, who preferred not to soil their hands or expose their persons in conflict with an adversary, to hire a bravo to

[1] *Il viaggio fatto in Spagna et in Francia*, etc., Venetia, 1563, p. 25.

[2] *Ibid.*, pp. 13–15.

do the business. Vengeance was wreaked and honor satisfied at a fixed rate, and paid assassination, taken over as a fine art from Italy, prospered. Officers of justice were powerless to suppress such organizations of *valientes*, and raids upon the watch by them and by the picaros were of frequent occurrence. Justice itself was thoroughly corrupt, and the severest sentence to be mitigated by a small bribe. Bands of robbers prowled in the mountain passes all-potent in spite of the Santa Hermandad, and the only safety for travellers lay in sheer force of numbers. A century after the observations of Cardinal Navagiero, matters had gone so far that Pedro Fernando Navarrete, in his *Conservacion de monarquias y discurso politico sobre la gran consulta que el consejo hizo al Sr Rey don Felipe III*, exclaimed: "Traverse the fields once fertile; you will see them covered with nettles and briers, for there is no longer any one who cultivates them. The largest part of Spaniards do nothing to-day, some under the pretext of nobility, others because they prefer to beg. The streets of Madrid offer a singular spectacle. They are encumbered with do-nothings and vagabonds, who pass their days in playing cards, in waiting for the hour to dine at the gate of convents, or to set out for the country to loot houses. What is worse, not only has this life of idleness been adopted, but the plazas swarm with adventurers and vagabonds whose vices corrupt all the town, and people the hospitals."

An era of famous deceptions seems to have been inaugurated at this time in the Peninsula. The pastry-cook, Gabriel de Espinosa, who in 1595 pretended to be King Sebastian of Portugal come back to his dominions seventeen years after his defeat and death at the hands of the Moors in Africa, was one of the most picturesque of these sharpers. He hoodwinked even the princess Doña Ana de Austria, a nun, and had for accomplice an ecclesiastic, Fray Miguel; but at last both he and his partner came to grief on the gallows in the Plaza Mayor of Madrid, while the princess and her maids were imprisoned and condemned to penitential fare and silence. Like other impostors, the pastry-cook king was celebrated in contemporary pamphlets, a play was written upon him, and so late as 1835 this Spanish Perkin Warbeck furnished the theme for a romance. Alonso Pérez de Saavedra somewhat earlier won notoriety in the same kingdom as a false papal nuncio, and besides the dramatic renderings of his story, his autobiography appeared, "written with his left hand after the right had been struck off." The credulity of the age made pseudo-science, too, a profitable field for fraud, and Juan Arias de Loyola and Luis de Fonseca Coutiño pretending to find the fixed point in 1603, or Lorenzo Ferrer Maldonado humbugging hundreds with essences and alembics until forced to flight in 1609, were but instances of historic picaros, only too common. The moral austerity which Protestantism introduced elsewhere in its attempt to revive the primitive simplicity of the Church, the Inquisition here successfully combated. Thus the seventeenth century in Spain found itself obliged to repent at leisure the mistakes of the sixteenth.

Yet in art and letters it was a noble period. Just as the romances of chivalry flourished when the age of chivalry itself had declined, so the literary blossoming of the first third of the century occurred when root and branch of the social organism had become diseased. Cervantes, from suffering personal privation, captivity, and disappointment, had been the witness of a series of national disasters that stung his patriotic soul to satire. As once in the heroic days men had spoken of Guzman El Bravo, so now in the days of anti-heroes, the merest beggar-rogue was for him ironically Cortadillo El Bueno.[1] The lofty genius of a Calderon might woo forgetfulness of actual conditions in religious mysticism, but the *Devotion of the Cross* has sometimes to give way to a *Mayor of Zalamea*, the picture of a lawless soldiery in conflict with ancient ideals of honor. Religion and morality had been divorced, and even in his *autos sacramentales*, Lope de Vega must express the perverted popular conception; for his Saint Diego of Alcalá, who has robbed the larder of a convent, goes undetected and with sanctity preserved from stain by the miraculous transformation of his booty into roses; while Moreto's comedy *El imposible vencido* shows a priest stabbing in jealousy the lover of his mistress. Of the literature of the Spaniards at this time, Sismondi's extravagant generalization

[1] Émile Chasles, *Michel de Cervantes*, etc., Paris, 1866, pp. 256 *seq.*

is perhaps approximately true,—"not only is dissimulation crowned with success in their comedies, their romances, and their descriptions of national manners, but that quality absolutely receives greater honor than candor."[1] And if serious works unconsciously reflect a distortion of truth and justice, which was only too genuine, what should the comic talent yield which proposed to immortalize the avowedly unjust and untrue picaro? This rogue in life has been shown to be a product of the decadence. But in literature he was a vigorous protest against it. And for that reason, the moral tone of the fictions of which he is the subject, is, after all, more honest and more healthful than that of the elegant efforts of the age. With all their pretence to be patterns of virtue there is greater danger in the company of Persiles and Sigismunda, invariable in their falsehoods, told for the sake of falsehood, than there is in rubbing elbows with the worst lying cheat of the *gusto picaresco*. The rogue of literature was only what he claimed to be. His creator brought him forward expressly to expose in effigy the

[1] Sismondi, *Literature of the South of Europe*, 4th ed., London, 1853, Vol. II., p. 269.

vices of the day. Taken from life, to be met with on the street at every turning, he was the best instrument for satire to be found. He was sure to be amusing, every nook and cranny of society was open to his exploration, and, best of all, his point of view was precisely the opposite of the ordinary observer's. What he praised was infallibly blameworthy; what he blamed was the really meritorious. This was understood by all, and constituted the humor of his life and story; but the values of the good and the bad, forgotten and confounded through mere usualness in the common view, by this new device stood forth again sharply defined. The rogue did what the artist in the course of painting often does; he inverted the picture. Turned upside down, the true color values reappeared in all their freshness; a finer appreciation was rendered possible for the chiaroscuro of vice and virtue.

Thus social conditions in Spain in the sixteenth and seventeenth centuries furnished an ample pretext for making the literary reaction expressive of a social one. The decadence presented all the material to inspire a corrective fiction; and the peculiar form of that fiction was determined both by the foregoing literary development from which it recoiled and by the social facts and failures which it emphasized.

CHAPTER II

THE SPANISH ROGUE

× THE picaresque novel of the Spaniards presents a rogue relating his adventures. He is born of poor and dishonest parents, who are not often troubled with gracing their union by a ceremony, nor particularly pleased at his advent. He comes up by hook or crook as he may. Either he enters the world with an innate love of the goods of others, or he is innocent and learns by hard raps that he must take care of himself or go to the wall. In either case the result is much the same; in order to live he must serve somebody, and the gains of service he finds himself obliged to augment with the gains of roguery. So he flits from one master to another, all of whom he outwits in his career, and describes to satirize in his narrative. Finally, having run through a variety of strange vicissitudes, measuring by his rule of roguery the vanity of human estates, he brings his story to a close. Sometimes he has attained the modest satisfaction of his desires and is ready to relinquish overt fraud; sometimes he is farther than ever from the goal; and sometimes, asking with Ginés de Pasamonte in *Quixote*, "How can my story be finished if my life itself be not finished?" he promises more when he shall have lived it.

The device is a simple one. The anti-hero is everything and nothing; everything in what he does, nothing in character. Yet weak and heartless though he be, his wit secures him immunity from contempt or condemnation. He has mirth and spontaneity, if he lack pity for the crippled, or if his sympathies respond only to exaggerated Castilian pride. Reprehensible in every way, we do not reprehend him, any more than we would Bardolph or old Jack Falstaff, although Falstaff is a lovable rogue where the picaro is often a clown. It is his nature and not his fault. For the Spaniard acts, but rarely feels; he passes and repasses upon the scene, but scarcely wills. There is in him still a good deal of the marionette operated upon a single automatic principle. And this principle is always avarice.

He makes no friends whom he would not betray for an advantage, and his highest conception of love is a profitable marriage. Even passion is seldom a motive with him, not because he esteems it less, but because he esteems material gain more. There are excuses for his initiation into roguery, inasmuch as starvation is the alternative. He must steal the sacrament bread if his master, the priest, will allow him only an onion every fourth day for fare, and when once he has acquired the method, it is natural he should test it by universal use. He lives in a land and at a time with the battle for individual existence waging relentlessly. The real foe is nature, though the incidental foe be his neighbor. In a struggle for the survival of the fittest avarice becomes a saving virtue, and the avarice of the picaro is not the miserable thing it is with Harpagon. It is active, not passive; not retentiveness, but acquisitiveness. There lies the humor of it; for stinginess is always mean, but thievery may often be noble. It depends solely on the magnitude of the theft. The rogue in every land holds up his head the higher and proclaims his kinship with Alexander. The conquering tyrant for Chaucer in the *Manciple's Tale* is a captain, while, as for the lesser rogue who—

> "may not doon so gret an harm as he,
> Ne bringe a contre to so gret meschief,
> Men clepen him an outlawe or a theef."

Just this idea of paradoxical kinship between the highest and the lowest is the core and centre of every satirical romance of roguery, from the most insignificant of Spanish *novelas* to Fielding's *Jonathan Wild the Great*. "At first only noble folk stole," declares Dr. Carlos García, "but in time thievery became an ordinary possession, so that the butcher and porter took it up."[1] The recoil of the anti-hero from the hero is here accentuated, and the Spanish rogue, who is precisely the porter and the butcher, or worse, for this reason can be only a rogue and not a villain. He may swagger and talk of killing, but he never kills. He does not rob on the highway or break into houses boldly. He is an artful dodger, with too much good nature and humor as well as too little resolution to wear the tragic mask. He may

[1] *Desordenada codicia*, 1619, Chap. VI.

be as coarse and as merciless as you will in his jests, but they are meant as jests to the last. Thus he stands midway between the mere jester and the villain; he is neither the court fool nor the pirate, but he has actual and literary affiliations with both.

In the earlier stories of his life there is in him no evolution of character. After he has entered the kingdom of fraud his progress is simply one of increasing opportunity; and nothing ever offered to the picaro can he refuse. It is as though he had been deprived of the function of choice. Sometimes he is up and sometimes down; to-day rich and to-morrow poor. But to him it is all one. The present alone is important; he must take what comes. He does not despair, neither does he hope. His gamut of emotion is woefully little. At defeat he shrugs his shoulders and plots how to make the best of a bad case. At success he snaps his fingers, gets drunk in the nearest *venta*, and loses everything by a throw of the dice, to begin all over again. It is no part of his avarice to harbor his resources; all his ingenuity is expended in getting. Here he has infinite patience and skill. Beyond that he has neither, and frugality is a butt for his ridicule.

His childish vivacity makes him an entertaining if a dangerous companion, when his pranks by themselves might weary. He is caressed by the great for the amusement he affords, and by the lowly for the genius he displays. He moves in the diplomatic circle at Rome with an easy effrontery, or bows before royalty at Vienna with the air of a visiting emperor. His unflagging ambition has been to get on in the world. Yet if he attain the honorable office of town-crier with Lazarillo, of silk-merchant with Rufina and Don Jaime, or of keeper of a card-house with Estevanillo Gonzalez, he asks nothing more. Or if in misfortune he find a way merely to evade ill-treatment in the galleys with Guzman, or to exile himself to the Indies from the pursuit of justice like Pablos, he will never complain. Life for him is a problem to avoid, not to solve. He is employed only in gathering data, crude sensations, common experiences, with which he does nothing. Should he think at all, the rogue would be a pessimist extending the sway of *desengaño* (undeceit, unveiling), a word forever in the Spanish mouth, from events of life to their meaning. As it is, he will now and again verge upon a conflict with orthodoxy, and in the next *Index Expurgatorius* find his story curtailed by the watchful Inquisition; but because he does not think, the picaro can afford to be inconsistent.

He may be seen kneeling in the *hampa* of Seville where Monipodio, king of the rogues, holds court, kissing the crucifix with deep devotion, and rising to receive instructions as to his province of beggary for the week, together with a list of knife-thrusts he is to administer for pay. And when alguazils pursue, he will be discovered in the church clasping the altar for sanctuary, while the civil and religious authorities wrangle over the right to his person. But what he really believes beyond the testimony of his senses, he himself can hardly say. Take him all in all, he is singularly free from the credulity of his age. For the most part, superstition is held up to scorn and turned against its disciples. The miracles of indulgence-sellers are mere shams for Lazarillo; Guzman declares he never pinned faith to astrologers, however tempted to do so in disaster; Marcos de Obregon prides himself on his exposure of magicians' tricks; Pablos pretends to supernatural power only to perpetrate a cheat upon his landlady; and Rufina and Garay, with false alchemy, wheedle a fortune from a seeker after the philosopher's stone. Still, the same Marcos who had been at pains to explain an apparition of the devil as produced by a black dog with a chain of bells about his neck, gravely describes a ghost seen by Don Pedro de Avila; and his friend, Doctor Sagredo, in his travels encounters enchantments and peoples that might have staggered veracious Sir John Mandeville. Pindaro and Francisco, too, have a pass with a witch, finding a wax image she had stuck with pins to enchant its living original, whom only the exorcisms of a village priest can rescue from the evil charm.

But whatever the rogue's opinions, they do not stand for much. His emotions and beliefs are at a discount, as well as his volitions. He is the sort of agent most efficient, not in what he does, but rather in what he suffers. He is the person to whom things happen. His vicissitudes are therefore more interesting than himself. They begin at the beginning, for we find him born into strange conditions. Lazarillo de Tormes is ushered into the world in the bed of the river from which he takes his name. His father is a miller, afterwards obliged to flee for bleeding his sacks, and his mother a lady who keeps an eating-house and becomes infatuated with a gentleman of color, the groom in a stable. Guzman de Alfarache sees the light as the result of an intrigue between the mistress of a rich ecclesiastic and a Genoese usurer so religious that he has beads as big as walnuts on his rosary. Don Pablos for father rejoices in a clever barber, afterwards hanged, who teaches the boy to cut the customers' purses while he cuts their beards; and both Pablos and Lazarillo de Manzanares are blessed with mothers noticed by the Inquisition for irregularities and witchcraft. Periquillo of the Poultry Yard is a foundling; and the Fortunate Fool, Ceñudo, is abandoned by his mother, a poor woman married by law to a reluctant Licentiate of Alcalá. The Ingenious Helen is the daughter of a Gallegan lackey and a Moorish slave, whose apostasy obliges her to keep one name for the house and another for the street; while Teresa, the Child of Frauds, is born of a laundress in the Manzanares, like Lazarillo in the Tormes. There is never a rogue of them all but finds the way paved for a cheating career. Nor does it take long to set forth upon it.

Lazarillo commences service with a blind beggar who has promised to treat him as a son; he receives the advice from his tender mother, "Look to yourself for the future, and farewell;" and the need of sharpness is made manifest when the blind rogue, asking the boy to listen to the strange noise within the stone bull carved on the bridge at Salamanca, knocks his head violently against it, and then bursts out laughing, telling him a blind man's boy should have more cunning than the devil himself. At which Lazarillo declares, "It seemed to me as though that moment had awakened me from the simplicity of childhood, and I said to myself, 'The old man speaks truly. I am now alone, and if I do not keep a sharp lookout for myself, I shall find none to assist me.'"

Others require no instruction at all. Periquin, born by a fortunate token feet first, as soon as he can walk makes friends with a neighboring tavern, where he receives and appropriates gifts. Justina, the daughter of the rascal innkeeper of Mansilla, is astute enough without any of the comprehensive counsels published by her father to guide his family in fleecing guests. Andrés, whose parents are honest people, but maligned, he says, by the wicked on the plea that they have cut off the silver hand of a St. Bartholomew, purchases his own reprieve on the condition of executing them, and does it with less compunction as there will then be left alive some one to pray for the deceased. Trapaza, whose mother is a widow before she is a wife, her lord having broken his neck in an attempt to escape jail, evinces admirable light-fingeredness as a babe, and as a boy becomes addicted to gaming, which with the reading of Martial constitutes his whole education.

Some of the Spanish rogues begin at school, where their pranks and their hardships, like those of the Witty Buscon, are capitally told. More set out like Marcos and Alonso by making for the university, presently to be drawn away by the temptations of a freer existence, or perhaps with Don Gregorio Guadaña failing to arrive at all. But most commence by going in quest of adventure, the recipients of maternal advice, "worth much and costing little," as one of them says, entering life immediately and through no academic limbo. Such in later years are likely to appear at Salamanca or Alcalá to study theology with Guzman, or to confound by riddle-answers the propositions of the Doctors, like Lazarillo. But beyond this, in youth or age, service, travel, and fraud divide the picaro's time.

Now the rogue is a soldier and forced into battles from which he takes refuge in a haycock; afterwards bragging of his valor with the best. Now he is plundered by the gypsies and left shivering at their forge-fires until dressed in the rags of the first deceased and inducted into the cheating mysteries of Egypt. At Valladolid or Madrid he is a courtier, and with ruse upon ruse all but wins the hand of a noble heiress or a rich widow, whose fortune, had he captured it, would have run through his fingers like water, and done him no more good. At Seville he is a porter engaged in unlading the caravels come from the Indies, or a charlatan peddling face-washes and dentifrices. Here he is an olive-picker and a mason; there a watcher of goats, and a water-carrier. Sometimes he is an itinerant actor and the veriest supernumerary, taking money at the door, writing posters, filling the rôle of the dragon in *autos* or that of the corpse in tragedies, mending the costumes between-whiles. Sometimes he is a poet, composing romances more ingenious than inspired, or else a barber's apprentice, inadvertently carrying off an ear by a flourish of the razor, in spite of having practised already upon long-suffering beggars. As silver-boy, cook, and major-domo he has fruitful expedients for enriching himself. As physician he goes about gravely on his mule telling people what they know already, but using long words to do it. He is familiar with the orders of knaves, — the Dacians, who maim infants with which to beg, the "drawers of wool" who snatch capes in the dark; and he himself crouches with painted ulcers before the church door, soliciting alms. As a hermit he receives the profit of a reputation for sanctity and of receipts from the sale of stolen goods. As a mock saint he parades the streets, crying, "Praised be the Holy Sacrament," asking contributions for those in prison, while his accomplices stitch sheets and pillows for the hospitals. But at night when the door is shut all are merry within to their hearts' content. Confirmed in his wandering, inns have an unfailing attraction for him, and half his life is spent within and between them. Although he may conclude that the tavern boy has a worse lot than the leader of a blind man, yet in the caravansary he is certain to become everything from hostler to proprietor. He can don a disguise or hide in a chest with the most consummate of Italian intriguers. He has devices for outwitting jealous husbands, learned in the school of experience, and taken from Italian *novelle*. New-born children utterly unknown are confided to his care, and mysterious caskets of treasure unexpectedly reached forth from doors for him to take. In the Mediterranean he never hoists sail but a fleet of Moorish corsairs bears down to bundle him off to Algiers, where his Mohammedan master's daughter will fall in love with him, and finally effect his escape. In the Atlantic, storms and pirates set him confessing his sins. He visits the Indies, and like Pindaro, the

Soldier, declares that all he saw is worth no more than a Guadix melon, or he pushes on beyond like Sagredo into unknown waters to the island of a new Cyclops. From Poland to the Netherlands and the Kentish coast his travels keep him busy. He wanders over the Peninsula, describing the cities and the shrines. He finds a favorite stamping-ground in Italy, at Naples, Rome, and Milan, and though he may be robbed by a Sayavedra at Siena, or tricked by a Doña Camila at Venice, he is alert and observant everywhere.

Through every adventure the rogue is subject to events. He is a bark beaten hither and thither by the waves of chance. Some he surmounts, others bear him down. Buffeted on one side, he veers to the other. Opposed in front, he falls back into the trough of the sea. He has never gained steering-way; he can have or hold no course, and the idea of will as conquering fate is never dreamt of by him. For such a voyager the most that can be asked is a fair wind and current to bring him sooner or later to his haven. Everything is dependent upon these, and nothing upon him. The rogue himself is therefore almost a convention, a pivot about which a description of society in classes and manners turns; and in the earlier Spanish romances of roguery we do not so much look at the rogue as borrow his eyes with which to look at the world.

The society, then, which the picaro traverses is the main thing; and although his satirical bent may lead to occasional caricature, the picture he presents of contemporary life must on the whole be faithful, for its very success arose from an appreciation of its likeness as a portrait. But in the description there is no order other than that induced by the order of the hero's adventures; and whatever sequence these preserve is rather a reversal than an observance of that in the mediæval satires. Instead of reviewing the social classes from the highest to the lowest, as had been the case in the *Dance of Death*, the picaresque novel was prone to lead from low estates to higher, where any scheme of progress is found at all. Thus Lazarillo, commencing his career as the leader of a blind beggar, the greatest rascal in the world, passes to a skinflint priest no worse than a miser, and then to a poor *escudero*, whose only fault is pathetic pride. Guzman de Alfarache, who serves an innkeeper and a cook, rises to be a cardinal's page and the petted favorite of an ambassador before falling to disgrace. Others, however, and most, change conditions without principle and by chance. In the *Desordenada codicia*, the hero, from a goldsmith's apprentice, becomes a professional rogue, and finally a convict in the galleys at Marseilles. The Bachiller Trapaza, too, must row for the king, being sent to the oar through the jealousy of his mistress, after impersonating a nobleman at Salamanca, engaging with an hidalgo as poor as an anchorite, and attempting a fraudulent match. Estevanillo Gonzalez, in all his life of chaotic variety, accepts whatever is presented to him, and his hurried adventures tread on one another's heels in a perfect rout of disorder. He is a barber, a sharper, a cook in the navy, and a cook on land, the surgeon of a hospital, a scullery boy, an alguazil, a robber, and a mock pilgrim. He plays the charlatan, the pedler, and the soldier. He is *vivandero* of a company, a court-buffoon, a mock dentist and physician, and a diplomatic envoy. From his younger to his elder years, the only advance made is a certain familiarity with the great, acquired through his office of jester. Alonso, the gossiping lay-brother, the servant of many masters, as the story styles him, goes through a range of similar vicissitude with no more reason. He bears arms, serves a sacristan and a nobleman, acts as secretary to a judge and aid to a physician, becomes in Mexico a rich merchant and at home a poor player. He is drudge to a convent, an accomplice of gypsies, the guardian of a love-sick maiden, apprentice to a painter and a wool-carder ; and taken captive into Barbary, after performing in a tragedy before the Moorish court, he is ransomed by the Santissima Trinidad, and returns to end his days as a hermit. In and out the shuttlecock of fate bore the picaro, weaving his story in haphazard design, although the warp and woof in the society described was practically uniform.

These artless romances of roguery in Spain, it is especially to be noted, were the work of men who were neither rogues nor yet essentially reformers. In England in the seventeenth and eighteenth centuries, by contrast, the authors *par excellence* of picaresque books were veritable rascals or those desirous of cautioning others against them and bringing the fallen to grace. Thomas Nash in *Jacke Wilton* did compose a story meant merely to amuse; but the great majority were actuated by practical considerations, from Harman, concluding his "bolde Beggar's booke" with the wish that its subjects might "amend their mysdeedes and so live unharmed," to Daniel Defoe, demonstrating to criminals condemned to transportation that repentance might yet bring prosperity overseas. As for rogue autobiographies, written by those who in the clutches of the law had turned penitent and yearned to guide others aright, they were innumerable in England, from the *Life and Death of Gamaliel Ratsey* of 1605 to the *Memoirs of James Hardy Vaux* of 1819. In Spain, however, the romances of roguery were distinctively *libros de entretenimiento;* their end was entertainment, and their creators, standing high in the state, the professions, or literature, simply assumed the rascal's rags for the moment. The Spanish tales, certain therefore to be more literary performances than the English, contemplated reform only indirectly, in so far as satire is always corrective. Yet, from the first, the Spanish picaresque author was fearful of being identified with his anti-hero, and often found himself forced to maintain his own integrity by declaring a moral purpose scarcely shown in his work. Aleman was careful to state that he had written *Guzman de Alfarache* for the common good, and Alfonso de Baros, chamberlain of Philip Third, in his eulogy upon the author, said pointedly that in Aleman's life was to be discovered the antithesis of his book. Espinel announced of his *Marcos de Obregon* that there was not a leaf that had not its particular purpose beyond what superficially appeared. Dr. Carlos García said of his *Desordenada codicia*, in the words of the English version of 1638: "This booke discourseth not so much of the antiquitie of theeves and of their cunning slights, as to teach thee to eschew them." Solórzano, in the preface to the *Garduña de Sevilla*, affirmed that to great princes had been offered works of this sort, acceptable less for what they set forth than for their aim, which must be to improve manners and advise the incautious. Picaresque productions were justified by Quevedo in his remarks prefixed to Tovar y Valderrama's *Don Raimundo el entremetido*, on the ground that vices seen in others cause greater abhorrence than those examined in one's self; and Ben Jonson expressed the same idea in the verses he wrote for Mabbe's English *Guzman*.

Beyond all this display of virtuous intent, the actual development of moral quality in the rogue story could keep pace only with the emergence of the anti-hero. The jest-books and lists of tricks had not touched morality, which can have no existence except with reference to a person; and when, as a matter of fact, that person began to be in evidence as set over against the things he did, the action attributed to him had little in it to arouse the moral sense. In the picaresque novel in Spain moral reflection may be encountered here and there inchoate in the narrative, but nowhere digested and become a part of its very life and tissue. Aleman confessed the moralizing scheme of most others when he admitted, "Nor is it any impropriety, or beyond our present purpose, if in this First Part I shall set before you some

Tracts of Doctrine." After him, readers of the romances of roguery were obliged to take the edifying along with the agreeable, unless a Le Sage would furnish, as he did for this particular work, an edition, "*purgée des moralités superfluës.*" Andrés Pérez, later, in the *Pícara Justina*, not content with so much of the edifying as he could distribute through the text, added profitable remarks at the close of each chapter, and a morally discursive style became the earmark of the picaresque novel. The acme of confusion was achieved by the *Donado hablador;* but as the *Lazarillo de Tormes* had escaped this besetting sin, so the late tales of the class showed an improvement from it, and an early one, the *Buscon*, was commendable for its straightforwardness.

In the romances of roguery, sentiment was impossible except as it might enter into interpolated episodes that were unpicaresque; and the licentious, which in Italy had stamped the *novelle*, left no trace upon these Spanish fictions. They were sometimes broadly coarse as with Quevedo and Pérez in quite the same manner that Eulenspiegel had been smeared with honest filth in Germany, but like him they were never obscene. The seasoning of Gallic salt was added to taste in a *Francion*, but only north of the Pyrenees; and even there it was not a popular condiment for this kind of fiction. The absence of sentiment on the one hand, and of erotic elements on the other, made the picaresque treatment of love and marriage distinctive. What constitutes so important a feature of the modern novel, then, in this, its forerunner, was almost lacking. Of real love there is none. Guzman de Alfarache, passing sleepless nights and dreamy days at Alcalá, believes he has matriculated in the school of Cupid, yet he admits that after all he is the creature of a blind instinct. The true creed for all rogue-affection is given by Justina in a couplet,—

Tanto crece el amor quanto la pecunia crece,
Que hoy dia todo á él se rinde y todo le obedece.

Love bears a direct proportion to wealth, and there are only three reasons, says the picara, for a woman's falling in love. First and foremost is interest; second is the joy of seeing a man her slave; and third is the fact that surrender is the readiest relief from importunity. Ironically, however, matrimony in most cases is shown defeating its own mercenary purpose, leaving the lover worse off in his wedded or widowed state than ever he was before. Guzman cries out, "I married rich, and married I am poor; happy were the days of my nuptials for my friends, and sad those of matrimony for me; they took the good and went to their homes, I was left suffering the evil in mine." This particular wife and her dowry he loses by death, and another, after keeping him in funds by playing her charms on generous admirers, runs off with his goods and a ship-captain; and still he is incorrigible, declaring that whatever wears a petticoat seems to him the goddess Venus. Alonso, however, has no better fortune, for married to a rich midwife with grown sons, she makes him wear her first husband's clothes which have gone out of style, assist her in trade by announcing to pleased parents the sex of their offspring, and when the lady dies, Alonso finds himself as destitute as before, for the sons snatch all of her property. Courtship for the picaro is rarely easy, and Marcos in this respect fares as badly as the rest, since, having arranged to summon a pretty Vizcaina at night with a cat-call, he is mistaken for a real cat and pelted with missiles, and, attempting a second interview, he is set upon by four men, who thrust him into the wheel-pit of a mill. In his devotion to another lady he is tricked and locked in a well-room, and his advances are so altogether unsuccessful that he continues single to the end.

The women are all fond of the window, and inconstant as the moon. Estevanillo's first mistress, when he gives her a room that does not look out upon the street, leaves him in dudgeon; and another, reproached with infidelity, steals all his belongings and departs. Rufina, who is married to an Indies merchant after an eight-days suit, tires of him because of his age, moderation, and economy. She accords her favors to others, among whom is a gallant who gives her a gown he borrows from a neighbor, and then dressed as a servant obliges her to return it to him in her husband's presence.[1] By her charms she defrauds a miser, an alchemist, and a hermit, who make advances

[1] From *Decameron*, 2d story of 8th day, and from a *fabliau*, *Barbazan* and *Meon*, Tom. 4, 181.

to her, and even outwits her faithful accomplice in cheats to marry another rogue. A lady with a reputation not entirely spotless is espoused by Lazarillo during his career in the sea, and on land he is the complacent husband of an ecclesiastic's mistress. The rascal hermit of Luna's Lazarillo continuation is only received in matrimony on agreeing to six articles, to the effect that he will not enter the house when he sees a vase at the window, by that token knowing his bride to be engaged, that he will hide should gentlemen come when he is at home, and that at least twice a week he will bring some friend to regale the whole household with a "*buen gaudeamus.*" The formality of seeing a curate is easily dispensed with, as the essential of marriage consists in the conformity of wills and mutual intent. Nuns seem to be the objects of a futile but common passion. Guzman condemns a friend for such an infatuation, finding him disputing with a nun on which is better in love, hope or possession. The Fortunate Fool overhears himself accused of talking so much that he must needs be a *devoto* of the nuns, and Pablos peers through the choir-grates at church, coughing to attract his love's attention. He waits about sanctuaries hopelessly, and in the convent courtyard he meets others as mad as himself, posing there only to gaze upon a woman through a grill or glass like some holy relic.

The picaro's true province in love, however, is best exhibited in the cheating marriages he plans and perpetrates. Pablos himself is adroit at this game. He pays suit to his landlady's daughter, pretending to be very rich, and counting over and over again the same fifty pieces where the jingle of coin will be certain to be heard by his mistress. He writes tender letters, and in disguise calls upon himself asking for the lord of so-and-so. Again, with the hope of securing a rich wife, he hires a horse and wedding clothes, and is devoted to an heiress, making a point of entering the good graces of her elderly female relatives, speaking of his great income, and declaring he will never marry for wealth. As an investment, he tenders a collation, begged and borrowed, which succeeds well enough until he is recognized. Then in spite of playing a strong game of presumption he is flogged. The Bachiller Trapaza tries similar tactics upon a beautiful heiress. At night he serenades her, but being no musician, hires another to do the singing, and unfortunately is exposed by a rival. At another time he employs a more elaborate trick upon a lady whose picture he has secured. He pretends to be robbed near her residence, is received there, and the picture and forged papers being found upon him, he tells a story of his noble birth and great possessions, and how having fallen in love with this miniature he relinquished all else to the robbers rather than be deprived of it. The deceived lady is about to reward him with her hand when, the fraud being discovered, he is scourged by farmer boys. These beatings are a frequent outcome of love-deceits, as Ceñudo discovers to his cost; for, only a page, he feigns to be a rich gallant with estates abroad, and makes a lady believe herself already queen of the Indies. When the truth dawns upon her, she lures Ceñudo to the Prado, where he is drubbed with wooden pattens for his impudence. Periquin, if he is not so punished, deserves it, for he pays court to the daughter of an apothecary, pretending to be of Mondragon, a town "where all are noble," and the nephew of his Majesty's physician. He writes a commendatory note regarding his own qualifications, but by ill-luck is recognized, and the apothecary, whose dreams are dashed, is as sorry as Periquin himself. The Sabia Flora Malsabidilla is chiefly occupied with attempting a marriage-cheat upon an old lover of hers by whom she had been known as a gypsy; and Teresa de Manzanares, the actress, befools a *perulero* returned from Lima into believing her the daughter of a Castilian hidalgo. Later, as a widow for the third time, she dresses up a slave girl, and passes as her aunt, fleecing two rival gallants who are kept at a respectful distance, although allowed to vie with each other in giving presents to the pretended niece. Cervantes, in the *Casamiento engañoso*, paints an admirable picture of a doubly fraudulent match, for Estefanía, a serving-maid who apes the fine lady, makes love to Lieutenant Campuzano, who appears rich, but whose jewels are imitations. They marry, each rogue deceived in the other, and Estefanía, when she hears that Campuzano knows of her cheat, comes off confidently with the false jewels, and Campuzano tells the whole story as a joke to a friend who dines with him. In the *Guia y avisos de forasteros*, Bonillo, a rogue, cheats a rich countryman and his daughter, declaring he will marry the lady and give her brother charge of his estates. The countryman, overjoyed, settles a dowry of half his fortune on the pair, and going to bed plain Sancho rises Don Sancho. To the daughter the picaro has promised she shall ride in a coach, and when tired of that in a chair of damask, all gold and azure, with two Barbary slaves to bear it. The girl's head is turned, but the rogue being just then arrested on an old score and sent to the galleys, Don Sancho becomes Sancho again, and Doña María, poor Marí-Hernandez. A widower accepts her child as his own, marrying her, but he uses a stick on her shoulders daily because her eyes will still be wandering after every foreign gallant passing through the village. Such is the unsentimental love set forth by the picaresque novel with no little humor, for humor is its necessary qualification. Where seriousness marks the handling, as in many of the inserted episodes in the various fictions, and throughout in the *Soldado Píndaro*, there the anti-hero is no longer to the front nor properly the theme; this treatment of love is simply the most comprehensive example of that of any passion or emotion.

These stories in Spain were studies of manners, not of character, and adventure served with them as a basis not for strong situations of heart and conscience, but rather for observation and description of externals. Almost exclusively, therefore, narrative prevailed, and even where dialogue was perforce the rule, as in the fictions dramatic in form, it did little to elucidate character. The anti-hero, who had all his attention diverted to the world without him, immoral and unfeeling, was barely conscious of himself or of his mission as an anti-hero. Berganza in the *Coloquio de los perros* might remark the difference between the shepherd of the pastorals and the shepherd of reality, who spent the day in shaking off his fleas instead of piping to a shepherdess, but the picaresque novels in Spain had little direct invective against the romances of shepherds and of chivalry. *Don Quixote* alone made an organized attack upon them; but the anti-hero, who was more closely allied to Sancho Panza than he was to the mock hero, Quixote, presented simply the reverse side of life, leaving the reader to draw his own inferences as to the absurdity of anachronistic knights and impossible shepherds. Moreover, Spanish authors of rogue romances were not so unflagging in their devotion to the picaro and realism that they could afford to carp at the heroes of idealism. Christóval Suarez de Figueroa, if he wrote the *Passagero*, had also written the dull and more famous *Constante Amarilis;* Alonso Castillo Solórzano by no means forsook romantic tales of intrigue when he patronized sharpers and vagabonds; Cervantes himself had composed a *Galatea* and was preparing a *Persiles y Sigismunda;* and the *Diversas rimas* of Vicente Espinel had nothing in common with *Romances de germanía*, or with the exploits of Obregon.

In France, however, the anti-hero as such came to full consciousness; for although Barclay, the author of *Euphormio*, fathered also the *Argenis*, and Sorel with his picaresque tales composed as well *Nouvelles choisies* of old erotic and heroic stock, still those who espoused the cause of reality there were consistent for the most part in maintaining its claims. *Don Quixote* had taken the lead, setting an example of direct onslaught that was aptly followed when the new exaggerated fictions, from

L'Astrée down, began to appear. In spite of their generally favorable reception, these heirs to the Greek and Amadis novels encountered powerful opposition, which minced no words, but declared its antagonism specifically in such works as *Le Gascon extravagant*, *Le chevalier hipocondriaque*, or the *Berger extravagant*, whose alternate title was nothing short of *L'anti-roman.* The anti-novel and the anti-hero attained their heyday, then, in France; for in Germany and Holland imitation did no more than take over the French fashion; and in England the emergence of the anti-hero from his deeds went so far that he became worth while for his own sake, without reference to the hero whom first he had arisen to combat. From a review of mere actualities in Spain, the story of the anti-hero led through a phase of self-conscious literary recoil in France to the beginnings of a study of anti-heroic character in England. With the English romances of roguery, accordingly, the interest centres usually in the individual actors, with the French in the formal and literary aspect of the work, while with the Spanish it is focussed upon the society so critically observed.

CHAPTER III

SOCIETY THROUGH THE ROGUE'S EYE

In the social world through which the Spanish picaro forges his way, the army, the law, the Church, and medicine share the professional honors; while students, publicans, robbers, gypsies, and *Moriscos*, hidalgos, and muleteers, barbers, players, and beggars are *dramatis personæ* of stock utility. These characters throng the romances of roguery. They come and go through the old tales with a careless and natural picturesqueness that succeeds in diverting attention from their lack of purpose or direction. The rogue knows them all, masquerades with them all, and they are the life and theme of his story.

The soldiers appear with their rodomontades and their tricks, lawless in youth, poverty-stricken in age, and needy always. Don Pablos meets one on the road, coming disconsolate from court, where for his scars he has gotten nothing but unprofitable litigation and the loss of his last *real*. Pindaro and his friends, hiding in a vineyard by night, are left unmolested by peasants who suppose them to be country-folk fleeing from the friendly foraging of companies on their way to Cartagena. Marcos tells of soldiers who stole a pig against orders, and expecting the censure of the sergeant, were rather forced to share with him heaven's bounty. The troop to which Alonso belongs is indefatigable in thievery, condemning to death any fowls that crow at night. Alonso himself, in climbing up a widow's chimney to pilfer a pudding, is discovered by the owner and smoked down; and his band comes to grief through its tricks and the captain's failure to pay proper respect to an alcalde. The townspeople rise in arms, the captain, bearing a flag of truce, is stoned to death, and the soldiers in retreat, stealing frozen beehives, shake out the powder from their flasks in order to conceal the honey there; but the attack being renewed they are dispersed defenceless, never to reassemble. A boasting soldier, when Guzman is page at the ambassador's, invites himself to dinner and gives the reason for his sitting down to table of his own accord, as, first, the quality of his person and noble lineage meriting all kindness and courtesy; second, his being a soldier, which renders him worthy of the table of any prince; and third, his great necessity. He takes everything as a matter of course, and walks off with a bow but without a word, for the Spaniard, as says the ambassador, is proud and never ashamed.

Estevanillo is the typical picaresque soldier. He joins the French army, and being paid at Villafranca goes over to the Italians. Here he makes profitable enlistment as previously he had done at Málaga, where, receiving his preliminary pay, he pretended to be wounded, took sanctuary in a church, and so escaped duty. In Naples he enlists once more, but is jailed for creating a disturbance in the barracks. And in Lombardy, Bavaria, and the Netherlands he is commissary, cook, or private sutler, travelling with a cart and a pretty wench to attract custom. At the battle of Nordlingen he distinguishes himself, seeking covert in a ditch, cheering on the Swedes and Germans when they are nearest him. When sent for by his master, he professes to be hurt, and then, fearing the advent of a surgeon, goes among the dead and wounded of the enemy, slashing here and there to show his bravery. One he had supposed to be a corpse rising up, Estevanillo in consternation takes to his heels; and after the battle he fights a duel with a comrade to settle which has shown the more valor, the two rascals cutting each other's shadows until falling down from sheer tipsiness. Altogether Estevanillo offers the keenest satire on the soldier in the romances of roguery, although he is so much of a knave in every profession that his commentary on this loses something of its force.

If the soldier gets his due from the picaro, the men of the law are not spared. As might have been expected, attention is chiefly bestowed upon the officers of justice. Immortal pleasantries at the expense of the lawyer are indeed in evidence. Guzman proves ironically that, although lawsuits be damaging, the lawyer is necessary. The soldier at the philosophical academy in the *Siglo Pitagórico* complains of the notary for snatching the profits of quarrels instead of being compensated with the delight of them. Lazarillo, suing his wife for over-intimacy with an archpriest, loses everything to the attorneys who espouse his cause; and Don Diego, come to Madrid on legal business, is advised by a wise old courtier and a *maestro;* 'Know yourself, do not covet the goods of others, and, above all, shun lawsuits.' Yet it is the more practical side of the legal administration that appeals to the rogue. His profession brings him into unending conflict with the criminal judge and his angels, the *escribano* and the alguazil. Not infrequently prison confinement is the outcome; but the picaro revenges by satire and tricks the discomfort he receives at their hands by force. He cannot say enough of his adversaries' bravery, integrity, and discrimination. The absence of these three qualities is made the pledge to fame of the Spanish police. Courage is the butt; for observe those puffing ministers of the law who, when Pablos, by accident, has tumbled on a notary's roof and is to be arrested for what he could not help, come blustering in, treading on their skirts that it may appear they were torn in the conflict; or witness the alguazils, who, interrupting Lazarillo's feast, stand about a frightened victim, crying, "Hold him!" making a show of capture, and each hiding behind the other. The bullying alguazil who confiscates every night a new guitar of Don Gregorio, as he is serenading his lady, is a bold one; but Gregorio gets even by means of a pulley and weight from the top of the house, which lifts the alguazil in mid air, only to drop him from a respectable height, leaving him to vow ever after that he was bewitched.

Palms are stretched forth at all occasions to be crossed with silver, and not only does the rogue himself, when he acts as alguazil, accept bribes from the family of his captive, but his most implacable foe among the officers of justice is thus to be propitiated when it is the rogue's turn to pay the piper. The way to comfort in jail, and the way to liberty itself, finds an open sesame in the prisoner's purse. The Buscon, in durance vile, after having kept out of the dungeon hole for a time by judicious expenditure, is thrust down there in the hope of squeezing more from him. Then he must give a garnish to his fellow-prisoners who are so thin they crawl into the cracks between the boards of their beds, and so famished that they fall upon him. Misery at last induces him to accede to the keeper's extortion, and he issues forth, even gaining the favor of boarding at the jailer's own house; a clerk who has promised to manage his discharge for money, after coming back a hundred times for a little more on this or that score, at last fulfils his word. But Pablos' companions are set in the stocks and whipped, receiving the deserts of poverty.

If Justice has not lost the sense of touch, she is more than proverbially blind, and against this lack of discrimination the satire of the picaresque novels as regards the civil administration is chiefly expended. Under no possible circumstances are the guilty detected or apprehended; the innocent, with the abuse and supreme contempt of their captors, are marched off, but the rogues, when they lodge in prison, most often go thither by error. Marcos de Obregon, taking the air one evening, encounters a friend who accuses him of being old, and as he agrees to run a race to disprove the charge, a young fellow in a doorway is given their cloaks and swords to hold. While they are running, he walks away with his booty, and a woman of the quarter happening to be stabbed at the time, the alert alguazils pursue the racers. In vain is their protest of innocence. Their cloaks and swords are not where they profess to have left them; and three months of prison ensue, where the only diversion is found in humbling a proud *valiente*, by cutting off half of his mustache, as he sleeps. Guzman, who has suffered a theft, when he prosecutes Alejandro for it, in Bologna, is himself confined by justice at the reliable instigation of the thief's father, and more than once he is arrested for robberies in which he had no part. Alonso, who reports to the authorities a murder committed in self-defence by his mistress, is imprisoned for complicity, although he can prove an alibi, and, languishing many days in chains, comes near hanging before anybody remembers him. After a fight over cards at which he is present, all are obliged to flee, knowing, he declares, that when the alguazils arrive nobody will be safe. Rufina and Garay, entering Córdova one night in a coach, get out to succor a dying man just wounded in a duel. At the approach of officers, the coach, with foresight, drives away, but the well-intentioned pair are seized upon as assassins and have no little ado to procure their release. Don Gutierre, entering the same town, has a similar experience, a stock incident, not only of the romances of roguery, but of all Spanish fiction. Gutierre is in even greater risk of his neck than Rufina and her lover, for a *perquisidor* employed to secure evidence against him, having taken the testimony of all the innkeepers from Estremadura to Córdova, finds one willing to perjure himself, whose lies are sufficient to cast suspicion on the truths of all the rest; and Gutierre, having expended large sums in bribes, the circumstance is turned against him by those benefited, although the money is not refunded. Trapaza, too, on the way to Seville with several others innocently falls into the clutches of the law, for the carrier has accepted for conveyance a box to be paid for on delivery. This is discovered to contain a corpse, and all the passengers are locked up except such as can hide in an inn cellar. Torture is resorted to, and Trapaza endures his share, only to receive sentence of banishment for two years, and the poor carter is fined two hundred ducats.

The insolence of the officer and his readiness to clap upon the first person met for his victim is partially balanced, however, by the ease with which he may be outwitted. He is a simple fool, after all, and needs only such devices as blocking up the door of a house with masonry, or disguise in beggar's rags, feigned madness, and assurance of demons pursuing, to throw him off the scent. Justina, with tears, makes an alguazil believe her the inheritress instead of the servant of a rich *Morisca*. Pedro de Urdemalas, having stolen a mule, befools the muleteer and alguazil sent after him, and in the guise of an astrologer informs the officer that the real culprit is the muleteer himself. In Italy, Marcos, having been attacked by peasants and wounding one in self-defence, is consigned to a credulous jailer into whose graces he enters by giving gold-pieces to his children and then pretending to the father to be an alchemist. He is relieved of his chains on the promise of confiding his secrets to the jailer, who furnishes apparatus for experiments, and having lit a brazier and produced a powder, is asked to smell it. The picaro thereupon dashes it into his patron's eyes and nose, strikes him down, and, with two convicts condemned to the galleys, makes his escape. The Gran Tacaño at the university, on a wager, agrees to disarm the guard, a feat readily accomplished by assuring them of the presence of six notorious criminals in a house where they have pistols and will fire if they see any enter with weapons. The officers, accordingly, hide their swords in a field, going in only with daggers, while the anti-hero, giving them the slip, makes off with their arms. Pindaro, who describes jail life vividly, is present at a fiesta, given by prisoners with the permission of the lenient *alcaide*. There is dancing, fencing, a masquerade, and a procession of twenty-four with wooden lances and gay trappings. This imposing train passes into a room opening out of the courtyard, where the chief keeper and his guests await its return. But delay exciting impatience, an investigation reveals the disappearance of all the performers. The wife of one of them had hired the adjoining house a month previous, and the wall, having been tunnelled, the party has marched away, lances and all.[1]

In downright roguery, the officers are rivalled

[1] That this trick had a basis of fact is probable from its occurrence in the *Relación de la cárcel de Sevilla* of Christóval de Chaves, 1585–97, Vol. I., col. 1358, of Gallardo, *Ensayo*.

only by the picaros themselves, and the miser, Marquina, who at the fancied approach of justice buries his treasure in the yard for fear of its being stolen, is wise in his day and generation, though he loses it straightway to sharpers. Lazarillo de Manzanares and his hermit are cheated by no other than a rascal alguazil who bursts in upon the hermit purposely left alone with a girl, and after listening to her false accusations demands reparation, in which both the hermit and his page are forced to join. And Lazarillo de Tormes serves the most astute alguazil in Spain, who, pretending to be seized with a fit for having wrongfully charged an indulgence-seller with fraud, is rewarded with half the profits due to the rise of value in holy wares when their merit has been miraculously attested. Like Pedro Ceñudo, the fortunate fool who becomes chief alcalde, the minister of justice believes that true discretion consists in being pliable and bending with the times. Ceñudo himself with the town is a lion, and with his alguazils a lamb. He goes where he pleases, imprisons the husband of a handsome woman, of whom he is enamored, like Bandello's Judge of Lucca, and, feared by the world, is the pattern for his underlings, aspiring to be as great cheats as he. In the romance of roguery, from the reverend judge to his upstart minion, the motto that serves for all of the profession, and insures their continuance in office is, "Set a thief to catch a thief."

The Church is gingerly handled by the picaro. None of that freedom of attack shown in Italy was evidenced in the Peninsula. Occasional satire there was, as appears in the works of the Archpriest of Hita, but a cautious reserve characterized literature. The restraint exercised by the Inquisition was too powerful to warrant meddling with orthodoxy. Juan de Luna in his continuation of the *Lazarillo* could speak of officers of the Inquisition, whom he had pictured greedy for bribes, as "folk as holy and perfect as the justice they administer;" but Luna was writing from Paris. In Spain, where the Church must extend its privilege to every book that entered the press, Castillo Solórzano could do no more than point the efficiency of the Inquisition as an instrument of private vengeance when he described a rogue getting even with a carter by accusing him before the Inquisition of swearing. The carter is apprehended and with his passengers detained three days and fined, while the virtuous plaintiff receives a reward and goes on his way rejoicing. Yet, if several of the romances of roguery did find a place in the *Index*, many rather daring passages were allowed to remain in subsequent editions, and others were never noticed at all. The satire on the Church, however, was less harsh than lovingly witty. In the main it was not seriously meant; and although it never hesitated to signalize inconsistencies, it does not often venture to suggest reform. The example of the first *Lazarillo*, which was only relieved from the ban put upon it in 1559 by the *castigado* edition of 1573, induced a greater show of respect for things ecclesiastic. At least, none of the other novels has so large a space devoted to the Church as this one, and none is so sharp in satire upon religious institutions unless it be the *Pícara Justina*. Here, however, by a system of morals appended to each chapter, the boldest utterances are given an air of respectability. The reader is advised that all the book contains is subject to the correction of the Roman Church and the Holy Inquisition, and that wherever a bad example occurs in the text, reference is to be made forthwith to the *aprovechamiento* at the end of the section.

Justina in Leon visits the cathedral, where she makes fun of the priests, and of the *cantadores*, who, professing to sing, really dance. Observing the few chairs in the place, she concludes that the prebendaries and the singing girls must go shares on them, and learning that it is required that the performers should be virgins, she marvels that after a season of these holy exercises any are to be found. Of this venturesome chapter the *aprovechamiento* complacently declares, "The evil-intentioned are insects that suck poison from flowers. Thus the holy fiestas profit Justina only in saying malicious impertinences." In such moralizing it is difficult to be convinced that the author was not putting into practice one of those profitable and pleasant hypocrisies which his own heroine had taught him. In her levity at sacred things Justina is indeed incorrigible. On a pilgrimage to the shrine of Nuestra Señora del Camino, she meets a vender chancing off hazel-nuts and calling them indulgences. At first she supposes him to be joking, but presently she learns that it is the custom to call everything connected with a pilgrimage an indulgence. She devises for the Humilladero, an oratory upon the road, a punning etymology, and has an admirer, the son of a washerwoman, who becomes a flagellant in order to win her favor. He is a great bully, supported by his widowed mother, whom he never addresses as anything but "my laundress," and to whom, after dinner each day, he relates a brief history of their greatness. On the fiesta of the Cross, arrayed as a *disciplinante*, he appears before Justina's house, followed by a crowd of boys, beating himself with a whip, and clad in a sheet of Justina's which his mother had taken to wash, thinking that what he was lacking in clothes would be made up in devotion. The picara, however, has cold water poured on him as he passes through her doorway, and the boys do the rest, driving the poor flagellant out of the *pueblo* never to be seen there again.

The priest served by Lazarillo is as much of a miser as Pablos' schoolmaster, and the boy's share of meat is so little he might have put it in his eye instead of his mouth, and been none the worse. At funerals his master eats like a wolf or a mountebank, and as this is the only occasion when Lazarillo himself does not starve, he prays continually that the Lord will take his own. One day, in the priest's absence, he calls in a tinker, who fashions him a key for the chest of sacrament bread, and the reverend father, missing his loaves, is made to believe that rats are the culprits. The chest is reënforced against these pests, but all to no purpose. The neighbors affirm a snake to be the offender, and Lazarillo, sleeping at night with the key in his mouth, and having made with it a low whistling in his breathing, the priest arises, sure that he hears the hiss of a serpent. Blows in the dark awake the boy, who is both rat and snake in one, and he is forced to seek other service. But the Church has a fascination for him. His fourth master is a friar, an enemy to psalm-singing and eager in the pursuit of every secular business and pleasure. From him Lazarillo receives his first pair of shoes, which are worn through in a week, so busy does the gadding friar keep him. Taking leave without asking it, the boy engages next with a *buldero*, a seller of bulls with indulgences attached, the proceeds ostensibly to go for the crusade against the Moors, already long at an end. This fellow is a barefaced rogue, who makes judicious presents to the clergy wherever he goes, and has a fund of deceits to play upon the pious. It is for him that the cheating alguazil feigns a fit, and Lazarillo declares, "If I, being an eye-witness to such an imposition, could almost believe it, how many more amongst this poor, innocent people must be imposed on by these robbers!" After a chaplain has hired Lazarillo as a water-carrier, his most intimate connection with the Church comes through the archpriest of Salvador, who gives the picaro his own maid-servant for wife. Evil tongues may say what they will as to the priest's motives, but Lazarillo accepts the scandal, together with his patron's advice, to think less of honor than of profit. Later, in the 1620 continuation of his adventures, when the anti-hero is being shown off through Spain as a marine curiosity, he has become rather more jealous. Uneasily enough, he overhears two old women commenting on his wife's devotion to the archpriest and its consequences; yet he endeavors to prove his own identity by begging the holy father to remember how one night, saying he was afraid, he came to Lazarillo's bed to lie down — an allusion which operates like a charm, for the priest concludes to recognize the picaro before he shall say anything more. On one occasion, engaged by a Franciscan to carry his luggage to a convent, Lazarillo, asking for his pay on reaching his destination, has the door shut in his face, and the last words he hears are, "Let it be for the love of God." Gypsies tell him that they are chiefly churchmen fallen from grace and come to lead a freer life; and a hermit's mistress confesses that her daughters can claim three fathers, who, according to the best conjectures, are a monk, an abbot, and a curate. She has always been enamored of the Church. She is nicknamed the ecclesiastical widow; and her daughters inherit her partiality for gentlemen of the cloth, whose recommendation lies in their being secretive, rich, and patient.

Guzman de Alfarache is gentler with the fishers of men than Lazarillo or Justina. At one time he hears a sermon which almost persuades him to turn friar, but having for several days frequented a monastery, toiling over grammar and Greek, he changes his mind. On the road he engages with a serious and honest priest who treats him well; and in the Cardinal's service at Rome he is honored and has nothing but praise for his master, although he tricks a chamberlain there by having a fellow in woman's clothes rush out of a closet at an inopportune moment. But Guzman's mother had been the mistress to an ecclesiastic who was outwitted with the lady's connivance by Guzman's father to be. Barbadillo's Elena telling her story says that her virgin favors through her mother's skill were bestowed not once, but three several times, and first upon a rich ecclesiastic, next upon a noble, and finally upon a Genoese who paid more and received less. Indeed, it is the charge of immorality which the romances of roguery bring against the clergy that constitutes the chief attack upon them. Even so, there is expressed less condemnation than merriment at their expense, and it is certain that deviations from the vow of chastity were looked upon with every indulgence.

Of other sins, avarice or lack of reverence are the worst. Alonso enters the service of a profane sacristan who makes no obeisance when he sets the church to rights. Alonso reproves him and some gossips who resort there to talk, but the sacristan dismisses his pious adviser. Afterwards in serving the nuns, Alonso's business is to dress the altars, and silence the whisperers at mass. With the picaro's curiosity he bores holes through the wall of his cell and hears the confessions of the nuns, duly impressed with their goodness. Periquin, engaged by a curate, through much drinking falls into a stupor and is thought to be dead. Reviving, he appears by night to his virtuous master, who thinks him a ghost come to rebuke him for withholding a bequest, and falls on his knees for pardon. Only Marcos so much as mentions the Reformation. Rainbound in an inn at Turin, he enters into dispute with a citizen of Geneva regarding the heretics, assailing roundly Martin Lutero and Juan Calvino. Blows being threatened, the hostess interposes, averting a quarrel; and later, when Marcos meets a party of Genevans in a coach, he has learned to continue friends with them by refusing to discuss Reformed tenets. Nothing more definite than these references would have been permitted by the Inquisition, which could afford to ignore pleasantries upon purity of ecclesiastical life, but never the shadow of heresy. For in Spain doctrine was all in all, and morality an incident, wherefore in part occurred the rejection there of Protestantism with its professed aim of reviving the simple moral asceticism of the primitive Christians.

Religion had too strong a hold upon the people, however, not to offer to the picaro a convenient handle for prosecuting his schemes. Religious cheats were certain to be profitable, from the mild hypocrisy of the lady whom Periquillo rebukes for cutting the finger-nails of the poor, already worn to the quick by hard work, to the systematic frauds of Montufar or of Molino. The latter, in Cortés de Tolosa's *La comadre*, is a lackey left behind by his master during an absence in the Indies. Molino with another rogue comes to Jaen, where they don ecclesiastic garb, pale their wine-red faces with an herb, and go about attending the sick and prisoners, asking alms, and reaping a rich harvest. The holy brothers, with feigned humility, calling themselves Peter the Sinner and John the Miserable, then perpetrate a cheat upon the lady betrothed to Molino's master and upon her mother, both of whom they seduce, rob, and desert. In Salas Barbadillo's *Hyia de Celestina*, Montufar, Mendez, and the heroine Elena are still more adroit in mock sanctity. They travel in the guise of pilgrims; and when in the midst of an admiring crowd in Seville, Montufar receives a blow in derision and the epithet "hypocrite," the enraged populace fall upon the assailant; but by a master move Montufar rescues this scoffer, publicly forgives him, procures him new garments and a sword, and sends him out of the city a believer; and the citizens remain more than ever impressed with the divinity of their saint. Montufar's humility exceeds all bounds. He names himself "Little ass, the little beast, the useless one." But of the alms for the poor which he receives, one-third is turned into gold and secreted, and when flight to Madrid becomes necessary, the saint with his gold departs at a moment's warning. Trapaza at the capital assumes the title of a Portuguese noble, puts on the habit of Christus, and wearing the great iron-bowed spectacles then in vogue, goes about without fear of detection. And in the *Guia y avisos de forasteros*, a rogue imposes upon a wealthy countryman by professing to be the canon of a cathedral, who on a voyage had lost his effects, which were thrown overboard to lighten the vessel when Moorish galleys pursued.

But the class of devotees most railed at for hypocrisy are the hermits. They were common enough in Spain in the seventeenth century, and if some went into seclusion as a result of disenchantment with the world, many were not so disenchanted that they ever lost sight of the main chance; and most chose the profession only as a cloak to roguery. Here and there a beneficent anchorite does appear. Marcos de Obregon relates the story of his life to one in an oratory on the Segovia Bridge during a storm that confines them there. The only fault this hermit exhibits is a tendency to fall nodding, with which, considering the length and discursiveness of Marcos' narrative, the reader may sympathize. Guzman, Micer Morcon, and a party of rogues listen respectfully to a sermon from an honest hermit without profiting by his advice. Alonso at the end of his career becomes a sincere recluse, and from that point of view relates the second half of his tale. In Loubayssin de la Marca's *Historia tragicómica de Don Henrique de Castro*, the hero, when his forces are defeated in Chili, seeks refuge with an anchorite who tells his own story after those of his guests have been heard; and Teresa de Manzanares, robbed in the Sierra Morena, is hospitably received by a hermit whose solitude is the result of a love disappointment. But the conventional hermit of the romances of roguery is as much a picaro as the anti-hero himself. Such an one Pablos and a soldier overtake riding on an ass. He gravely reproves the soldier's swearing, and crossing a pass together, they come to an inn at night. Waiting for supper, a bout at cards is suggested. The hermit professes to know nothing of the game, but in a trice both his adversaries have not enough left to pay the reckoning. Pedro de Urdemalas in Granada refuses an alms to a hypocrite hermit held to be a saint by the people, but Pedro is beaten by the angered anchorite, to whom, in sheer self-defence, he is obliged to be reconciled. To the picaro's relief, this Brother Llorente finally departs on a pilgrimage, really eloping with a girl; and he is next heard of scouring Italy in a troop of soldiers. Lazarillo de Manzanares is taken into service by a *santero*, with whom he leads a merry life, his business consisting in gathering from the rich more than they give.

Lazarillo de Tormes, in the third account of his life, meets at a church door a hermit who dilates upon the joys and satisfactions of his trade. At the hermitage the two dine together, but the proprietor is seized with a sudden and fatal illness. Lazarillo, fearful of being accounted his murderer if no witnesses are at hand, hunts out some shepherds; but when they arrive all the hermit can say is "Yes." So Lazarillo, who never neglects an opportunity, asking if he be not the sick man's heir, the poor fellow can only give assent to this and all other queries, while a shepherd takes down the testimony with charcoal on the wall. The hermit is interred, and Lazarillo after a search finds his money beneath the altar in a pot. Crowds come to visit the dead saint's grave, every appearance pointing to his canonization within six months, and Lazarillo, who has accepted the hermit's mantle with good grace, secures from these pilgrims enough to live sumptuously. But going through the city and begging at the doors for diversion, at one he is drawn in, being mistaken for the original Padre Anselmo, and he finds himself confronted by a family that proves to be no other than the wife and children of the sainted dead. They weep on learning of their lord's demise, but when they hear he has left them nothing, tears turn to blasphemy. Lazarillo, however, thinks to assure possession of the money he has gained by proposing marriage to the daughter of the household. But he is sadly out of count with his host; for his new friends fetch everything from the hermitage, and despite his protestations search for the treasure, discovering where he had removed the earth beneath the altar, and finally the holy pot itself. The next morning when he goes to be married according to arrangement, he is tricked, tied down to the bed, and hot and cold water is poured over him until, having suffered much, and lost all, he is content to escape with his life from the pious hermit's pious offspring.

But Crispin, the anchorite of the *Garduña de Sevilla*, is the arch-rogue among hermits. Rufina and Garay, overhearing robbers speaking of him as their receiver, determine to outwit him. At night Rufina lets herself be bound to a tree and sets up a great outcry, Garay galloping away as though afraid. The hermit releases Rufina, who with all the picara's arts makes him believe she was about to be slain by a jealous brother, and so wins his favor that he consents to hide her in his cell. The next morning, during the absence of Crispin on a begging tour, Garay leaves a sleeping-potion to be administered to the hypocrite on his return, and then the two depart with his plunder, informing on him and his clients by an anonymous letter. Crispin is arrested, and the robbers are hanged, but the hermit, falling ill, justice in his case is long enough delayed for him to escape from jail in woman's clothes. Digging up a bag of doubloons he had hid in view of disaster, he takes a servant, Jaime, with whom he proceeds to Toledo. Garay and Rufina are already there, and he proposes to get even with them by introducing Jaime into their house as a fugitive from justice and enacting the alguazil himself. But Rufina and Jaime become enamored, and during the absence of Garay, Jaime secures large sums from the hermit, robbing him of what he cannot beg of him, after which the two flee from Toledo, informing on the unhappy Crispin. The hermit is captured and hanged; yet like a good Christian he forgives his accusers on the scaffold.

Although, in comparison with Massuccio and the Italian novelists, the picaresque romancers were considerate of religion and religious institutions, these instances of satire gleaned from their works comprise the most daring attacks upon the faith to be found in Spanish fiction, and perhaps in Spanish literature. And yet it must be manifest that the faith itself was less the object of attack than the abuses to which it might be put. There was indeed a spirit of Protestantism through these romances of roguery which has led to the suggestion that the authorship of their first exemplar should be attributed to some one of the coterie gathered about the brothers Valdés, but as Protestantism itself in Spain never got beyond the stage of inquiry and occasional adverse criticism, so its expression there was negative, not positive. All the leaders upheld the Church, however they might disapprove specific methods. From Lope, who countenanced with his official presence the burning of at least one heretic, and Góngora, who lamented at an *auto* that no more than one was burned, to Cervantes and Quevedo supporting the expulsion of the *Moriscos*, although aware of the ruin that must ensue, there was no wavering of loyalty. The demand for union against Mohammedan arms and dogma had kept the Church intact. And those who might have scoffed would not permit themselves to doubt. Only the rogue who doubted all save things of sense, and scoffed at all where laughter could result, coddled no scruples. With the candor of impudence, he declared his mind, but the restraint of habit from within, and the restraint of the Inquisition from without, tempered his dealing with religion.

If peculiar conditions in the Peninsula were concerned in the treatment of the clergy in national letters, the physician of Spain offered no vantage point for ridicule that his brethren elsewhere could not present. The sign of his trade here was the ass, astride of which the Castilian *médico* still ambles through the romances of roguery as in life he was wont to swing down the sunny streets of Seville or Toledo; but pedantry, ignorance, and consummate play upon his patients' credulity were traits that marked him in Spain as in France.[1] Sorel, Molière, or Cyrano de Bergerac were to give him harder raps than any he should get farther south, but the theory on which this assault was excused was always the same. The physician seized folk at a disadvantage. In their weakness he persuaded them to outlandish courses of regimen or medication, contrived with no view to effecting a cure, but rather to prolong the malady. If recovery came, the sufferer praised him; if death, none could blame. God's will had been done, and the defunct at least might not rise up to deny the alleviation of his pains. Opposed to this destructive theory of the physician's functions was a constructive theory for nature's. Let alone, nature would accomplish more, it was

[1] See Maurice Raynaud, *Les médecins au temps de Molière*; and the *Journal de la santé du roy*, edited by M. J. A. Le Roy, Paris, 1862.

argued, than all the doctors of the faculty, for nature was the reservoir of vitality from which the rogue physician would shut the patient off. Considering the state of medical knowledge at the time when the ridiculous *Medicina española contenida en proverbios vulgares de nuestra lengua*, written by Dr. Juan Sorapan de Rieros in 1616, is vouched for as having served at the Academy of Medecine in Granada as a text-book, and when copious bleedings were resorted to on every pretext, and water either interdicted altogether or forced upon the unhappy victim in floods, it is not to be wondered at if longevity did prefer the children of nature to those of a barbarous science. At all events, the picaro believed with Louis Fourteenth, who, on being asked to forbid the representation of Molière's *L'amour médecin*, made reply, "*Les médecins font assez souvent pleurer pour qu'ils fassent rire quelquefois.*"

In Zavaleta's *Conde de Matisio*, the anti-hero's father is hastened off like the man who ordered his epitaph to be *los muchos médicos me mataron.* Guzman has a poor opinion of the faculty. He tells of a patient getting well in the course of nature who went to mass against orders, and being met there and reproved by his physician, paid him a fee to discontinue his advice; and when Guzman's hostess is ill he doctors her himself. His verdict on the honesty of the faculty is given masquerading as a beggar in Rome, where with a painted ulcer on his leg he sits by a church door until he attracts a cardinal's attention. The benevolent cardinal arranges for the picaro to be cured at his own expense, and Guzman, brought before the best physicians of the city, is fearful lest his sore fail to withstand the tests of professional scrutiny. He confesses his cheat; the doctors listen gravely, and compact with him to share the cardinal's bounty. Thus the painted and profitable ulcer is cured by degrees to the mutual satisfaction of the artist and the healers. As a physician, Marcos de Obregon is proclaimed aloud to be a fraud, and when a patient asks why he makes no retort, Marcos is content with explaining that as the remark was not addressed to him he has nothing to say. The same rogue serves Doctor Sagredo whose books are fencing swords, and whose wife is no more devoted than is that of the physician with whom Trapaza engages. When the doctor wishes to bleed the lady, Marcos takes him to task for his expedients and his technical circumlocutions, recommending instead methods of cure based on common-sense. At Salamanca, Marcos falls ill, and a physician forbids his drinking any water, but orders a bath to reduce the fever. After the bath, Marcos in delirium drinks the water, and then on its disagreeing with him returns it involuntarily to the basin. The next day he is well, and the doctor, seeing the water apparently as he had left it, begins to extol his treatment. Informed of what had happened, he only crosses himself and departs, mumbling, *rectum ab errore.* Less successful in error is Estevanillo; for, serving as surgeon at the hospital in Naples, he gives a draught of water to one to whom it had been forbidden and sends the patient grateful to his grave. From beneath a dying student's pillow he filches a purse, and becoming a charlatan, vends useless concoctions at outrageous prices to make them esteemed. With four Jews he plays the itinerant dentist, three of his assistants pretending to have the toothache and purchasing his lotions, while the fourth lets himself seem to be operated upon. The rabble is deceived, and trade thrives, until as a joke Estevanillo draws not only a tooth, but part of the jaw of his astonished accomplice; and when the latter and his three comrades clamor thereat, the rogue denounces them to his audience as heretics, and they are driven off without hope of reparation. For a carnival the buffoon prepares a satire on the faculty, with a cart upon which is placed an ass in bed. Officials with cupping-tools and syringes, the rogue himself in robes, a weeping wife for the ass, and violinists to soothe his last moments, complete the outfit, which is drawn about town in triumph, the ass dancing on the bed from the pain of the flax burned on him when he is cupped, but breaking loose finally to create havoc among his attendants.

Yet nothing could shake the faith of the common people in the physician, and the rogue was not slow to avail himself of such confidence. When Sancha Gómez, a fat, enormous creature with a well-provided larder, falls ill, Justina becomes as loving to her as a monastery cat, and arranges with a foolish barber to play physician. He feels Sancha's pulse, examines her tongue, talks gibberish, and after deliberation prescribes a poultice of pork, the patient's body to be rubbed with new bread, and subjected to applications of eggs and honey. Poor Sancha is delighted at the coincidence of having all these things in the house, and gives up the storeroom key unsuspectingly. But when she is poulticed and covered over head and ears with blankets, the false physician and Justina sup sumptuously, helping themselves to all the place affords; and this barber is not more lacking in knowledge than most of the faculty. Teresa as an actress feigns illness in order to be revenged on her manager, and physicians who are called in, being shown wine for water, pronounce gravely upon her case. Lazarillo de Manzanares tells of a similar trick, and Ceñudo perpetrates it, the physicians prognosticating such dreadful things he might almost believe them, but for realizing that it was they who were weak and not he. There is scarcely a rogue without something to say or to do at the physician's expense, not excepting those who, like Gregorio Guadaña, have a medical ancestry. The mother of this anti-hero brings people into the world, while his father takes them out of it, the one a physician, the other a midwife; his relatives on both sides are apothecaries, surgeons, dentists, and barbers; yet he cannot spare the profession. The only picaro to do so, indeed, is the Donado Hablador, loud in his praise of disciples of Esculapius. He cannot say enough of the fatigues of the physician's life and its small recompense. He complains of such as demand that the doctor shall predict the hour and moment of his patient's demise, and tells of one called to a village to minister to a dying man, who all the way there was abused by the messenger regarding his pay, and arrived only to be accused by the widow of having killed her husband. In short, declares Alonso, the physician is successively an angel, a man, and a demon, as the patient is sick, convalescent, and recovers. This eulogy, as the single exception, not only in the Spanish romances of roguery, but in the French or German as well, might merit more comment were it not that its author, Gerónimo de Alcalá, was himself a physician, the writer of medical works, and for twenty-six years a practitioner, he tells us, before the publication of his novel.

The students of the romances of roguery are a motley crew. Little study and much carousing is their portion, although some meet hardship in lieu of good cheer. Marcos at Salamanca, cold and hungry, hunts for fuel, and with his companions can find only the leg bone of a mule, which will not burn. When the students fail to salute the *corregidor* they are taken up for lack of respect, and toils and fatigues await them from morning to night, until the hero rejoices at being withdrawn on receiving a legacy. Rios, in the *Viage entretenido*, on the way to Madrid to visit his mistress, meets a starved student who greedily eats up all his private provision, swearing by the Delphic Apollo, and boasting of amours with the very lady Rios is going to see. Alonso at Salamanca, though he does not starve, has no easy time of it. Having run away and joined a party of students, on arriving with them at the colleges, he is surrounded as a novice, spit upon, asked how his mother and brothers do, and if he cried at leaving them, or has brought with him any goodies. At this he can only marvel, but learning it to be the custom, he cleans his clothes and says nothing. His friends ere long spend their all in dissipation and are forced to seek other employment, as a last resort entering the Church, where they get a good living, while Alonso joins a company of infantry for Italy to find a bad one. Not dissimilar to the Donado's experiences at Salamanca are those of Pablos at Alcalá. At his advent he is cornered in a courtyard, buffeted, and spit upon, and the very fellow who, pretending sympathy, persuades him to uncover his face, uses him worst. Escaping, he dashes home and crawls into bed, only to be scolded by his young master, Don Diego, and to be told he must take better care of himself for the future. That night in the dark he is flogged and shamefully abused, and when in the morning he finds it expedient to pretend illness, the students drag him forth from the bed, bind him with cords, and pull his middle finger until it is out of joint as a remedy for his feigned fit. Then he breathes grim counsel : "Look to yourself, Paul ; stand on your guard !" and resolving to begin a new course of life and be a knave among knaves, he becomes fast friends with his tormentors. There is no roguery after that in which he is not concerned. Capturing pigs that stray into the *patio* and roasting them with straw from stolen beds, he excuses himself on the plea of hunger, and because the animals appeared so much at home there he thought them his own. He outwits the cheating old housekeeper, steals from the shopmen, and when sought for to be punished for his pranks by the governor and vice-chancellor, he seems to be dying, his companions praying by his side, tapers burning at his head and feet, and an extempore priest administering unction.

In boyhood, too, at school, Pablos is always in scrapes. A councillor, Poncio Aguirre, he calls after as Poncio Pilato, and is spared only on the schoolmaster's promise to the offended councillor that he shall never call Poncio Pilato again. So the next day, in the creed, when the sentence, "And he suffered under Pontius Pilate," is to be repeated, Pablos says it, "and he suffered under Pontius Aguirre," to the diversion of the schoolmaster and the boys. At twelfthtide he is elected by the scholars as their king, and mounted on a blind jade that in hunger gobbles a cabbage in the plaza, a fight with market-women is precipitated; the king lands in a kennel, and his retinue is dispersed amid a volley of vegetables. Sent to boarding-school at Segovia to attend on Don Diego, Pablos finds a house of famine, and in the master, Cabra, "a skeleton, a shotten herring, a slender cane with a little head on it."[1] When one stray turnip is brought in at meals, Cabra cheerily bids his charges eat, but exercise lest it disagree with them; and at night scraps of roast goat, and broth so clear that ten fathoms of it must have been transparent, are served, with rules for avoiding indigestion. Sometimes Pablos must question Diego if already, having been killed in the battle with the market-women, they be not dead and in Purgatory. In declining nouns they eat half their words from hunger. Pretended illness brings only fresh griefs, for Cabra's aunt administers horrible potions as restoratives. Presently she comes to rule the kitchen to their chagrin, and in her blindness drops her beads in the dinner-pot to be mistaken for Ethiopian peas. At last a student dies from hard usage, the physician declaring

[1] A letter from Adan de la Parra to Quevedo in 1639 (cited in note to p. 489, Vol. XXIII., *Bibl. de aut. españoles*), establishes the real existence of the miserly master, one Don Antonio Cabreriza.

that for once famine had forestalled him in his trade, and Pablos and Diego are brought away. They must be gently handled, the dust wiped from their mouths with fox-tails, and no one allowed to speak aloud lest their empty stomachs return a painful echo. Burlesque as is this treatment, it is parent to a whole family of school scenes in modern fiction, not the least among which are those in *Oliver Twist* or *Nicholas Nickleby*, where the caricature has not yet been entirely abandoned.

In imitation of scenes in mediæval jest books, here and there the student is presented standing before the doctors unabashed, responding to enigmatical queries with easy assurance. The Fortunate Fool is taken to Salamanca, where the servants of some gentlemen students conduct his mock examination. Arrayed in their robes, they propound to the poor page a series of questions to test his mettle. What is the most discreet folly? they ask him. Love, he replies. How may a fool cease being foolish? By knowing that he is so. Why are there so many fools in the world? Because nobody believes himself one. And urged to give his critical belief, he exclaims, "The precepts of poetry are like the precepts of the law of God, which all know but few keep." Lazarillo de Tormes, after his fantastic adventures in the sea, comes to Salamanca desirous of setting up as a professor of the mackerel language. The rector of the university and the doctors ask how many hogsheads of water there are in the ocean, and he answers that he will quickly compute it, if they will first get it all together. They ask how many days there have been in the world since the creation of Adam, as if, says Lazarillo, I had been in it always myself, pendulum in hand; yet he responds only seven, since those are the days of the week which after the first one were repeated again and again. But where students have not crude wit, they rely upon open roguery; and well might William Lithgow, who travelled in Spain in 1620, refer to Salamanca as "the sacerdotall University of Spaine whence springeth these Flockes of Studientes, that over-swarme the whole land with rogueries, robberies and beging."[1] Trapaza on the road to that very uni-

[1] *The totall Discourse of the rare Adventures and painefull Peregrinations of long nineteene Yeares Trauayles*, London, 1632.

versity more than pays his way by gaming. With the surplus he fits himself out in gay attire, assumes spectacles, and changing his name, cuts a dash as the son of a wealthy noble of the Grand Canary. He affects the society of rich Mexicans, is always at cards, and fleeces Genoese of large sums in gold and jewels. He learns too that other students may be successful if less elegant thieves, for one night a party in masks, having sung and danced before his bed, loot the house. Trapaza can only complain to the authorities, but he dare not state his actual loss for fear of exposing himself. Later, when he has left the university, sleeping at Jaen, he is robbed by a student and a muleteer, and awakes so destitute that he has to enter service to recruit. Guzman at Alcalá finds only rogues for his comrades. At eight in the morning they go to chapel at San Ildefonso, attendance being required, but they simply enter one door to pass out at another, and at night they are merry in their cups. During the more than seven years that Guzman is in Alcalá for arts and theology, although sometimes he goes to the schools, he understands nothing that is said or done in them, and is chiefly impressed by the scant fare to be had; yet, in a rash moment, he marries his landlady's daughter. Rogue students in the *Dia y noche de Madrid* run off from a wine-shop without paying their reckoning, and the proprietor hearing his maid upbraiding them, mistakes some inoffensive customers for the culprits, and rushes out sword in hand. A chestnut vender's stand is overturned in the fray, the wine-merchant is arrested, but the students as usual go free.

Justina, however, shows the rollicking student crew at its best. For on her first wandering expedition to the fiesta at Arenillas a band of students toward night encounters the picara. Disguised as canons and archdeacons and with their chief as bishop, they clamber upon a cart and begin to dance, while one sings a *romance* with the refrain:—

Yo soy palma de danzantes,
Y hoy me llevan los estudiantes.

Then Justina is seized, and in the singer's robes made to chant the same ditty so that she is readily carried off in the cart, her cries for help being mistaken for the refrain of the song. Lamenting, Justina can only compare herself to all the characters in history who have been ravished; but left alone with the bishop, she preserves her virtue by strategy, demanding a public feast and her installation as queen of the company. The bishop acquiesces, and commands his students to scour the country for provisions. They return so laden down that Justina wonders that they have left the dead in their graves, and a wild carouse follows. When they are all drunk in the cart, Justina lays the driver low with a blow of the whip and guides the mules home to Mansilla. There in the plaza she cries out for the alguazils and drubs the awakened students, who dash away half clad through the grain, looking, as the heroine expresses it, like Samson's foxes with their tails afire. The bishop is deposed from office as disgraced, and Justina is held to be more chaste than Lucrece and braver than Semiramis. After this the picara can never overcome her enmity to students; she rails at them all, though few dare address her on account of her fame; and one whose love for her has conquered his fear, she tricks by sending him to an inn, where she had not paid her bill, to look for a box of honey which does not exist.

The innkeepers of the romances of roguery are both publicans and sinners. Whatever pretence they make of serving their customers is mere pretence and nothing more. The food is bad, the hostelries are filthy, and the landlords not only dishonest, but frequently in collusion with road-knights. If by any chance an innkeeper prove honest, the satire is emphasized by his ill-success. Guzman at his second marriage has such a father-in-law, one who does not permit his servants to steal barley from the beasts or moderate the meals of the guests. But for these unusual virtues Guzman has to suffer, since the innkeeper goes into bankruptcy and his family is turned out of doors. Pindaro, the Soldier, tells of the honest son of a dishonest father, both innkeepers. The latter, by dint of false measures and baptizing the wine, had left the former an inheritance; but the son, in order to repair his father's faults, used measures that were larger instead of smaller than the standard, and gave overweight. Happily he was saved from ruin by a stranger who, dying at the inn, willed him a fortune. But the usual recommendation to inn service is a penchant for roguery. Periquin secures a place because the hostess remarks that he has the figure of a great thief. Teresa, through her personal attractions and her discretion, is kept at a caravansary to draw custom. Even Guzman, who is none too good, and who on that account has gained the readier acceptance as a tavern-boy, cries out against the "robbery, tyranny, and shameful deeds of inns where there is fear neither of God nor of His ministers of justice." On the very first day of his wanderings he meets an amorous old hag who gives him eggs that are half chickens, and crockery and linen in deepest mourning, so that having got away from the miserable place, he falls ill at the thought of it. At Cantillana he has his best-known adventures of this character, where a rogue of a landlord passes off mule on his guests as new-dressed veal, and discourses meanwhile of his own honesty. That night Guzman is half devoured by fleas, and in the morning his cloak disappears with the landlord's connivance. In his search for it the picaro by accident discovers the hide and hoofs of the mule, and a sharp quarrel brings the host to confessing his guilt in this and other matters, even to his villanies on the highway. Indeed, the information given by the landlord to footpads and the part he takes with them in robbing-adventures are included in his common functions. Don Gregorio and his friends in the Sierra Morena are so served by a landlord; for when all are sleeping, thirty *bandoleros* by his advice appear, and relieve the company of their valuables and most of their garments. In the Guadarrama a surly innkeeper who has refused Pindaro anything, even for money, further up the pass attacks him, but is wounded and sent to the galleys.

Where such open violence is not employed, ruses are tried; and Alonso on the way to Seville has a narrow escape in a little *venta* from the landlord's daughter. She proposes that he espouse her, and on his demurring, she raises a cry at which seven men pounce upon him. The parents pretend he has been there often before, showing the lady marked attention; and Alonso, realizing that he is trapped, can only appear to accede to their demands. Preparations for the wedding festivities are made, but, when momentarily unguarded, the bridegroom-elect takes to his heels and succeeds in regaining liberty. At Madrid, Lazarillo de Manzanares and his master have a similar experience with a landlady and her daughter, but release is secured for a financial consideration. Sometimes the innkeeper is discovered robbing his guests, and outwitted when he thinks himself safest. Marcos, at Ventas Nuevas, hiding in a tavern stable, finds the host and his wife entering at night to open a trap-door into a cabinet, where some guests on the other side of the wall have locked their treasure. The innkeeper, mistaking Marcos in the dusk for his wife, hands him the booty, with which the picaro is not long in departing. The wife of Rodrigo — a rogue innkeeper of the *Engaños deste siglo* — makes her thief-of-a-lord believe that her gallant's mantle is one she has stolen from a guest, and so escapes suspicion. The general counsel for the innkeeper is best arrayed by Diego Diez, Justina's father, an astute member of the trade. He advises that the barley be kept at a distance, where its purchaser may not see it mixed, and that a hand properly applied in measuring will be worth half a peck. If the beasts be good, he says, they will eat anything, and if bad, they do not deserve even the worst. When a guest asks what there is for food, he is not to be told what already the house affords, but a pretence of fetching it is to be made, that the favor may appear the greater. More graces than words are to be bestowed upon the traveller, and all demonstrations should take place before meals, as then he will exchange anything for his hunger. On a feint of feeding the poor, the leavings are to be given to the landlord disguised as a beggar. Everybody is to be honored, but especially things that cannot speak for themselves. Thus a dead cat is to be called a hare, a cock a capon, and a jay a pigeon. The fruits must be affirmed to come from afar, which will add to their flavor. When a guest requests wine, she who serves him is to ask in a loud voice how much, for pride will then cause him to order more than he otherwise would; and a pretty girl, well kempt, is to stand at the door as a signboard, especially toward evening. Despite his wisdom, the author of these rules comes to an untimely end. In a dispute with a *caballero* over the mixing of grain, he is felled by a blow from a half-peck measure and dies outright, having the sense not to waste a caraway seed in illness. As much of a rogue too, and more varied in past experience, is mine host of *El passagero*, of whom one of the characters exclaims: "Wonderful ups and downs has this man known thus far in his life,—farmer, soldier, priest, go-between, ruffian, and publican; and the last dignity to which infallibly he must attain is either the galleys or the gallows." But the innkeeper never troubles himself with forecasting, and most, like this one, might declare that in the publican's trade is to be enjoyed more liberty than in Geneva itself.

From the innkeeper of the Guadarrama or the Sierra Morena, robbing, or in league with brigands, it is an easy step to the *bandoleros* themselves, who figure through the romances of roguery as the picaro's enemies rather than as his friends. They are never as interesting as the rogues, for with them the place of wit is supplied by force. Sheer bravado carries off the day, and ingenuity is at a discount: nor are they essentially Spanish types. Celestina, Elena's mother, loses her life at the hands of bandits when on a journey. Teresa is set upon in the Sierra Morena and becomes the bone of contention among her robber captors. As they are fighting over her, she escapes, and later brings them all to justice. So, too, the outlaws with whom Periquillo robs in the mountains are taken when disputing concerning a fair captive. They are not villains for the joy of it, however, as the picaros are rogues, but have retired to wreak vengeance upon an unkind world. Sometimes the picaro becomes their unwilling agent, like Lazarillo de Manzanares, who is seized and forced to enter a house ransacked by robbers, serving for their scapegoat, or like Juan in the *Passagero*, who is used as a tool by grave-robbers to hand up jewels from a tomb where presently he is left immured. Rufina and Garay in a wood overhear robbers planning an expedition, and one of them, a young man of good family who has left his studies to follow this profession, that night relates a story to pass the time. But Rufina, although she is entertained, does not scruple to get him and his fellows executed. There is small love lost between rogues and robbers always, although Marcos tells of a student returning from Salamanca with empty pockets who was encountered by brigands as he went singing on his way. They took him to their den, and were for killing him lest he inform upon them; but one set him free, whom long after he was able to save in return by securing a commutation of his sentence from death to the galleys. Marcos himself, however, is held up by bold *vaqueros* near Ronda, and with Doctor Sagredo only escapes at their flight before troops.

More picturesque, but performing a similar office of plot complication, the gypsies of the romances of roguery are all cheats and importunate beggars; and their life as mirrored by these novels hardly differs from that of to-day. Occasionally, however, assemblies of rogues seem to have been mistaken for the genuine gypsy. Lazarillo comes upon such a band by whom he is well received, and among whom he finds an attractive girl who describes her early career. She was first preferred by a priest, then fallen in love with by the jailer set to guard her, and finally, an alguazil was also her slave, whom she befooled by arranging a quarrel in which blood from a bladder gave the appearance of real slaughter. When Lazarillo asks if all her companions were indeed born in Egypt, the prompt rejoinder is, "not one; they are friars, clerks, nuns, or thieves escaped from solitude, convents, or prisons, and the worst among them are the friars, who have exchanged a contemplative for an active life." But no mere renegades are the gypsies overtaken by Marcos in the Sierra de Ronda, half-clad and wicked-looking, some afoot and some on limping mules. True *gitanos* of the tribe, they begin by asking alms, and end by demanding them. Marcos dispenses wine and bread and finally money through fear, but at a narrow pass with a mountain above and a precipice below, where he trembles lest they push him off the trail, one seizes his mule. The picaro, never failing in wit, is equal to the emergency. He professes to have left a comrade behind, whose steed has failed from being overladen with treasure. At this, the gypsies cannot too quickly turn about, and Marcos is relinquished in the confusion. The same mule he so nearly loses here was earlier stolen by a gypsy whom the hero found offering it for sale. An hidalgo, intrusted with the matter, pretended he would buy it, but must first test its qualities. He took it home; but the fumes of the wine it had been given to induce docility being dissipated, the animal returned to its former maliciousness, and the *gitano*, who had vowed it to be a pattern of all gentleness, on showing how it was shod, received a kick that more than compensated Marcos for his loss. The wiles of Egypt are further exposed by Pindaro, for whom Julia, a foolish girl, has so great a passion, that she consults a gypsy witch how to secure its requital. Promising much, the hag, by night, leads the girl to a distant part of the town, while gypsy accomplices enter the door Julia has been persuaded to leave unlocked. The heroine of the *Sabia Flora Malsabidilla* is herself a *gitana*, the daughter of gypsy rogues of Cantillana, and known as the "Sun of Egypt." Of her father, who was hanged and quartered, she says delicately to one ignorant of the facts, that he died of a pain in the neck, which lasted but briefly, and so humble was he in spirit that he would not accept a tomb in a chapel, but his body was parted because he owed much to many. Had he lived another year he would surely have attained a title, meaning, of course, that of *el conde de gitanos*, chief of the band. Her mother, she declares, was a wonderfully penitent lady, who for mortification went barefoot, slept on the earth, and received the whip-lash frequently. Flora herself is seen busied with attempting to compass a cheating match in which she is to pass for a fine lady. A contrast to Flora is Cervantes' heroine, Preciosa, of *La gitanilla*, the prototype of all romantic gypsy girls. She has nothing in common with her cheating sisters, and proves indeed at the last to be of better blood than they. With the author of *Don Quixote*, she is as much the *gitana* idealized as with Victor Hugo in *Notre Dame de Paris*, or with Longfellow in the *Spanish Student*. A charming figure, she has not the life of the real gypsy, as the picaresque novels portray it. But with the genuine nomad the most intimate if an involuntary acquaintance is made by Alonso.

Dismissed from the convent where he has been *donado*, Alonso is laid hold of by gypsies, dragged before their *conde*, and stripped of his money and clothing. An old woman demands even his last rag for her son on the plea that he suffers from a cold stomach. The gypsies' only fare is a goat they steal from a shepherd, which they wash down with cold water. Alonso is allowed to stand by their fire, but all night his teeth chatter, and a skin which he finds and wraps about him is taken away by a hag who declares she has used it for two generations as a couch. So he goes naked several days until he secures the rags of an ancient *gitano* who dies opportunely. As one of the crew, he works at a forge and accompanies the women on their begging and thieving expeditions. They tell fortunes, teach their children to flatter, and playing the rôle of astrologers and diviners, rob wherever they can. Once a rich widow is persuaded by *gitanas* to put all her jewels in a jar on the floor surrounded by candles, being told that as riches attract riches, a hidden treasure will so be forthcoming. All kneeling down, the *gitanas* in altered voices issue divine commands to the widow to dress herself in her finest, and while she is gone upon this errand, they make off with the jar and its contents. Alonso himself becomes skilled in deception. He discovers a thief in an hidalgo's house by giving to each of the servants sticks of equal length, and assuring them solemnly that on the morrow the thief's stick will have grown four fingers longer than any of the others. The culprit apprehensively cuts her stick four fingers shorter to allow for the growth, and thus is exposed.[1] At another time Alonso pretends to have found a purse of money, and taking it to the priest has it announced after mass. A gypsy accomplice claims and identifies it, and Alonso, who has posed as a destitute pedler, through his seeming honesty gets credit for being a saint, and receives a contribution from the appreciative worshippers, and a dinner from the *corregidor*.[2] But even success cannot for long reconcile the rogue to so dangerous a life where the prison is sure and the galleys probable. At the first chance, therefore, he forsakes the calling, richer

[1] This story, slightly altered, with rouge in a bowl placed on bells in place of the sticks, occurs earlier in *Marcos de Obregon*, Rel. I., 16; and later in Charles Sorel's *Histoire comique de Francion*, in Livre ix. (Livres viii.-xi., 1631), where blowing on a candle-flame is substituted.

[2] This story is in *Guzman de Alfarache*, Pt. II., 3, 7, where the same trick is used to impress a widow's reverend counsellor with Guzman's probity; but it comes direct from Massuccio's *Il novellino*, where it is the 16th *novella*.

in experience and pocket than when he entered it.

A deeper enmity than any against the gypsies was that borne by the rogue in common with all Spaniards against the *Moriscos*. Islam had met open defeat in the Peninsula, but Islam was not dead there, for the Arab peoples who remained behind kept to themselves, and would forsake neither habits nor beliefs. Outwardly they conformed to the pressure brought to bear upon them, but inwardly they were unchanged in thought and custom. All Spanish authors of the period or travellers in Spain cry out against these infidels who retained their language, and were Christians merely by force. The frequent resort to baths was unfavorably construed as a reminiscence of washings before entering the mosque. The retention of Arab names in spite of orthodox christenings was a theme for abuse. Don Francisco Bermudez de Pedraza, a canon and treasurer of the cathedral of Granada, declared: "The *Moriscos* are not Moors admittedly, but heretics in secret, in whom faith is lacking while baptism abounds. They go to mass for fear of paying the penalty, work on fiestas behind closed doors with greater gusto than on other days, and Fridays they observe more rigorously than Sundays." To which charge he adds that they wash themselves though it be December, that they christen their children, but straightway with heathen ceremonies remove all trace of the sacrament, and that they delight in stealing Christian infants to carry to Barbary.[1] In the romances of roguery, although the rôle of the *Morisco* is an unimportant one, altogether subordinate in interest to that played by Moors in Algeria or renegade Spaniards there, still it adds not a little to the characteristic stage setting. The mother of the Ingeniosa Elena was a slave called María by her masters, but Zara by her parents. Each year she fulfilled the obligations of the Church through fear, but she was as good a *Morisca* as any in Granada, and something of a witch and go-between besides, whence her nickname of the Second Celestina. The Donado Hablador tells of a *Morisco* boy called Juanillo abroad, and Hamete within-doors; and shows a *Morisco* stealing from his masters and sending back a satirical letter from Barbary. Rojas in the

[1] *Historia eclesiastica, principios y progressos de la ciudad y religion católica de Granada*, 1638, cap. 82.

Viage entretenido is mortified at being claimed by a *Morisco* of Ronda for his son, and Justina finds it difficult to conquer her aversion when she goes to serve a Moorish hag who is made to appear in league with the devil. This witch is a spinner of wool, associated with two others of the faith as sinister as she. From these three graces, Justina learns many cheats, and by carrying their wool, and keeping it in damp places to increase the weight, she ekes out a living, winning the title of marchioness of the woofs. The old *Morisca* promises to be a mother to Justina, but her religious views, which are evident from her calling prayer the conjury of abbots, inspires the picara with fear. One night during a tempest, Justina finds her mistress dead, and realizes that the elements must be celebrating. She binds the corpse with cords and rifles her treasure, but no masses are said for the soul of the deceased, Justina remembering her aversion to them in life. In the *Soldado Píndaro* among the roguish tricks played by Pero Vasquez of Seville is one upon a merchant with a reputation of being more affianced to the crescent than the cross. Pero Vasquez goes to his shop one evening, and, pretending to look over some cloths, hides a box among them. Visiting the shop again the next morning with his friends, he pulls forth the inlaid box, at which the *Morisco*, hopeful of gain, professes it to be his. At this Pero Vasquez opens it, drawing forth what he himself had arranged there, a gilded Mohammed with the moon beneath his feet and the Koran in his hand. The friends crying out in feigned horror at this discovery, the trembling *Morisco* begs them to be quiet lest the Inquisition seize him. A bargain is struck, and Pero Vasquez and the rest depart enriched. And so through the picaresque novels the conclusion with regard to the *Moriscos* drawn a century earlier by Cardinal Navagiero is upheld: "They are enemies of the Spaniards, by whom, however, they are none too well treated."[1]

But Islam in Spain to the picaro was less a circumstance than Islam in the Mediterranean and in Barbary. Captivity in Algeria and fights with Arab pirates were matters of everyday occurrence in life, and of frequent use in fiction. The southern seaboard was never secure from sudden inroads, and no embarka-

[1] *Viaggio fatto in Spagna*, etc., p. 25.

tion took place from those shores that the chances of attack by the Moor militant were not weighed. In Algiers the number of captives was immense. For three years thirty thousand Christians had toiled as slaves in the building of the mole there, and the system of piracy, introduced by the Turkish rover, Aruch Barbarossa, and reënforced by the advent of the expelled *Moriscos*, was constantly supplying new recruits from the captured, as the old died, turned renegade, were ransomed, or escaped. France, England, and the Venetians, exasperated by the Algerine corsairs, might fling fleet after fleet against them, all more successful than the unhappy expedition of Charles Fifth, yet the Mediterranean was still the province of Moslem depredation. The horrors of Algerine captivity found faithful presentation in such serious works as *La historia y topografía de Argel*, brought out in 1612 at Valladolid by the friar, Diego de Haedo, even if these horrors were glossed over sometimes in the general comedy of picaresque fiction.

But among the picaros the father of Guzman de Alfarache, making a voyage, is taken, and carried to Algiers, where he becomes a renegade and is married to a rich wife. Biding his time, however, he collects her portable wealth on a plea of entering commerce, and decamps to Spain. Alonso, embarking at Alicante for Barcelona with some comedians, is storm driven, his bark beached on the shore before Algiers, the elements having done the work of the pirates. The viceroy himself appropriates Alonso and the players, but the hero can only remark the poor food and unremitting labors of all captives. Everybody is flogged at short shifts, and a rower in the galleys, suspected of laxity in effort, has his arm struck off as a warning to others. When the players are bidden to perform before the viceroy they unfortunately select for their piece *La rebelion de Granada*, and meet martyrdom on account of its anti-morisco sentiments; but Alonso, who has acted as corpse, and as page to the Moorish king, is spared and ransomed. Pindaro engages in a naval battle with seven Turkish ships off the island of Iviza, where a storm disperses the vessels and the hero is wrecked. The surviving Spaniards band together on shore with a company of Moorish captives, defeating their enemies. A Moor, whom Pindaro befriends here, turns out to be really a Spaniard, Figueroa, his boyhood companion, captured while mackerel-fishing near Cádiz and taken to Algiers. There he had married his master's daughter and become a renegade, acquiring riches through piracy. Now he is reconciled to the Church by Pindaro and dies a good Christian. Most of the captured, however, from the first only feign conversion to Mohammedanism, and are plotting escape through securing the favor of their masters or making Moorish marriages. Marcos de Obregon's Algerine tells him of a Moor who captured on the Spanish coast a beautiful girl that he brought back to Barbary treating her kindly, and making her his wife. For seven years she seemed reconciled to her new life although always planning to get away. At last during the absence of her lord on a piratical expedition, she escaped in a brigantine, eluding the pursuit of the galleys sent after her, but falling in with her husband's own ship. The lady ordered that her sailors don the Turkish habit, so their continued flight was taken by the Turks aboard the husband's ship, all of whom were in Spanish dress, to be the result of fear, and an excellent joke, and the lady reached Spain safely, where she expended her infidel lord's fortune in charity. Obregon himself is not reduced to such ruses to secure his liberty, for it is presented him by his renegade master. Wrecked off the Balearics, and taking refuge on Cabrera, Marcos had been wont to frequent a cool cave on the island, from which he was warned because of the Turks who would often replenish their stock of water there. One day surprised by pirates in this cave, the hero believed them his companions in disguise, but was disabused of this idea when carried to Algiers. There he becomes the tutor of his master's son, and the renegade's daughter falls desperately in love with him. She is strangely dejected until at length he makes her gay by a pretended spell, simply repeating sweet words in Spanish which no one else understands. But his fame for this cure grows troublesome, as all the women in Algiers are at his heels to be relieved of melancholia. Upon one lady he tries his Salamanca logic formula, *Barbara*, *celarent*, *darii*, *ferio*, *ıralipton,* and although she has no idea 'hat it means she is made to laugh. The ənegade is so proud of Marcos that he treats im rather as friend than as slave, and promises im freedom on the condition of discovering ıe thief of the viceroy's treasure. Marcos :arns that Hazen, the vizier, is suspected, but o one dares accuse him. Accordingly he rocures a thrush which he teaches to say, Hazen stole the money." The bird being ıosed when the viceroy goes to the mosque, egins its cry from the top of a minaret. Everybody listens breathless, taking it for a gn from Mohammed, and by means of astrolo- ers and torture Hazen finally confesses. So Marcos, after he has paved the way for the onversion of his master's son and daughter, carried back to the Balearics by the rene- ade himself. Later, in Spain the *escudero* nearly recaptured; two brigantines land- ıg suddenly, he is seized and taken aboard; ut the Turks in the midst of rejoicings ashore re attacked by the Spaniards, whereupon the əw on the vessels unbind the prisoners as the nly chance of saving their own lives. A res- ue by Spaniards, too, spares Doctor Sagredo, whose ship, returning from the Pacific, is waylaid by Turks in sight of Gibraltar. But the hero of the *Dia y noche de Madrid*, like Marcos, is well treated by Algerines and freed from captivity by a kind master that he may satisfy his dearest wish of viewing the Spanish capital. Cervantes in his *Trato de Argel*, and its reworking, *Los baños de Argel*, in the story of the *Captive* in *Quixote*, as well as in his *El gallardo Español* and elsewhere, has given graphic pictures of Islam in conflict with the Spaniard, needing to go no farther afield than his own bitter experiences during those five years of captivity in Algiers, when indomitable courage alone sustained him, and death was constantly threatened.

That this peculiar phase of life offered, too, an opportunity for fraud was appreciated by at least one rogue, Teresa de Manzanares, who passes herself off as the daughter of Don Sancho de Mendoça, taken in infancy by the corsairs and now returned to Spain full grown. From a servant who has lived in Algiers, she learns the customs and some words of the language, and in Moorish clothes the two present themselves before Don Sancho, having forged a notary's statement of their landing at Valencia with a band of refugees. Unluckily the impostors are no sooner installed with the overjoyed father than the real daughter appears, and Teresa is obliged to relinquish her pretentions. For other peoples and in later years, Moorish captivity and piratical adventure might become a romantic episode of fiction, but for the Spaniard at this period it was a fact only too real and terrible.

The hidalgo, or petty nobleman, of the romances of roguery for the most part escapes the satire of the picaro, and is a lay figure, a master to be tricked or served, except in two or three notable instances. Even here, a kindly feeling is displayed by the sharper for the threadbare gentleman, quite unusual in the rogue, and to be accounted for on the ground of common poverty. But where, as in *Lazarillo de Manzanares* or *Marcos de Obregon*, the hidalgo is merely a beneficent agent, and indeed wherever he is not poor and proud, he is uninteresting. The classic prototype of all proud hidalgos is he with whom Lazarillo de Tormes engages as page. Well-groomed and walking with an air of ease and consequence, he is followed about all day by the boy, who gets nothing to eat, the gentleman declaring he breakfasted early and never dines until evening. Lazarillo is famished, and on his pulling forth some crusts got in his begging career, his master shares them with him, only asking if the bread were made with clean hands. When evening comes, the hidalgo concludes that the market is too distant to visit till the morrow; besides, he holds that nothing will insure length of life so much as eating little. Lazarillo prepares their hard bed, where the slats show through an old coverlet like the ribs of a lean hog; and in the morning cleans his master's clothes, which have served as a pillow through the night. Buckling on his sword, which all the gold ever coined might not buy from him, and throwing the corner of his cloak over his shoulder with a jaunty air, the hidalgo saunters forth to hear mass, or to flirt with veiled ladies, who are charmed until they find he can indulge them in no luxuries. The starving page in the meantime is obliged to revert to his old trade of begging, and the gentleman, returning at night, professing to have dined, is again persuaded to eat of the store his servant has brought in. So they live, Lazarillo foraging, and the hidalgo swelling with pride and shrunken with hunger. A law is passed forbidding beggary. Matters go from bad to worse. One day in the street, seeing a funeral and hearing a widow complain that they are taking her husband to the dismal habitation, where there is neither eating nor drinking, Lazarillo speeds home and bars the door, sure that it is the hidalgo's house that is meant. The gentleman himself still struts magnificent with a waist as slim as a greyhound's and a straw between his teeth to make it appear he has dined. To the boy he explains that he has ample properties in Castilla Vieja, a stock of houses and an old dovecot, but that honor will not permit him to live there because of a quarrel with a count, who demands that in salutation he shall tip his hat first. Finally, the poor hidalgo, being dunned for the rent of his bed and room, on the pretence of going out to change a gold piece disappears, and Lazarillo, who has consideration for nobody else, declares that never again does he see a gentleman like his master, moving in state as if the street were scarcely wide enough, without pitying him from his heart "to think that with all his apparent greatness he might at that moment suffer privations equally hard to endure." And he adds, "All that I blamed him for was the extravagance of his pride, which, I thought, might have been somewhat abated towards one who, like myself, knew his circumstances so intimately.

Beyond this, little can be added to round out the rôle of the hidalgo. Although later writers rang the changes on the theme, none could approach its earliest presentation. Gerónimo de Alcalá shows Alonso engaged in Toledo to a proud but improvident gentleman, dependent upon his parents, and married against their wishes to a shrew. Presently, bread and money giving out, love follows suit, and the hidalgo and his bride even come to blows. The household's only resource lies in the verse and prose effusions of the gentleman, all of which are tried upon the long-suffering page, who would much prefer edibles. Don Tomé, whom the Bachiller Trapaza serves, is such another poetizing hidalgo, and even more strongly suggestive of Lazarillo's master. Elegant in his personal appointments, he lives in poverty, which he relieves by playing the parasite, his seat being paid for at the comedy and his presence allowed at the houses of the great because of his wit. But, as if the real hidalgo were not proud and miserable enough, sometimes he was aped by the rogue gentry, who descending to the depths of infamy retained recollections of better days. An hidalgo of this least fortunate class Pablos overtakes on the way to Madrid. To begin with, the pícaro believes him to have alighted for a moment from his coach, so imposing is his manner; but on closer inspection the gentleman proves to be threadbare, and his garments falling to pieces. Out of compassion, Pablos mounts the stranger upon his own mule, and as both are bound for the court, they journey on together, the hidalgo declaring that in Madrid wit can turn all it touches into gold, and describing the dodges of his trade, whose professors flatter to live. The mock hidalgos dine at the tables of the rich. In dress they are careful only of what shows, using the same garment in forty different ways. Once a year they attend church, and profess to know everybody; the names of all the dukes and counts they can reel off like prayers, claiming acquaintance with the dead and distant, but women they eschew unless profit be concerned.

Because the rogue is an inveterate wanderer, muleteers are often in evidence in the picaresque novels of Spain, but they rarely play other than an insignificant part. The typical muleteer is a taciturn, negative character, as little concerned at what passes as the one who, accompanying Alonso, plods forward undisturbed when his client is seized at an inn, but welcomes the picaro back when he has effected his escape. This lack of concern disappears only in the muleteer of Barbadillo's *Pedro de Urdemalas*, who being charged with stealing his own beast, is put to the rack, and confesses what he never did. As a rule the professional wayfarer is none too good. Elena's muleteer passes the time singing *romances* composed on famous thieving gentry. Trapaza's carter when accused of blasphemy avows that he never thought swearing matter for the Inquisition, but rather a requisite of the business, believing he was forced to swear on the pain of being a bad carter; and Marcos de Obregon has a muleteer, who in order to be left alone with the only lady in the party he is conducting, pretends that a bag of money has been filched from him, and that he will have all the rest given over to alguazils on suspicion. At this they all flee, but the lady has enough spirit to resist him and inform an *alcalde*.

A distinctive Spanish figure is the barber, everywhere satirized in the romances of roguery, sometimes on account of his trade, and sometimes for his simplicity or amorousness. Bertol Araujo, whom Justina uses to befool her sick hostess, is a barber of the latter class, who cries for fear of his wife when he has broken some cupping-glasses, but at night having performed a mock cure upon the hostess wishes to try another upon Justina. Marcos de Obregon's friend, the guitar-playing barber who reappears in *Gil Blas*, is a simple and unfortunate lover. He serenades Doña Mergelina, Doctor Sagredo's wife, and arranging a meeting with her is almost discovered at her husband's unexpected return. The barber hides beneath a table, where a dog persists in sniffing at him, and the good Doctor's attention is only diverted from this circumstance by a false cry of thieves, which allows the lover to come forth and assume the rôle of the thieves' victim. Hospitality being extended to him for that night, Doña Mergelina and he both suffer discomfort and are effectually cured of their love. Another barber lover, patterned undoubtedly upon this one, pays his devotion to the wife of a one-eyed sacristan, the master of Lazarillo de Manzanares. Here, when the barber is on the verge of being detected, resort is had to the old Eastern expedient of the lady's covering her lord's good eye by a ruse while the lover beats a retreat.[1] Simplicity in other things is also a trait of the barber; for Trapaza, as a student, tricks one of the fraternity, by pretending to be a rich Peruvian exceedingly exacting, and demanding that the barber wash his hands at each moment; finally he sends him off with a copper which he never looks at, supposing it after so much ceremony to be gold. With the rogues, however, not with the simple, is connected the chief satire on the trade itself. Pablos' father is adroit in cutting in more ways than one. The Licenciado Periquin is apprenticed to a barber, robs the customers, and makes

[1] This was the 8th story of Petrus Alphonsus, the 6th of the *Heptameron*, the 16th of the *Cent nouvelles nouvelles*, the 23d of the 1st Part of Bandello, the 2d of *Sabadino degli Arienti*, and is to be found in the *Gesta Romanorum* and elsewhere.

way with his master's lancets and razors. Alonso describes a poor student who allowed himself to be shaved gratuitously by a beginner, and hearing a dog baying, judged that it, too, must be losing its skin. Estevanillo is a hopeless blunderer with the razor. While his master is called away one day by a street quarrel from an hidalgo whose mustache he was dressing, Estevanillo tries his hand, and saves his life only by flight. Sometime afterward he is placed with another barber, his father agreeing upon a forfeit if his year be not served out. His first experiment is upon a beggar, and his new master, returning from a bleeding, finds the shop filled with an angry crowd, and the beggar's wife disclaiming him, so hacked is he. Put on probation, before another month has passed the picaro has nearly severed the ear of a merchant's son, and before the year is done his father has to pay the forfeit and large damages as well, since Estevanillo, with the best of his master's tools, decamps to Naples.

The players and affiliated poets of the romances of roguery are entertaining Bohemians, and itinerant companies come in for their share of attention. The *Viage entretenido* of Rojas, although lacking in unity as a story, gives the best description of the life of these strollers, so careful indeed as to prove a valuable commentary on the Spanish stage at the end of the sixteenth century. The eight orders of companies and actors are described, from the *bululú*, a single performer who, mounted on a box, recites a whole comedy before the curate, the barber, and the sacristan of a village, with the curate taking up the collection in a sombrero, to the *farándula*, with three women, eighteen comedies, two trunks for costumes, and muleteers or carts for travelling. Here the actors put up at good inns, eat apart, wear feathers in their hats, twirl their mustaches, and live content, except such as are in love; while in the full-fledged *compañia* there is a repertoire of as many as fifty comedies, with palfreys, coaches, and litters for transportation, "thirty who dine and heaven knows how many who steal." Rios and Solano in the *Viage*, recounting their adventures, describe evading a bill at an inn by means of escape with a sheet from a window, on this occasion running off with the advance sales of an advertised play on

Cain and Abel. At another time Rios, in the same comedy, forgetting the knife with which to kill Abel, was pursued by the incensed audience. The two rogues live by helping muleteers at taverns and playing for carters in courtyards until they are going about almost naked, and the *autor* of a company in pity receives them. Here for a month they journey from town to town, bearing the manager's wife in a hand chair when it rains, the *autor* himself and two others carrying the goods, and a boy the drum and the baubles. Sometimes the lady wears a mask or false beard to protect her complexion in travelling, and these artists do not disdain to forage by the way. In their favorite piece, *La resurreción de Lázaros*, the *autor*, playing the part of Christ, one day cries in vain to Lazarus "*Surge, surge!*" and thinking Solano asleep in his tomb, finds in dismay that he has fled. But the foolish people take it for a miracle, and deem him translated to heaven at the very least. So the actors lead a varied life, some borrowing mantles for costumes which they forget to return, some collecting bread and eggs and sardines as entrance fees, and some sleeping on the earth with arms crossed to keep warm when lacking capes. With the best the toils are excessive, because of the lines to be learned and the roads to be traversed, and on the whole the actor must experience more changes than the moon and more perils than the frontier.

Guzman de Alfarache, charmed at first with the notion of the stage, is soon disillusionized. He has read profane books, and for love of Isabela, an actress, determines to join a troop of performers. The free and vagabond life of people to-day at the court, to-morrow at Seville or Toledo, appeals to him. They may always enjoy a new world, content with the present, without care for the future. "And this exterior fully satisfied me," says the picaro, "although afterwards I saw how bitter sometimes is what outwardly appears delightful." Alonso enters a company of comedians, where he is given disagreeable tasks off the stage and silent rôles upon it, and he, too, is impressed with the difficulty of the profession. If the summer be hot, he complains, nobody attends the play, if the winter be rainy nobody ventures abroad, if one of the royal family die representations must cease. To a curate he defends the drama and approves the return of women after Philip Second had banished them from the boards, for it seems to him out of place that boys should take female parts. A candidate for a professorial chair at Salamanca, Alonso declares, was opposed by a rival on the score that he had been a player, but carried the election readily by asking for the votes of such students as had acted also. Teresa de Manzanares joins comedians at Granada, where an old lover of hers, marrying her, advises the step. By her acting and singing she wins fame, and when her husband grows remiss, a prince is doubly devoted, and the *autor* of the company would be so too did she permit it. At Seville crowds attend the performances; but to be revenged upon this *autor* Teresa suddenly refuses to play, and the physicians who attend her are tricked. Sarabia, her lord, writing an *entremés* upon them, entitled *La prueva de los doctores*, is waylaid, the *autor* is imprisoned for debt, and the company breaks up. Such is the end, too, of the troupe to which Pablos for a time is attached. He meets the strollers at an inn, and finding among them an old companion of

Alcalá, is permitted to join their ranks. Making love to one of the actresses, he unwittingly confides the whole matter to the lady's husband, without, however, incurring any displeasure. In Toledo he ventures upon a part, which fortunately requires him to be clad in armor, since he is saluted with volleys of rotten oranges from the audience. The author of the play is blamed, but explains that he has only made a patchwork of other men's effusions, and Pablos takes the cue and sets up as an author himself, earning reputation for a piece all godliness. Blind men flock to him for ballads, and lovers for laudatory verses. He hires a house and writes his plays in the garret in emulation of genius. But when most of the insolvent company are arrested, Pablos concludes to forsake a bad calling. The same rogue meets a clerical poet who rails at the learned of Alcalá for lack of appreciation, and professes to have stanzas for each of the eleven thousand virgins of Saint Ursula, a comedy patterned on Æsop, and nine hundred and one sonnets and twelve *redondillas* on the limbs of his mistress, conceits which he admits in the last instance are not descriptive, but merely by way of prophecy. At every remark from the picaro the poet is reminded of some piece of his, and at Madrid he is greeted affectionately by a host of blind ballad-singers, against whom Pablos reads a mock proclamation. These blind men seem to have been closely allied with the scribblers, and used by them sometimes as instruments of revenge; for a poet in the *Pedro de Urdemalas*, quarrelling with a gambler, has a ballad-singer chant scurrilous verses which bring down condign punishment. All the poets of the romances of roguery are tedious folk, from Justina and Estevanillo with their rhymed conceits, to the bard whom Trapaza meets on a stage-coach, reciting his *entremeses* and recounting the hardships of getting comedies accepted. Poetical academies like that of the *Diablo cojuelo*, and philosophical academies like that of the *Siglo Pitagórico* were in fashion as an elegant social diversion, brought over from Italy in the sixteenth century, and early patronized by such men as the *conquistador*, Fernando Cortés. Usually satirized, these polite conventions for discussion and entertainment had a marked influence in the picaresque novel, and determined the form of many of the lesser works of Salas Barbadillo and Castillo Solórzano. But of all the poets, perhaps the most successful is Don Jaime of the *Garduña de Sevilla*, who is only a feigned one. He pretends to be the author of a comedy which he reads aloud to a company of players; and on its poor reception, as if in anger, he oversets the candles, and then in the confusion departs with two thousand *escudos* provided for a fiesta.

In the society scrutinized by the picaresque novels, amusing as are the pictures of most estates, and valuable to-day for their faithful record of forgotten manners, none naturally are so interesting as those that paint the mendicants and rogues themselves united in a body-politic. Among the mendicants, Lazarillo de Tormes' blind master is a veritable patriarch. More than an hundred prayers he knows to repeat in a pleasing voice, with an air of profound piety. He has charms and prognostics for every occasion, and is sought after by women as a quack. His adroitness brings him more in a month than an hundred other blind men might get in a year, and Lazarillo, having imbibed the begging instinct with his mother's milk, and studied it as an art under this, its greatest master in all Spain, becomes an adept himself. With an humble voice, his hands folded on his breast, and the Lord's name on his lips, he goes from house to house, and so can live in a town which, he says, has no more charity than would save a saint from starvation. Later, when parted from his wife, he begs on the way to Madrid; wine abounding that year, he receives drink where he can get no food, and is soon more merry than a girl on the eve of a fiesta, and bursts forth into an encomium upon beggary. "To tell the truth," he declares, "the picaresque life is life, and no other merits the name." If the rich would taste it, they must forsake their riches as did the ancient philosophers; indeed, the philosophic and the picaresque life is all one, the only difference being that the philosophers attain this ideal existence in leaving what they possess, and the picaro possesses it without leaving anything.

Still more intimate and infatuated with beggary is Guzman de Alfarache. Departing from Genoa, he is now in one place, now in another, asking charity in all. He studies to please the rich, to arouse pity in the lowly, and awake the pious to a sense of duty. Arrived at Rome, he learns the ordinances of the mendicants in which it is laid down that each nation shall have its own way of begging, the Germans singing in chorus, the French praying, the Flemish making reverences, the gypsies importuning, the Portuguese weeping, the Tuscans haranguing, the English abusing, but the Castilians proud and suffering. The beggars are to assemble at certain inns, ruled over by their ancients; they must carry substantial staves, wear nothing new, and communicate fortunate tricks and discoveries to the whole fraternity, with the privilege, however, of a three-months monopoly for the finder. The infirm are to go two by two on opposite sides of the street, one beginning to complain where the other leaves off. Alms must be received only in the hat, although hidden purses and pockets are permissible. Those who use begging dogs are not to interfere with those who ask at church doors. The childless may hire as many as four little ones five years of age or under, but at least one is to be carried in arms. The maimed beggars are not to haunt the quarters of the healthy, nor should the latter club with those of special trades, as redeemed captives, false soldiers and sailors, field-preachers, and musicians. Guzman is further informed by an expert Córdovan how he should conduct himself in Rome, refraining from disturbing the siesta of the rich and from grumbling at hard usage. He is taught the knack of raising swellings, false leprosies and ulcers, and of feigning pallor. At evening the rogue and his friends dispute on exclamations they invent to draw money from the pitying or the flattered. On fiestas they occupy the choicest stations in the churches, or scour the suburbs for the produce of compassion. To the traveller descried at a distance they call out woefully in time for him to get his hand to his pocket; when a number approach, they assume different rôles, falling suddenly halt, blind, and mute. Pretty women Guzman looks in the eyes, and on kissing their hands with fervency, his pleasure in the caress is mistaken for the overflow of gratitude. He tells of a mendicant of Florence who willed his ass to be sold to bury him, and the saddle to be given to the Grand Duke. The prince was offended until a fortune was discovered concealed in his bequest, the profits of a busy life. At Gaeta, with an artificial scab on his head, Guzman befools the governor into bestowing gifts upon him, but disguising anew, and with a painted ulcer on his leg, this time he is recognized. The governor in apparent good faith promises the picaro a shirt to his back, which proves to be woven from sound blows; but undiscouraged, the rogue tries a similar deception upon a cardinal and meets with more success. Micer Morcon, king of the mendicants, and a friend to Guzman, is a jolly fellow, fat and happy, although bare of foot and head. He orders his subjects to quit asking as soon as the day's necessities are satisfied, arguing that no beggar should allow himself to think of the morrow; and like Guzman he is never weary of dilating upon the beauties of the art which for most becomes a darling habit. One poor woman in Rome, having subsisted all her life upon charity and then receiving a bequest, is unable to break off this trade, falling ill of the desire for begging. Finally as a nun she is able to continue, pretending she does it to acquire humility. "No condition of life is so happy as that of a beggar," says Guzman, "and fortunate were it indeed if every one could know when he is well off."

All of the anti-heroes are not of the same opinion, however. Periquillo, who turns leader to a begging blind man, because he had heard that the life of the picaro is a fine one, after enduring all the discomforts of the trade, finally counsels himself thus, "Leave the guiding of the blind to Lazarillos and Alfaraches, for you have some good in you yet which will be ruined in this roguish life." No such scruples trouble Estevanillo, who in Paris frequents the Spanish embassy, blistered and bandaged, demanding money for his restoration until a stipend is actually promised him. Flattery never comes amiss in the profession, as Periquin understands, who, going from door to door and meeting one enamored of his own hands, asks that they be laid upon a bruised pate since such pretty things must serve as a cure. Instead of a *real* he receives four for this diplomacy, and the ladies with whom the gallant is talking bestow eight more when he thanks God who made him neither a stone, nor a tree, nor a marquis, nor a count, but simply a suppliant to them. Begging is an expedient by which every picaro may retrieve his fortunes or pass in disguise. Lazarillo de Manzanares takes to it when robbed and left destitute, and in the *Dia y noche de Madrid*, conversely, robbers ply as beggars. Marcos de Obregon, pursued by justice and seeking sanctuary in a church, evades capture through the sacristan's posting him as a beggar among the rest at the church door; and Justina, anxious to raise money to purchase a coveted jewel, exchanges her fine mantle for a faded one, and hiding her face, begs at a church, doing a good trade with young men who admire her figure, one of whom on that account goes to his devotions seven times. Don Pablos, after having been beaten as punishment for his love pretensions, procures rags, goes on crutches, and joins the begging trade, where he finds that saying *Jesu* takes better with the commoners than *Jesus*. His boon comrade is a fellow who uses cords to swell his arms, flatters all who pass, and has children to beg and steal for him; and Pablos adopts the same means to carry on his business. Finally both attain prosperity by kidnapping children and returning them for a reward, claiming to have saved them from disaster. In the *Ardid de la pobreza* Andrés de Prado shows four poor rogues meeting in Saragossa, who on adopting beggary elect officers and portion off the streets into begging districts, with a code of laws, according to which one of them, for merely walking with a lady through the captain's questing territory, is fined for trespass.

Besides the rogues who are anti-heroes and anti-heroines of the picaresque novels, there are other notable cheats and bands of sharpers in these stories, some of whom have already figured under special captions as gypsies, hermits, or innkeepers, but most of whom are professional frauds. Sayavedra, who becomes Guzman's lackey after having robbed him, is such a rogue. He commences as adventurer, embarking for Italy, where he is sneak-thief, cuts ladies' girdles, prowls about stables, enters houses boldly, but if encountered, asks alms, and attends churches and comedies in order to rifle pockets. In journeying through the country, he and his companions are never at expense, living on appropriated fowls by the way. In Naples he brings his cheats to perfection, and practises schemes of defence, a member of the band always waiting in readiness to buttonhole a pursuer. Linen out to dry is his booty, and anything else that comes to hand. He enters the service of a more ambitious rogue of Bologna, son of a professor in the university, whose method is to commit depredations away from home, returning for safety, where his reputation remaining excellent protects him. Marcos de Obregon meets two rascals whom he detects playing an old trick that the English conny-catching pamphlets term that of the ring-faller.[1] At night, through a wall, he hears the pair plotting, and in the morning one of them goes ahead with a fine ring, while the other makes friends with Marcos and a couple of merchants, the intended victims. All journeying together, the sharper excites the thirst of the company with dry cakes, so that on arriving at a deserted *venta* they stop to drink, and at the fountain find the ring left by the accomplice. In order to decide who shall have it, they agree to play for it that night, and accordingly all bring up at an inn, where of course is the accomplice with a stacked pack of cards. Not

[1] This same story in altered form appeared in the *Histoire générale des larrons*, 1623, as the 19th of the 1st Part, a false diamond taking the place of the ring.

only the ring, but all of the merchants' money is played for and won by the two rogues, although Marcos later outwits them and returns the property to the victims. A boy whom Obregon encounters in his travels is a less sophisticated rogue than these because younger, but his adventures which he relates constitute a picaresque tale in little. Beginning by stealing four *reales* from his father, which he lost at play, and afraid to go home, he slept on a bench in the rain, was beaten by mistake, wandered to Córdova, and with a boy friar tramped to Alcalá, begging. At the university he nearly starved, but had a way of snatching bread and running with it to his room, sticking it on nails he had driven in the slats of his bed. As nobody could find it, he always went free until discovered by a master who was scratched on a nail. After this he ran away, and as the two lay-brothers, sent to pursue him, knew the country better than he, the boy hid till they passed and then followed their lead. Wearied with dodging, at length he appeared to them in a bee-farm, and as they dashed after him he upset the hives, whereupon they were so badly stung that they relinquished the chase. Other minor rogues rove through the picaresque novels, from the Frenchman who travels with Estevanillo, donning ragged garb at the entrance to towns and making lamentations, to the picaro, Pernia, who passes for the Monja Alférez, the original of Belmonte Bermudez' comedy of that name, a noted woman who turned soldier to win glory in the Indies. A cheating alchemist gets the best of so sharp a picaro as Lazarillo de Manzanares; and Teresa's mother, left a widow, consoles herself with a guest in her lodging-house, only to lose all her savings by his flight. The rascal innkeeper of the *Engaños deste siglo* delivers his spoil to a friend "most skilful in metamorphizing and disguising all sorts of garments in order that they may be sold again even to those who have lost them"; and a more pretentious "fence" is Periquillo's master, who keeps servants to hire out into rich houses from which they steal.

A distinct class of rogue and the most typically Spanish of all is the *valiente* or bully who is employed in playing the enraged husband or else in inflicting punishments for pay. As a "badger," or cross-biter, as he was known in sixteenth-century England, the *valiente* clamors for reparation from the innocent victim found with his pretended wife. In the *Guia y avisos de forasteros*, Mendez of La Mancha visits a lady whose favors he prefers to merit, not to purchase, but as he is taking leave of her, he is seized by her bully. Don Martin in the *Novelas morales* of Agreda y Vargas has a similar trick played upon him in Seville, although his accuser fortunately dies in good season. Such a bully is Lazarillo de Manzanares' most prosperous master. If this gentleman were present when his wife was serenaded, forth he would go to the street, and provided the singer were weaker than he, demand gold for his wounded honor; but if the gallant were the stronger, then the *valiente* would bring him in with caresses and eyes on his purse. Ruffians are hired to pursue Trapaza, who has written a satire against a miser that bled himself to escape giving a banquet; and more desperate ones receive ten thousand ducats for an assassination, the blame of which they fix upon Filardo, a stranger in Madrid. A braggadocio bully, an old friend of Don Pablos at Alcalá, is met by that anti-hero scarred, and eloquent of battles. He deals in men's lives, selling cuts and slashes, bearing the sign of his trade on his face, and introduces the picaro to his gang, fellows with a smith's shop of swords and daggers about their waists, their beards like brushes, and their eyes staring. Pablos is bidden to rumple his neck-band, thrust out his back, make faces, talk big, swear, and be rude. They all dine on food highly seasoned to promote thirst, and lie along the ground to drink out of a half-hogshead on the floor until they no longer recognize one another. Then they quarrel, jargon, weep, and laud the deeds of a hanged companion, finally swearing to suck up the blood of the officers responsible for taking off so brave a man. Although these bullies in their maudlin bravery do kill two of the guard, most are cowards, who bluster but seldom act. The *Sabia Flora Malsabidilla* depicts two *valientes*, Cespedos and Calvete, hired to put a gentleman out of the way. They swear *por Christo* continually, and all their talk is of blood and asking confession. Yet they tremble to draw a sword. They ask wine and are all vinegar; the chronicler of their achievements is the wind. They bow to a superior, who gives directions and has handed down a decree that from the money for each death inflicted they shall pay for three masses for the defunct, thus satisfying all scruples of conscience. Although these two fight as to who shall be privileged to kill their intended victim, both at the critical moment take flight, leaving their cloaks and swords behind. Two other *valientes* in the *Dia y noche de Madrid* fight, but allow themselves to be separated, content with the appearance of bravery. One had wounded himself with a pin, telling a fine story of his heroism, and the other equals him with a tale of robbers, the first going home unable to sleep through fear. A similar bloodless quarrel is incited by Pedro de Urdemalas between a *corchete* of the chief alguazil and a *valiente*, both proud of their fencing, but their only warfare consists in tearing down abusive posters, put up by each other. Juan of the *Passagero* for a while is a bully, famous at first through feigned valor and then on reputation; but, stabbed in the exercise of his profession, he abandons it. That Seville was the favorite stamping-ground for this kind of rogue there can be no question. Most of their exploits occur there, and Ramirez in the *Viage entretenido*, when lamenting the free-list the comedians are forced to allow in the capital of

Andalusia, says that one-third of the people enter without paying, either *valientes*, who push past the gate-keeper, or those who have seen their entrance and demand admittance as well.

Seville, too, is the scene of the *hampa*, the congregation of rogues handed down to posterity by Cervantes in his play, *El rufian dichoso*, and in his tale, *Rinconete y Cortadillo*. In the latter, the two *valientes*, Chiquiznaque and Maniferro, are as genuine bravos as any, with their memoranda for cuts, cudgellings, ink-throwings, and the nailing of horns over the doors of cuckolds; and other rogues are scarcely less interesting. There are elderly gentlemen with rosaries, who, by their venerable appearance, gain entrance to houses, appraise the value of the booty to be got there, and mark the means of access. There are mock students, boys with baskets to act as thieving porters, blind men, pretty girls, and a pious old lady, to say nothing of Monipodio, lord of all, examiner of novices, apportioner of labors, and court of last appeal. As in the begging fraternities, so here the streets are divided into territories assigned to different picaros, each to be held responsible for whatever may be stolen in his district. Somewhat similar rogue societies are described by Pablos at Segovia and at Madrid. In the former town, Pablos is entertained by his uncle, the hangman, together with a band, including a beggar of charity for the poor at church doors, a swineherd, and a mulatto *valiente.* They all drink immense quantities of wine, pour the soup without instead of within them, bless the souls of those who have gone to make mince-meat for bakers' pies, and, eating salt to provoke them to drink more, fall into a stupor, as fine rogues as ever lived. At Madrid a more notable company is found, presided over by an old woman, the picaros coming in one by one from their sharping expeditions, the first with a begging-letter for a poor family, another with a set of false missives upon which he collects postage, and two others who have put up a trick on a child at church, one having pretended to be the owner of handkerchiefs the child was sent to deliver, and his companion having affirmed him to be so. Now their dispute to the property is decided by the old woman's gathering the handkerchiefs into ruffles to represent shirt sleeves for all; after which, they turn in, packed closer than tools in a tweezer case. In the morning, the scoundrels help one another dress, and Pablos is made a strange outfit from his scholar's robe, his hat band being of cotton picked from ink-horns, his stockings only meeting the tops of his boots, and the rest in keeping. Assigned to a ward to operate in, Pablos has for conductor one who evades a creditor by letting his hair fall about his face, clapping a patch to one eye, and talking Italian, and who at noon sprinkles his beard and clothes with crumbs, that he may be thought to have dined. When Pablos at night returns to headquarters he finds that his instructor has been beaten for trying to cheat beggars at a monastery, that the soldier has stolen the candle given him to hold at a funeral, that one who pilfers cups at nunneries has secured a new cape by retiring early from a billiard game and leaving his old garment behind, that another has spent the day pretending to heal diseases by incantation and prayer, and that still another with a false beard and a cross has gone about crying for folk to remember the dead, taking up alms for masses, and thieving. But this life does not last long, before they all get into custody.

As the *Guzman de Alfarache* gives the best account of beggary, so the *Desordenada codicia* of Dr. Carlos García is most explicit as to organized roguery. Here the thieves are divided into categories as they were in the *Liber vagatorum* in Germany and in its English, French, and Italian heirs. According to this classification [1] there are above a dozen orders of rogues in Spain. *Salteadores* steal and kill on the highway; *estafadores* single out rich men, and showing them daggers threaten death unless a stipulated sum be forthcoming by a certain time; *capeadores* snatch cloaks in the night or go in lackey's clothes to places of entertainment, where they carry off plunder, saluting those they meet; *grumetes*, deriving their name from boys who, cat-like, scale the tacklings on ship masts, are thieves provided with rope ladders hooked at the top; *apóstoles*, like Saint Peter, bear the keys, and are picklocks; *cigarreros* haunt public places, cutting off the half of a cloak or a gown; *devotos* are religious thieves who spoil images and rely upon the moderation of Church laws for a light

[1] *Desordenada codicia*, Cap. VII. *De la diferencia y variedad de los ladrones.*

punishment if detected; *sátiros* live in the fields and are cattle thieves; *dacianos* kidnap children three or four years of age, "and breaking their arms and legs, lame and disfigure them that they may afterwards sell them to beggars, blind men, and other vagabonds"; *mayordomos* steal provisions, and trick inn-keepers; *cortabolsas* are cut-purses, the commonest thieves of the republic; *duendes*, or hobgoblins, are sneak thieves; and the *maletas* are such as are made up in bales or barrels like merchandise and so effect an entrance to houses. Besides these, the *liberales* slander for pay, inflict punishments, throw ink, dirt, and acid, and hang chaplets of horns at doors. As to the organization of thieves itself, there is a captain to direct enterprises and before whom once a week all the thieves meet to make reports and receive instructions for the days to come. Novices have three months in which to acquit themselves of difficult tasks, such as stealing a horse from beneath his rider or snatching a courtier's sash among an hundred people. Then the acolyte is assigned to one of the thirteen orders of knaves according to his abilities. Of all thefts the fifth part goes to public officers who spare the whip, banishment, the galleys, or hanging to such as are condemned, and a certain part is devoted to pious uses, to succor the sick and needy of the fraternity. The thief himself shares equally with the captain; his accomplices have one-third, and mere spies one-fifth. Women are not admitted to privileges in the society except in cases of necessity, because they cannot keep secrets. The only quarrelling allowed is a pretence to draw a crowd and give occupation to the cut-purses. Two are not permitted to dine together more than once a week in taverns, and all have their badges of office, the *salteadores*, a glove hanging by one finger; the *capeadores*, their doublets buttoned alternately; the *estafadores* stroking their beards, and the little finger inserted now and then in the nose. To a woman who marries, each of that order gives a portion, but a hobgoblin's daughter must wed a hobgoblin, else her husband pays the *duendes* a fine. In each of the districts of a town is left a die, and when one thief arrives there the ace is turned up, when another, the deuce, and so on, no more than six being allowed to operate in the same quarter. No thief may wear or dispose of his booty in the town of its stealing, and all must carry the paraphernalia of disguise, patches and false beards. In religion the rogues are half Christians, concludes García, loving God, but not their neighbor, allowing two parts of penitence, confession and contrition, but never the third, which is restitution.

In this fashion society was reviewed by the picaro, minutely, fearlessly, mockingly; and of all classes, the nobles alone were spared. The hidalgos, indeed, received some little admonition, although mollified with a certain display of sympathy; but Berganza, in the *Coloquio de los perros*, tempted to attack folk of high estate, and checking himself as on the verge of an impropriety, no more than voices the sentiment of Spanish literature in general where plebeians have alone been the target of wit. In a novel of rogues, necessarily, low life must absorb the major attention, yet the opportunities for administering blows higher aimed was early appreciated abroad, and Charles Sorel, in the *Ordre et l'examen des livres attribués à l'auteur de la Bibliothèque Française*, is found distinguishing the *romans comiques* of the French from the picaresque fictions of Spain on precisely this ground. Nevertheless, so thorough a canvass of society for its own sake as the Spanish romances of roguery offered was scarcely again to be had. The novel of manners refined meant the study of manners already beginning to succumb to the personal interest, and for that reason the picaresque tale of the Spaniards in its very crudity is a mine of curious detail, and of value chiefly as such.

CHAPTER IV

CRUDE FORMS OF THE PICARESQUE NOVEL

FROM Seneca and Martial to the Archpriest of Hita, Spain excelled in satire, and the Archpriest himself, Juan Ruiz, was the first Spanish ancestor of picaresque fiction. In parody and burlesque he found his element, and the same confused formlessness, ironic observation, and love of autobiography that marked his verses, reappeared in prose in the romances of roguery. His Don Furón is the archetype of so familiar a figure as the poor and proud hidalgo of the *Lazarillo de Tormes*, and Ruiz was copied in the *Celestina* still more closely. There the lovers Melibea and Calisto were patterned upon Doña Endrina and Don Melón of the *Libro de cantares*, and Celestina, mother of iniquity, revived the procuress, Trota-conventos. This *Tragicomedia de Calisto y Melibea* was the most important Spanish precursor of the *Lazarillo*. First printed at Burgos at the end of the fifteenth century in sixteen acts, and subsequently extended to twenty-one and even twenty-two, it was a dialogued novel, or novelistic drama, not adapted to representation, yet wholly dramatic in build; but its influence, although large on the stage, was larger still in the novel. Whoever wrote it, and Fernando de Rojas, in spite of his repudiation of the first act, was probably the author of the whole, the *Celestina* did in a more serious way what the picaresque novel was to attempt restrictedly; that is, it laid hold upon reality. Simple life and passion was its subject, not extravagant adventure, and observation its instrument; but in emotion it attained a deeper reality than any sought by the romances of roguery. The low life centring about the wily Celestina had all the traits of the best picaresque fiction, while the higher life involving the lovers entirely transcended anything in the tales of anti-heroes. The trenchant, never superfluous, dialogue, the restraint in expression, so unlike either the Archpriest of Hita or the romances of roguery, and the feeling for character were sufficient to stamp this tragi-comedy as a masterpiece. In the sixteenth century it was as popular as *Quixote* in the seventeenth. A philosopher like Ludovico Vives might decry it as *nequitiarem parens, carcer amorum*, yet even he must finally reverse his verdict, when the chief personages of the book and their sayings had passed into common proverb, and editions, additions, and imitations were mounting up prodigiously. Both Cepeda and Velasco brought it upon the boards, the one in prose, the other in verse, and before them Feliciano de Sylva had resurrected from her grave the wise old bawd in his *Segunda Celestina* of 1530, Domingo de Castega had added a second part in 1534, and Gaspar Gómez de Toledo a third in 1539. The *diabolica vieja* Claudina of the *Tragedia policiana* in the next decade, and the religious but infamous Marcelia of the *Florinea* of 1554 were amplified Celestinas, and the same year, which was also that of the appearance of the *Lazarillo de Tormes*, found still another echo in the *Comedia Selvaggia* of Alonso de Villegas. Translations into Latin and the chief languages of Europe were a matter of course, as were early verse transcriptions and later dramatic renderings in Spanish. Of the latter, some like the Portuguese *Comedia Eufrosina*, composed in

1566, but done into Castilian in 1631, were less picaresque than their original; while others, with the *Segunda Celestina* of Agustín Salazar and the *Escuela de Celestina* of Salas Barbadillo, were rather more so. Of the actual romances of roguery, Barbadillo's *Hyia de Celestina* and his *Sabia Flora Malsabidilla* have been referred to as lineal descendants of the *Calisto y Melibea*, but for all picaresque novels Celestina was recognized as godmother. The curious frontispiece to the 1605 and the 1608 Medina del Campo and Brussels editions of the *Pícara Justina* shows that anti-heroine in the allegoric ship, *La nave de la vida picara*, side by side with a bespectacled crone, *La madre Celestina*. Sempronio, Parmeno, and the ruffian Centurio, with Areusa and Elicia, the roaring girls, as Middleton would have styled them, were folk from the stews, but full of truth and vigor. They were part and parcel of the picaresque clan, although scarcely careless and witty enough in fact, if in theory they could state the picaro's philosophy to a nicety.

Elicia in James Mabbe's archaic English declares: "As long as we have meat for to-day, let us not thinke on to-morrow; let to-morrow care for itselfe ; as well dies he that gathers much as hee that lives but poorely; . . . we are not to live forever, and therefore let us laugh and be merry, for few are they that come to see old age; and they who doe see it, seldome dye of hunger. I desire nothing in this world but meate, drinke, and clothing, and a part in pleasure. And though rich men have better meanes to attaine to this glory than he that hath but little, yet there is not one of them that is contented, not one that saies to himselfe, I have enough. There is not one of them with whom I would exchange my pleasures for their riches." That was ever the rogue's reasoning; and that is why actually Lope de Vega, at the age of fourteen, as Montalván assures us, turned pícaro for pleasure, and in fiction, Don Diego Carriazo and Don Tomás de Avendaño of the *Ilustre fregona* did as much, going tunny-fishing to the *finibus terræ* of picaresque life, as Cervantes dubs it. The *Celestina* might be punningly scoffed at as the *Scelestina*, but it stood and still stands a faithful study of the human heart and of external reality, and the model of innumerable lesser works, among which, in part at least, may be ranged the romances of roguery.

Another Spanish antecedent of picaresque fiction was the Lucianic satire, which as early as 1528 had come to life in Spain in the *Diálogo de Mercurio y Carón* published anonymously, but due to Juan de Valdés, and perhaps as well to his brother, Alfonso. In spite of their heterodox views and secret allegiance to the Reformation, the brothers Valdés were tolerated by Charles Fifth; and, ready to perceive abuses in the Church and State, Juan, at least, was not chary of attacking them. That he possessed the critical faculty was attested by his *Diálogo de la lengua*, where the theme was literature; and that his satiric power lent something to the *Lazarillo de Tormes* is probable. So, too, the Lucianic *Crotalón*, supposedly from the pen of Cristóval de Villalón, must have had its influence, for the infancy of Alexander as depicted there bears an analogy to that of the Salamanca picaro. Yet the lumbering and learned style of the satire was in contrast with the fresh, free swing of the rogue story, and the most obvious heirs of such productions as the *Cro-*

talón and the *Mercurio y Carón* were the *Sueños* or the *Diablo cojuelo.*

It is in vain to seek more definite origins for the picaresque novel in the Peninsula. Clemencin, and after him Ticknor, asserted that the *Breve suma de la vida y hechos de Diego García de Paredes* was a romance of roguery in little. Paredes died in 1533, and his short autobiography was printed by 1559 at Saragossa, and again in 1584 at Alcalá de Henares, with the *Chrónica del gran capitán Gonçalo Hernandez de Córdova y Aguilar.* This very book the curate and the barber in *Quixote* contemplate, and the curate declares that so great was Paredes' strength that with a finger he could stop a mill-wheel in the midst of its fury. Mendoza in the *Guerra de Granada,* and Lope in the *Dorotea,* paid similar tribute to the "Samson of Extremadura," as he was nicknamed. But the autobiography is simply that of a brawny rascal who went to Italy, joined the papal halberdiers, was forced by poverty to thieve at night, cut off the head of a captain who reprehended him, killed his jailer, and performed impossible feats in combat. Except for manifest boastings, it was matter-of-fact, and devoid of humor, of tricks, and of style. The subject's actual life, indeed, was more picaresque than this narrative, for desertion and piracy were features of it, as was better shown in the account written by Tomás Tamayo de Vargas and published at Madrid in 1621. But at best no reliance is to be placed on García de Paredes as an elder brother to Lazarillo. The *Celestina* alone among early Spanish fictions was worthy to rank with it in art or in kind, and with these two nothing could compare in style save the *Epistles* of Guevara.

The claim of the *Lazarillo de Tormes* then to be the first romance of roguery and the originator of a literary species is unshaken. In 1554 at Burgos Juan de Junta published the earliest edition known, and on the twenty-sixth of February of the same year Salzedo, a a bookseller of Alcalá, brought out the tale with two slight changes. Martin Nucio in Antwerp gave a repetition of the Burgos edition the same year, and thenceforward the success of the little novel was never in doubt. In 1559, when the Archbishop of Seville and Inquisitor General, Fernando de Valdés, had placed it in the *Index Expurgatorius*, the *Lazarillo* continued still to circulate beyond his jurisdiction and even surreptitiously within it, so that Philip Second was merely politic in ordering his secretary, Juan López de Velasco, to amend and print it with the similarly revised *Propaladia* of Torres Naharro and the verses of Cristóval de Castillejo.[1] The *Al letor* of this *castigado* edition of 1573 states that while not of the same consideration as its companion pieces, this story "is so lively and faithful a representation of what it describes with such wit and grace that in its way it is estimable and has always been relished by all, whence, although prohibited in these realms, it has been commonly read and printed abroad." The emendations of the Inquisition were not so considerable as might have been expected, and because the *Lazarillo* was a daring book, too daring seemingly to have first been tried

[1] This *castigado* edition was also issued with the *Galateo Español* of Gracian Dantisco, and the *Destierro de la ignorancia* from the Italian of Horacio Riminaldo Boloñes, in 1599, at Madrid, and often later and elsewhere. From this circumstance Navarrete, in the *Bosquejo histórico sobre la novela española*, Vol. XXXIII. of the *Bib. de aut. esp.*, erroneously supposes Dantisco the expurgator.

in Spain, arose the myth of an Antwerp *editio princeps* of 1553, although its existence was never more than rumored.

The controversy as to the authorship of this anonymous fiction has resulted negatively in leaving the field, as it was at first an open one.[1] The most successful candidate for the honor of this romance of roguery's paternity has been Diego Hurtado de Mendoza. It is not probable that his name will ever be entirely dissociated from the tale, and yet no claim for him was put forward until half a century had elapsed, and with the publication at Mayence in 1607 of the *Catalogus clarorum Hispaniæ scriptorum . . . opera ac studio Valerii Andreæ Taxandri.* There a brief passage devoted to Mendoza concluded succinctly, "he composed

[1] For this argument at greater length see Alfred Morel-Fatio's Preface to the French *Lazarille de Tormes*, 1886, and his *Études sur l'Espagne*, Paris, 1888, Vol. I., p. 121 *et seq.* As purely negative criticism, M. Morel-Fatio's conclusions have not met general acceptance, although they are inevitable unless new facts can be adduced. Such an authority as Don Pascual de Gayangos dissents, however (State papers, Spanish Series, Henry VIII., Vol. VI.), and H. E. Watts in his essay on Quevedo and the picaresque novel mistakes Morel-Fatio's decision, supposing him to be urging the Ortega claim.

also poems in the vulgar tongue and the pleasant little book, entitled *Lazarillo de Tormes*." Two years before this the question of authorship had been raised for the first time by José de Sigüenza in his *Tercera parte de la historia de la orden de San Gerónimo* published at Madrid, and Juan de Ortega, a general of the order, had been accredited with the work, said to have been composed while a student at Salamanca, the proof resting upon the asserted discovery of the manuscript in his cell after his death. Curiously, the two traditions were straightway merged, for Schott in his *Hispaniæ bibliotheca* of 1608, affirming Mendoza to be the author, added that he produced it during his student days at Salamanca. But the *Lazarillo* could not have been written earlier than 1526, since reference is made to the Toledo *Cortes* of 1525 after the battle of Pavia, when Mendoza, probably a soldier, was certainly not a student. This was as firm ground as the attribution to either Ortega or Mendoza ever had to stand upon. Succeeding bibliographers upheld the title of one or of the other, and Nicolás Antonio in the *Bibliotheca hispana nova* of 1783 presented both, but neither the 1610 collection of Mendoza's works at Madrid, nor the 1627 biography of Lisbon, paid heed to suggestions of his connection with the *Lazarillo*, whose popularity would have recommended its ascription if possible. A late and still more chimerical hint proceeded from an Englishman, Dr. Lockier, dean of Peterborough, who, in conversation with the Rev. Joseph Spence, saddled the *Lazarillo* upon bishops of the mendicant order who were said to have composed it during their journey to the Council of Trent.[1] Neither Juan de Luna, the 1620 continuator, nor López de Velasco, the 1573 expurgator, had known the *Lazarillo's* author, although both recognized that the second part could not be by the hand that wrote the first. It is probable therefore that the need for giving the book the sanction of a well-known name, and Mendoza's indisputable gayety and wit shown in his *redondillas* and burlesque verses, was what established the tradition. If, however, the brilliant author of the *Guerra de Granada* has never been successfully identified with the undeclared author of the

[1] *Anecdotes, Observations, and Characters of Books and Men*, London, 1810, pp. 59–70.

Lazarillo, neither required the lustre of the other's name. With his authentic achievements in letters and statecraft, Mendoza could rest content, as could little Lazarus of roguish memory with his literary influence.

Lazarillo told his tale with a verve and directness that his imitators might well have copied. For him there was no beginning *in medias res.* With the very first sentence he gives his name and the names of his parents, and with the second sets the scene of his birth. Unimpeded, the narrative moves forward, tracing the rogue's adventures from master to master in the order of his service, and with never a backward glance. When one employer is left for another that is the last of him. Of his first master Lazarillo says, "What became of the old man afterwards I don't know, and neither did I ever give myself any pains to inquire." In the seven *tratados* of the original work, only four episodes were wrought out in detail, corresponding to four degrees of service, the first with a blind beggar, and the others with a miserly priest, a poor hidalgo, and an indulgence-seller. Beyond these, Lazarillo's masters were figures in outline, a busy-body friar who ran the boy's legs off, a painter, merely mentioned, who consigned him to color-mixing, a chaplain who hired him as water-carrier, an alguazil who drew him into the train of justice, and finally and best of all the royal government itself. In the office of public crier he forgot his past anxieties and pains, for if only as auctioneer and the publisher of the misdeeds of criminals flogged about town, he was still in the service of the king and emperor, whither, with the breaking up of feudalism, was tending the ambition of all classes. Of scoundrel stock, the picaro had come up somehow, from the bed of the river, through blows, and by supplementing chance with cheating tricks, to a position of comparative ease. The archpriest of Salvador, whose wine he had cried, gives him his own housekeeper to wed, and Lazarillo, after one brief misunderstanding with his patron and the lady concerning whispers of scandal, agrees that the bride shall resort as frequently as she please by night or day to the archpriest's house. Nor does he regret his complacence. To all the world he vows that his wife is as good as any in Toledo, conferring on him by the grace of God more benefits than he can hope to deserve. And so, with a touch of self-irony, the book ends.

In the plan of the whole, and in the treatment of the four main episodes, however, inheres the chief originality of the story, for it seems as if the early portion alone had been completed, and the rest laid down simply in a scheme for farther elaboration. There the masters are catalogued, but barely described or satirized; while with the initial portion they are drawn and rounded out. The blind beggar, who first relieves the virtuous Antonia Pérez of her hopeful son, and undertakes to teach him the ways of life in return for guidance about the country, is a Spanish type second only to the decayed noble with his suave graces and gnawing hunger. Jests of blind men and their boys had long circulated not only in the Peninsula, but through Europe. The mediæval conscience saw nothing repulsive in barbarities practised upon the infirm, and the primitive stage had abounded in pieces of rude wit quite in line with the pitiless war waged between Lazarillo and his beggar. One of these, indeed, a farce entitled *Le garçon et l'aveugle*, recorded as played at Tournai in

1277, is identical in spirit with the amplified Spanish account;[1] and this, together with the discovery of early fourteenth-century drawings of scenes afterwards included among Lazarillo's cheats upon his *ciego*, places beyond question the dependence of so much of the first romance of roguery upon previous dramatic representations.[2] Still, the narrative of the anti-hero of the Tormes for once and all fixed these stray jests about one character, and extended to every leader of a blind man thereafter the name in good Castilian of *lazarillo*.[3] The first bearer of that name, from the moment that his head is knocked against the stone bull of the Salamanca bridge, understands that he must cope with cunning and avarice by counter-cun-

[1] *Jahrbuch für rom. und eng. Litteratur*, Vol. VI., pp. 163–172 (1865).

[2] In Brit. Mus. MS. Roy. 10 E. IV., beginning at fol. 217; see *Athenæum* for Dec. 29, 1888, article by J. J. Jusserand.

[3] This fact has led even Brunet into error. In his *Table Méthodique*, under the caption of *Romans Espagnols*, he includes *El Lazarillo de ciegos caminantes desde Buenos-Ayres hasta Lima* . . . por Don Calixto Bustamente . . . en Gijon, 1773. Yet the book was not a novel at all, but simply a guide, as was more obviously the eighteenth-century Madrid publication, *Lazarillo ó nueva guia para los naturales y forasteros de Madrid.*

ning. All his endeavor is to get enough to subsist on. Sometimes he intercepts the coin given as a return for the beggar's prayers, changing it for smaller pieces in passing; but usually meat and drink is his spoil. He steals from the beggar's provision-bag, sucks wine from his jar through a straw, or drinks from a hole conveniently stopped with wax between draughts. The blind man may batter out the little rogue's teeth with blows from the jar, but Lazarillo will still be a thief. Grapes that the two have agreed to eat share and share alike he pilfers, and substitutes a cold turnip for a warm sausage on the roaster, only to be detected by its aroma on his breath. To pay for the cruel drubbings he gets, he leads his blind man over every stumbling-block in the way, and the climax of his vengeance is reached when, bidding the old man jump with all his might to clear a stream which does not exist, the victim dashes head-foremost against a stone post and falls back senseless. "How did you smell the sausage and not the post?" cries Lazarillo tauntingly before running off, and *oler el poste* ever since has been a Spanish locution; while in Shakspere's *Much Ado About Nothing* the speech of Benedick, "You stroke like the blind man; 'twas the boy that stole your meat, but you'll beat the post," probably refers to this incident.[1] As an acolyte, Lazarillo falls from the frying-pan into the fire, for the priest whom he serves is a miser, compared to whom the blind man for generosity was an Alexander. The old struggle for food never flags, but with new inventions to aid it, the sacrament loaves are now subject to hungry assaults until the assaulter, discovered at last, is dismissed.

At Toledo he meets his hidalgo, the happiest creation of the book, and the truest to the time. Here famine pursues him still, but no longer is it famine due to avarice. The noble, who by his airs and his dress seems lord of all, has nothing save his pride; and, as hungry as the boy, he is unutterably more miserable, since he dare not admit it or beg for relief. If broad farce marked the picaro's passes with the blind man, true comedy marks those with the jaunty

[1] A claim made by Aribau in his essay in the *Biblioteca de autores españoles*, Vol. III., but disputed without proof in *The Spanish Comic Novel*, in *Cornhill* for June, 1875. A somewhat similar blind-man trick, where the victim is lured off a precipice, occurs in Giacinto Nobili's *Il vagabondo*, Venetia, 1627, chap. 11, suggestive, too, of *King Lear*.

and starving esquire. In him all Spain was satirized, the Spain of early decadence that preferred to seem rather than to be. In the pitiful shifts and the desperate clinging to the gentlemanly ideal the light of a softer humor plays over this part of the story, where surely some chord of sympathy was touched in the heart of the writer. The rôle of the poor, proud gentleman braving it out in his stately way was altogether too exquisite not to be noted at home and abroad, and even brought upon the stage. The closest transcription for the latter was Gerbrand Adriaensen Brederoo's *Spaansche Brabander* in Dutch of 1617, printed the following year. There the Junker Jerolimo Rodrigo stalks down the streets of Amsterdam, as Lazarillo's fine master through those of Toledo; but even Brederoo never thought to alter his hero's nationality along with the language. To the bone the hidalgo was Spanish, a type of the people and country; and Spanish he remained. Of less consequence than the other three principal episodes was Lazarillo's service with the *buldero*, since it was little more than a refurbished tale from Massuccio's *Il novellino*, where in the fourth *novella* Fra

Girolamo of Spoleto makes the people of Sorrento believe that a bone he exhibits is the arm of Saint Luke. An accomplice contradicts this statement, whereupon Fra Girolamo prays to God for a demonstration of the truth of his words by the working of a miracle. Then the accomplice feigns to fall down dead, and Fra Girolamo by prayer restores him to life, collecting through the fame of this double miracle a great sum of money, becoming a prelate, and thereafter leading a lazy life with his comrade.[1]

In style as in matter, simplicity and naturalism distinguished the *Lazarillo de Tormes*, and in both it was strongly contrasted with productions of the *Amadis* cycle. Juan de Luna, in his 1620 revision, might criticise the language as French in construction rather than Spanish, but Luna overlooked the fact that only by his day had the use of pronouns been sloughed off in the southern idiom, as well as certain expressions formerly common to the two languages. By authorities in general the little novel has always been regarded as

[1] This was also the 1st story of the 26th chapter of *Il vagabondo*, 1627.

a monument of pure and idiomatic Castilian. Indisputably the first of the romances of roguery, it differed somewhat from the rest. What they often possessed, it certainly lacked. No breath of moralizing marred it, no pedantry or anecdotal ornament rendered its aimlessness tedious. Its anti-hero stole from necessity, while later rogues acquired the habit and the art of stealing from sheer delight. The satire, which was fierce, and especially so upon the clergy, had not that inclusiveness which later it attained, and Lazarillo himself as to emergence from his actions was only a step removed from Til Eulenspiegel. Yet these differences were all to be accounted for by the long interval between this work and its true successors, and the unevenness of its performance, in part, by its barely assimilated materials. The crude farce element at the start, the milder farcical passages regarding the ecclesiastic, the fine comedy of the hidalgo overtopping everything else and fairly modern in spirit, the reworked *novella* of the *buldero*, and then the reach of merely personal, fragmentary episodes ensuing, down to the last laughing fling at the archpriest and his mistress,—

these things constituted a narrative strangely mixed. The pace was never twice the same, leisurely at first and beating off hurriedly at last, it galloped, trotted, or walked at caprice, and the quality of the ground covered was even more changing. Such as it was, however, the *Lazarillo de Tormes* must rank as one of the most celebrated and influential of Spanish fictions.

The anonymous continuation which appeared in 1555 from the press of Martin Nucio was printed with a permission for four years, but was issued there at the same time by Guillermo Simon, who published the first part as well, notwithstanding Nucio's ostensibly exclusive imperial privilege. For this continuation, however, the booksellers of Antwerp or any other town need never have quarrelled, since its merit was not disproportionate to its bad success, and in the Peninsula it did not attain the dignity of print until 1844. Cardoso, from whom Nicolás Antonio took his cue, attributed it to a Fray Manuel of Oporto, but no sufficient interest was manifested in the story to make a claim to its authorship a particular honor. Curiously that fraction of *La segunda parte de*

Lazarillo de Tormes: y de sus fortunas y adversidades destined to achieve a semblance of renown was just what of it had perhaps least worth. This was the short initial chapter entitled "Lazarillo's account of the friendship he formed in Toledo with some Germans, and of what passed between them." In the earliest French translation of the *Lazarillo* in 1561 by Jean Saugrain at Paris, this chapter was appended to the first part, and usually, when the original story has since been published alone, this insignificant section of the anonymous continuation has tagged along.[1] Except in quantity it was no addition to the book, and the accident of its first inclusion seems slight justification for retaining it where, however, it has come to stay, even in English translations.

The fable of the sequel may have been inspired more directly than its parent part by the *Golden Ass*, but at all events a metamorphosis no less remarkable than that of Lucius

[1] M. Morel-Fatio, in his *Études sur l'Espagne*, implies that *all* editions of the first part after 1561 contained this chapter, but among others, those of Saragossa, 1599, and of Lisbon, 1626, did not have it, and Barezzi's Italian version of 1622 and 1626 ended as did the original.

is applied to the picaro. After his good fellowship with the Germans, he embarks in Charles Fifth's expedition against the Barbary Turks, and during a terrible tempest, fortifying himself against the elements with drink, sinks unharmed with his ship to the bottom of the sea. Surrounded by multitudes of fishes determined upon his destruction, he retires to a cave and puts up so fervent a prayer to heaven, and vows so many pilgrimages to the Virgin, that for his benefit a miracle is performed, and he becomes a tunny-fish. In this guise follow his chief adventures, which are not particularly roguish, and in which his sword, happily retained, enables him to take a prominent part in the politics of the water world. He weds a fish, has three fishes for children, but, after intriguing experiences at the court of the tunnies, is drawn forth in a net by fishers off Gibraltar. In wresting his sword from him, they find it grasped by a human hand and arm proceeding from his mouth, and hearing themselves addressed in the Spanish tongue, they convey their treasure-trove to Seville to be shown to the Duke of Medina-Sidonia. Here the fish cerements are peeled from Lazarillo, and as man once more he proceeds to Salamanca with the intention of founding a school for the study of the tunny language. Accordingly he is examined by the doctors of the university as was Pantagruel by those of the Sorbonne, and answers precisely the same questions earlier proposed to Eulenspiegel at Prague.

It is needless to dilate upon the fact that except for the name there is nothing in common between this sequel and its original. The essentially Spanish and picaresque service of masters was absent, the fantastic story out of hand had replaced the careful observation of actual life, and while satire of real men and women lurked beneath the fish's scales, as it had too beneath the impossible shepherd's cloak, only a retrogression to the old style was apparent, and no further development of the new. If success at court through the medium of feminine influence was secretly attacked here, the whole manner of this poor fiction was more closely that of the heroic than of the anti-heroic genre; and even the sword of the transformed Lazarillo savored of Excalibur. The decision of Velasco in 1573 that this second part was *muy impertinente y desgraciado* has never been disapproved, and Juan de Luna sixty-five years later avowed the chief incentive to the composition of his sequel to have been to replace an account so devoid of truth, — *sin rastro de verdad*.

In translation, this continuation had little vogue. In 1596 it appeared at London published by John Oxenbridge and Englished by William Phiston. In 1598 it was issued at Antwerp by Guislain Jansens with the first part done into French by Jean Vander Meeren. The Italian version of 1635, by Barezzo Barezzi of Venice, added a second part based on this, but a thing of shreds and patches with hundreds of pages of irrelevant discourse gathered from miscellaneous authors and put into the mouth of Lazarillo. Not until the thirty-second chapter, indeed, did the picaro get to the point of embarking against the Turks, and even then the discursiveness was scarcely mitigated. The original *Lazarillo de Tormes*, however, was deservedly successful in other languages, if not altogether immune from alteration. In 1561 it was printed in French as *L'histoire plaisante et facetieuse du Lazare de Tormes*, and again in Antwerp in 1594 and 1598 by Jansens. In 1601 Nicolas and Pierre Bonfons brought it out with the Spanish and French texts, the latter the work of P. B. Parisian, or, as the later reprints had it, of M. P. B. P. After 1620, Juan de Luna's sequel was usually included in all translations, but the first part appeared alone in 1653 done into French doggerel by Le Sieur de B. In Dutch, *De ghenuechlijke ende cluchtighe historie van Lazarus van Tormes wt Spaingen* was published at Delft as early as 1579; and in England the *Marvelous dedes and the lyf of Lazaro de Tormes* had been licensed in the Stationers' Registers in 1568. Possibly it was published then, and very certainly it was printed by 1576; for in the copy of *Howleglass*[1] given to Gabriel Harvey by the author of the *Faerie Queene*, the former in a manuscript note on the last leaf spoke of having "received of Mr. Spensar" "this Howleglass, with Skoggin, Skelton, & Lazarillo," on the twentieth of December, 1578, undoubtedly referring to *The pleasaunt historie of Lazarillo de Tormes a Spaniarde* . . .

[1] This unique copy of the English *Eulenspiegel* is in the Bodleian Library.

drawen out of Spanish by David Rouland of Anglesey, described by Bagford as published by Henrie Binneman in 1576, and re-issued in 1586 and 1596. Of the many English editions that ensued, the most altered was that of 1688, printed by J. Leake at London, and adding to the first part, both a variation upon Luna's sequel, Englished separately as early as 1622, and *The Life and Death of Young Lazarillo, Son and Heir to Old Lazarillo de Tormes.* The latter was a compilation of rogueries from Aleman, Quevedo, and the authors of the *English Rogue*, but hopelessly poor. In Germany, in 1617, Niclas Ulenhart issued his *Zwo kurtzweilige, lustige, vnd lächerliche Historien, die erste, von Lazarillo de Tormes einem Spanier*, translating Cervantes' picaresque tale, *Rinconete y Cortadillo*, for the companion-piece, with the title *Isaac Winkelfelder und Jobst von der Schneid.* The Italian *Lazarillo*, published by Barezzi as *Il picariglio castigliano*, with a second edition by 1622, and a third in 1626, appropriated still another *novela* of Cervantes, *La gitanilla*, giving it to the hidalgo, Lazarillo's third master, to tell.

While the original *Lazarillo de Tormes* had

attracted sufficient attention to lend its name to the Flanders extravaganza of 1555, and by 1559 in a comedy of Timoneda's was spoken of as already widely known, the latter year saw both parts banned by the Inquisition, and picaresque fiction, just launching out, forced back upon the ways. For a long time, then, it must have seemed that the first romance of roguery was to be also the last. Fear of the ecclesiastical censor could not alone have been responsible for the failure of Spanish authors to emulate the example of the cynical unknown. It is rather to be supposed that the anti-hero's hour had not yet come. For the romances of chivalry, if waning somewhat in charm, were reënforced now by pastorals. In the latter half of the century the *Diana* was followed up by such works as *Los diez libros de fortuna de amor*, the *Fílida*, the *Galatea*, the *Desengaño de celos*, the *Ninfas y pastores de Henares*, and the *Pastor de Iberia* down to Lope's *Arcadia* of 1598. Readers were not yet prepared to behold their aristocratic favorites ousted by low-lived picaroons. Nor had social conditions come to that crisis which presently was to furnish not only the substance for a continuous fiction of rogues, but the public for its appreciation. Timoneda's *Patrañuelo* of 1566 here and there in its tales might instance the picaresque manner, and the same author's *Sobremesa y alivio de caminantes* of 1569 follow suit in its shorter anecdotes, but beyond this and Christóval de Chaves' *Relación de la cárcel de Sevilla*, composed from 1585 to 1597, nothing was ventured in rogue fiction until the *Guzman de Alfarache* of 1599. It is true that Ginés de Pasamonte in *Don Quixote*,[1] lauding his own autobiography, cries, "Woe betide *Lazarillo de Tormes* and all of that kind that have been or shall be written," seeming to imply the existence at that time of at least several works of the picaresque series. Yet this was penned before 1605, when, as far as is known, only *Guzman* was printed. The *Pícara Justina* of the same year, but licensed earlier than the *Quixote*, had mentioned Cervantes' masterpiece along with choice company in truncated sextillas:

Mas famo — que doña Oli —
Que don Quixo — y Lazari —
Que Alfarache y Celesti —

[1] Pt. I., 22.

so that the *Pícara* itself could scarcely have been included in Pasamonte's reckoning. If Guzman, then, had any immediate predecessors, they have gone the way of all things perishable; and to Mateo Aleman of Seville belongs the fame of being the first openly to avow the authorship of a romance of roguery.

Aleman was a conscientious, hard-working government official, for nearly twenty years a *contador de resultas* to Philip Second, and generally a man of affairs. He conducted himself so uprightly that he fell into poverty and was obliged to retire to a life of less estimation, his painstaking studies having hurt both his estates and health. "Let the tongue of men be listened unto, and ye shall hear nothing so common as the publishing of his praise, no less in Spain than in Italy, France, Flanders, and Germany, which mine own ears and eyes can truly testify and avow," said his eulogist, the lieutenant Luis Valdés; and a further tribute he paid to the novel itself, declaring, "We are all beholding to Mateo Aleman. . . . For we must acknowledge him to be the first that till this very day hath in such a kind of style as his, come to discover and excommunicate vice."[1] From the immediate and immense success of the *contador's* venture in fiction, however, he could have derived little benefit, and his alleged preference for being a poor philosopher rather than a rich flatterer was to be gratified to the letter. Of his own accord he left office and went over to Mexico, where in 1609, from the press of Jerónimo Balli, he issued the *Ortografía Castellana*, begun before his departure from Spain. He translated the *Odes* of Horace; and a *Life* of Saint Anthony of Padua, undertaken to accomplish a vow, was written between the appearance of the first and second parts of *Guzman*. Employed all day in other concerns, Aleman would reel off enough in the watches of the night to keep the printers occupied until the next sundown. Such facility, however, had its dangers, as was proved by the prolixity of the adventures of the picaro no less than the miracles of the saint.

The *Primera parte de Guzman de Alfarache*, dedicated to Don Francisco de Rojas, Marqués de Poza, first appeared at Madrid, published by

[1] *The Rogue: or, the Life of Guzman de Alfarache*, James Mabbe, 1622, preface.

the Licenciado Varez de Castro, in March, 1599. Within a few months a Barcelona and a Saragossa edition had followed, and in 1600, Portugal, France, and Flanders gave Spanish reprints, and Gabriel Chappuys, a French redaction at Paris. Mateo Aleman had pleased the popular fancy; adopting the ground plan of the *Lazarillo* in satirizing society through the experience in service of a merry rascal, he had broadened the social field reviewed, as well as the function of the picaro himself. Like Lazarillo, this younger anti-hero tells his own story, beginning with birth, and even in the fashion of Laurence Sterne entering into prenatal detail. Of illegitimate but not mean origin, the picaro had for father a Genoese with an adventurous past, for mother the mistress of a rich old priest. The name Guzman descends to him maternally from an amour with one of that famous family, and the title Alfarache from possessions of his father at San Juan de Alfarache, close to Seville. Thus equipped for pedigree, the picaro, at the age of fourteen, leaves his widowed and impoverished mother, to seek his fortune in the world. The *Primera parte* of 1599 is presented then in three books, the first relating Guzman's early experiences which make plain to him that he must trick others or himself be tricked, and particularly satirizing inns; the second describing his initiation into active roguery in Spain and his cheats in service there; and the third, showing his ups and downs in Italy, from his life among the begging fraternity of Rome, to his happier days as buffoon with a cardinal and page to the French ambassador. At the end of the first book is inserted the romantic story of *Osmin y Daraxa*, as told by a priest met on the road; and at the end of the third book, a gentleman at the embassy recounts the tragic tale of *Dorido y Clorinia*, — the one in the manner of Italian *novelle*, the other in that of the then popular Moorish histories, whose fountain-head was the *Guerras civiles de Granada*, of Ginés Pérez de Hita, published in its first part only four years previously. Except for these episodes, *Guzman de Alfarache* was as essentially a romance of roguery as the *Lazarillo*, and very much more thoroughgoing in treatment.

In the opening book, Guzman himself is often victimized, from his misfortunes at the miserable inn of Cantillana to his false arrest upon the highway. But after that he can give points to the devil if need be. Not only has he become convinced of the theoretical efficacy of roguery, but he is adroit in its practice. Serving an apprenticeship with a dishonest innkeeper, he repairs to Madrid, becomes a mendicant and scullion to a cook, with whom and from whom he steals all he can. Similarly, he serves an apothecary, who is cleverly defrauded while the picaro escapes with the proceeds to Toledo, setting up for a man of fashion, and growing unaccountably older in the short interval. His love intrigues are not altogether fortunate; for once he is obliged to take refuge from his lady's brother in a washtub, and again he loses a considerable sum by his devotion to a scheming charmer. On being reduced to service once more, military life claims him; and, enlisting with a company at Almagro, there is no sharp practice up to highway robbery in which, with the connivance of the captain, Guzman is not engaged. At Barcelona, his best exploit before embarking for Italy is tricking a goldsmith whom he accuses of robbing him of an *agnus dei*, for which the jeweller has just paid him a round sum. Dismissed at Genoa as too dangerous a companion, the rogue seeks out his relatives, but is badly received, and resorts again to begging, travelling to Rome, and leading a vagrant life there among the infamous Italian rogues, the *bianti* of *Il vagabondo*. In the cardinal's service, the practical jokes played by Guzman are rather diverting than malicious, resembling Lazarillo's devices for provision-getting, except that Guzman does not pilfer from necessity. Dismissed for inveterate gaming, he is engaged by the ambassador as a likely agent to manage his gallantries; and so closes the first part of this romance of roguery, the plan for all of which was already conceived by Aleman, for in a preface to his 1599 publication, he announced that Guzman was writing from the galleys, after having, on his return from Italy, studied with the intention of becoming a churchman, but by reason of frequent backslidings, abandoning that course for new rogueries.

Upon this suggestion, and probably upon something more definite in the way of actual access to Aleman's unpublished second part, Juan Martí, the Valencian lawyer, issued his sequel intended to deceive the public.[1] This must have appeared at Valencia in 1602, as the later editions of Juan Flamenco in Madrid in 1603 and of Roger Velpius in Brussels of 1604 testify. Martí's very *nom de guerre*, Mateo Luxan de Sayavedra, was meant to suggest Mateo Aleman, and the literary pirate, like Aleman, signed himself *natural vezino de Sevilla*. Taking up the story where Aleman had left it, Martí sent Guzman to Naples. There a priest becomes his master and treats the picaro well. As fashionable as ever he was at Toledo, Guzman makes love to several ladies, one of whom, getting what she can from him, has him set upon and beaten. He is mistaken for a thief, and coming out of jail turns steward to recruit; these incidents obviously echo those in Aleman's first part. Guzman, descanting at tedious length upon cookery, is assistant in the kitchen of the viceroy, with whom he returns to Rome and finally to Spain. At Barcelona, one of his quondam mendicant friends, Micer Morcon, reveals the secrets of the begging trade, and the picaro goes to Alcalá

[1] See Fúster, *Biblioteca Valenciana*, Tom I., 198, for identification of Sayavedra with Martí.

to prosecute his studies in theology and the arts. When he is wearied of this, and on the way to Valencia to seek service, a lackey of Vizcaya holds forth through three whole chapters upon the nobility of that province and its people. From first to last, discursiveness is a chief ingredient of this sequel. Lawyers and divination are harangued against. An entire sermon on the duty of forgiving enemies is included, and the anti-hero, hearing it, determines to become a friar. But resolution never counts for anything with him or any other rogue, and presently he joins a company of comedians instead, having fallen in love with their leading lady. Of the triumphal entry into Valencia of Margarita de Austria, the bride of Philip Third, Guzman can scarcely say enough, but unable to resist the temptation of stealing amid the confusion of these festivities, he is apprehended and sent to the galleys.

The sequel concludes promising a third part, which fortunately never appeared; for although no romantic episodes were introduced here, every blemish of the original was magnified, and not many of the virtues retained. Aleman, if at times he had been coarse, had remained always virile, and his satire irresistible. Martí without coarseness, and with satirical intention, was nevertheless dull and weak, his irony of little value, and the only new element he provided, the view of student life, taken at best on his predecessor's hint. In style, Aleman had been so discursive as to try the patience of the most indulgent reader, and his moralizings unnecessary and out of place; but Martí in this respect was intolerable. He expanded Aleman's most fatiguing tirades, and lacked even the piquant seasoning of proverbs which had enlivened the other's narrative. Like its original, Martí's sequel was portioned off into three books, but upon no particular principle. The first half was the better, and as absence of invention seems to have been Martí's prime trait, it is probable that here he was most dependent upon Aleman's manuscript, and in the latter and poorer half of his story most dependent upon himself.

As a sequel, however, the book was certainly more of a success than had been the Antwerp continuation of the *Lazarillo*, remaining true to the plan of the romance of roguery, and possessing some merit in its details even where its anecdotal character was prejudicial to fresh observation. In view of the bold plan of Martí to emulate the tactics of his picaro and defraud Aleman, the latter's forbearance was admirable. Forced like Cervantes at Avellaneda's *Quixote* forgery to publish a second part in self-defence, Aleman in 1605, in the prefatory remarks to his authentic *Segunda parte*, admitted that he had been too prodigal in communicating his papers, but added, "I must acknowledge in this my competitor . . . his great learning, his nimble wit, his deep judgment, his pleasant conceits, and his general knowledge in all humane and divine letters, and that his discourses throughout are of that quality and condition that I do much envy them, and should be proud that they were mine." The injured novelist did not intend, however, to submit quietly to imposition. His title-page bore the caution *Y advierta el letor que la segunda parte que salió antes desta no era mia, solo esta lo es;* and in the text he resorted to a more effective expedient still, making the plagiarist a prominent character of the story, and of course a rogue.

Guzman in this second part is found where the original had left him, acting as *gracioso* and master of intrigues for the French ambassador. In the latter capacity he is shut out in the rain all night by a lady and run away with by a pig to the diversion of the whole town, so that unable to endure the ridicule heaped upon him he turns his back on the Eternal City and goes to Florence. This is done on the advice of one who previously befriended and now seeks to fleece him, no other than Sayavedra, the author of the spurious continuation, with whom Aleman proceeds to deal according to his deserts. At Siena, Sayavedra's gang steals Guzman's luggage, but Sayavedra himself is caught and banished, and heaping coals of fire on his head, Guzman takes the thief into his service as lackey. Arrived at Bologna in search of his goods, Guzman is falsely jailed, but on being released, merits the punishment already suffered by practising with Sayavedra a gambling cheat which enriches them both. On the road, Sayavedra tells the story of his roguish life, and in order that no doubt may be left as to the blow aimed at Aleman's rival, Sayavedra is given a brother named Juan

Martí, of Valencia. Guzman robs a merchant by wit, and visiting his inhospitable relatives at Genoa pays them back by cheating his uncle with an imitation gold chain before sailing for Spain. On the voyage in a storm, the final ironic touch is administered to Sayavedra; for he goes mad, and calling himself Guzman de Alfarache, springs overboard to death. At Madrid, Guzman sets up in trade and marries, but living too high and counting too confidently upon the wealth of his father-in-law, he fails, his wife dies, and her dowry reverts. Like the Guzman of Martí then, this one attends the University of Alcalá. He marries his landlady's daughter, and with his wife cozens a merchant and others. A judge pays the lady profitable attentions, but wearying of her, banishes the faithful pair from the metropolis, and in Seville this true helpmeet elopes from her lord with a ship-master. Guzman, obliged to seek service as of old, tricks a widow and her priestly counsellor and is retained as the lady's steward. He steals right and left in office, and attempting to escape in women's clothes he is captured and sent to the galleys. There he has various successes, but finally gains his freedom by betraying a convict plot to give over the ship to the Turks, and the story ends promising a third part, said to be already completed, but never printed, and probably not penned.

Throughout, the parallelism with Martí was evident, and Aleman confessed to having incorporated some of his rival's choicest ideas, vowing to do the same in his third part if forced to it by the false Sayavedra. The division into three books was retained, and Aleman here reverted to his scheme of interpolated episodes, closing the second book with the Italian *novella* tale read for diversion on the voyage to Spain and entitled *Bonafacio y Dorotea*, and in the first book in the anecdote of *Don Luis de Castro y Rodrigo de Montalvo*, told by the same gentleman who related *Dorido y Clorinia*, borrowing direct from Massuccio.[1] The style of this *Segunda parte* was more discursive and involved than that of the original, but far less so than Juan Martí's continuation. The satire was keen, the incidents following in fairly rapid

[1] This story, the 41st of *Il novellino*, reappeared in Scarron's *Précaution inutile*, and in the sub-plot of Beaumont and Fletcher's *Little French Lawyer*.

succession with greater coherence in plot than Martí could boast. But a significant difference from either of the preceding parts was the slighter relative importance here of the service with masters. The rogue himself as an individual was coming to the fore, his personal adventures and his roguery being almost as much the subject as the society described. Aleman had called his book *Atalaya de la vida humana*, the beacon-tower of human life, but the public would not take kindly to the name, persisting rather in styling it simply *The Rogue*, from him in whom the interest centred.[1] Although the entire novel was incomplete, and this continuation in many ways inferior to its original, the reception that both parts met with was not only gratifying, but beyond all expectation. The statement of Luis Valdés, that already by 1605 the number of printed volumes exceeded fifty thousand, and the number of impressions twenty-six, is to be taken with a large grain of allowance, but there is still no doubt of the fiction's

[1] Aleman even complains of this, saying of his work, *que habiéndolo intitulado Atalaya de la vida humana, dieron en llamarle Pícaro, y no se conoce ya por otro nombre.* Parte II., Libro I., 6.

having many editions from the start. In translation its fortune was no less remarkable. First taken over into French by Gabriel Chappuys in 1600, it was retranslated by Jean Chapelain in 1619 as *Le gueux*, and the second part in 1620 as *Le voleur*. In 1695 at Amsterdam, Gabriel Bremond, himself almost a rogue, gave an arrangement of it, with attacks on the police, and added observations; and in 1732 the definitive translation by Le Sage appeared, omitting the moralizing of the original. In Italy, Barezzo Barezzi, the indefatigable adaptor of other men's works, brought out the initial part very faithfully for him in 1606 at Venice, and the other parts followed in 1615 and 1616.

In Germany, Ægidius Albertinus in 1615 at Munich published *Guzman* with a decidedly Teutonic twist. Indeed, in its latter half, the book of Albertinus is practically an original production, resembling and contributing to the later *Simplicissimus*, but greatly its inferior. As if the Spanish had not been discursive enough, Albertinus foisted upon it interminable dissertations, to admit which the fiction proper was much abridged. Aleman's first part was compressed to a hundred pages, and it is noteworthy that Martí's continuation, not Aleman's, was the basis for what followed. But grave alterations were made, Guzman's ecclesiastical master becoming an Italian count, and the picaro devoting himself to study as the result of the religious warnings of a hermit. He marries in Turin, turns innkeeper, enters a Swiss Benedictine cloister, and as a comedian appears in Germany with his company, travelling to Amiens in France, and back again to Spain, where he is condemned to be hanged, but has his sentence commuted to the galleys. After three years there, he is released, and receives above one hundred and sixty pages of edifying advice from another hermit to prepare him for a pilgrimage of repentance. The promised third part was issued eleven years later at Frankfort by Martin Frewdenhold with a still stronger analogy to Grimmelshausen. For Guzman's pilgrimage, which is here the theme, takes him to the East in a career not unlike that of the Spessart hero. He is captured by Turks, steals from his masters, and as a bath-attendant at Cairo escapes with a German count's valuables. He visits Jerusalem and Sinai, becomes a charlatan, wanders to the

Euphrates, Babylon, and Nineveh, and returning passes from Tripoli to Venice. Cheated out of all his wealth by an alchemist, he turns gondolier, robs a Jew, and sails for Amsterdam with an accomplice who defrauds him. Enlisting as a marine aboard a man-of-war, a detailed voyage is made to Japan, and Guzman returns, to be in succession a calendar-writer, an apothecary, a ruffian and pander, a cheating miller, and even an enchanter, with no less than a dozen chapters of reflections on soothsaying, dreams, and witchcraft. At last, on his recalling the instructions of his hermit, repentance sets in afresh, and "*Gusman bekompt Rewe und Leyd dasz er sich so weit eingelassen, vvnd fängt an sich zu bessern.*"

In England, Aleman's fiction met with a better fate than in Germany; for James Mabbe, the able translator of the *Celestina*, was also the foster-father there of *The Rogue: or, the Life of Guzman de Alfarache*, printed for Edward Blount at London in 1622. This excellent folio edition contained Aleman's two parts with his prefaces faithfully rendered and with copious marginal notes added by Mabbe; some of which, it is true, were sententious moral reflections, but most of them critical aids. Reëditings followed, the translator's *Celestina* being bound up with the Oxford 1630 series, and also with some copies of the third edition of London, 1634. Abridged translations with Mabbe's for a basis were forthcoming, and the lives of Osmin and Daraxa were separately published along with Cervantes' *novelas* in 1723. Before the appearance of the Latin version of the *Celestina*, Gaspar Barth's *Pornoboscodidascalus Latinus*, Guzman had found his way into that language through the patronage of Gaspar Ens, a literary hack of Cologne, who in 1623 published there the first part as *Vitæ humanæ proscenium.* A *Pars secunda* was issued by Ens in 1624; but the brief third part did not come out until 1652 in the edition of the whole *Dantisci, sumptibus Georgii Forsteri.* The first part in its main events coincided with Aleman's original, although compressed and with intrusions here and there, such as a long description of the city of Rome, and discourses backed up with quotations from Horace, Seneca, and Plutarch. Its most remarkable feature, however, was the inclusion of Lazarillo de Tormes as a character. He is met on the road by Guzman and tells his own tale where in Spanish occurs that of *Osmin y Daraxa*. In the Latin sequel, Aleman's second part was followed, but in place of the story of *Dorido y Clorinia* was another, while the episode of *Claudio y Dorotea* was not touched. This volume fell short of ending with the Spanish, for Guzman, getting no further than his second marriage and his removal to Madrid, breaks off abruptly; —*Sed expectas forte ut narrem que mihi Madriti evenerint? Narrabo tum quum mortem meam ipse narrabo. Nunc valete & plaudite.* In the third part, which did appear when Ens if not Guzman was dead, the picaro after his release from the galleys turns actor and finally becomes a hermit, a conclusion manifestly drawn from the German redaction. In Dutch the novel was anonymously translated as *Het leven van Gusman d' Alfarache 't afbeeldsel van't menschelijk leven.* The first edition was of Harlem, 1655, and the second was published in the same year at Rotterdam by Abraham Pietersz with a third under the same auspices in 1658. Although shortened, and the romantic episodes rejected, this work embraced the chief incidents of Aleman's original, and the same divisions into parts and books. Other editions followed, and as Brederoo had written the *Spaansche Brabander* from the *Lazarillo*, so Thomas Asselijn in 1693 evolved from this novel his comedy *Gusman de Alfarache of de doorsleepene bedelaers.* Through Europe, indeed, Guzman became a popular hero like Eulenspiegel, Gargantua, or Harlequin, and the commonest criminal pamphlets in England blazoned forth his name with unfailing regularity, assuring the public "that our English Gusman is as famous in these times as ever the Spanish in his time."[1] No other Spanish picaresque novel ever attained the same general celebrity or exercised so broad an influence as this one.[2]

In the same year with Aleman's true sequel to *Guzman de Alfarache* appeared the *Libro de entretenimiento de la pícara Justina*, published at Medina del Campo by Christóval Lasso Vaca, and professedly written by the Licenciado Francisco de Ubeda, *natural de* Toledo. The real author seems to have been a Dominican friar, Andrés Pérez of Leon, anxious to

[1] *The English Gusman, or The History of that Unparallel'd Thief, James Hind*, by G. F(idge), London, 1652.

[2] For the indebtedness of Grimmelshausen to *Guzman*, see *Eine Quelle des Simplicissimus* by Rudolf von Payer, in *Zeitschrift f. deutsche Phil.*, Vol. XXII., 93 *et seq.*

conceal his identity for professional reasons and because of his works of a different character. In 1601 he had published a life of San Raimundo de Peñaforte, and there were yet to come from his pen a series of *Sermones de Cuaresma y de los santos.* *Justina* is accounted for as produced during the pious Pérez's student days at Alcalá, as *Lazarillo* in the Mendoza and Ortega tradition was soon to be ascribed to student leisure at Salamanca. And certainly there was little ecclesiastical ring in the book in spite of its assiduous moralizings. Guzman de Alfarache was the principal model proposed, although the *Celestina* and *Lazarillo* were included with others in specific mention. In the *Prologo sumario*,[1] the description of Justina by herself is said to be that sent by her to Guzman on the eve of her marriage to him; and at the end of the story, in promising a sequel, Justina declares herself already the spouse of that re-

[1] Justina says here, *No hay enredo en Celestina, chistes en Momo, simplezas en Lázaro, elegancias en Guevara, chistes en Eufrosina, enredos in Patrañuelos, cuentos in Asno de Oro, y generalmente no hay cosa buena en romancero, comedia ni poeta español cuya nota aquí no tengo, cuya quinta esencia aquí no saque.*

doubtable picaro. That she must have been a worthy companion to the rogue, all who read her story will admit, although the sequel and her actual relations with Alfarache were never further exploited. As with other novels of the class, this one was autobiographical. The heroine, after elaborate prologues, and addresses to pen, ink, and paper, rambling and ejaculatory in style, gives her genealogy; for a rogue should prove roguery a heritage, she says. Her father's father was a gambling barber, her great-grandfather a dwarf and a puppet-showman. Jugglers and tumblers, costumers and bagpipers, were ever her ancestors. As daughter of a rogue innkeeper, she treats of that trade, and of the death of her parents,— her father who was killed by an irate customer he had cheated, and her mother who choked on a stolen sausage. Justina's adventuring begins after these melancholy events with a journey she undertakes to a fiesta at Arenillas. This ends with her capture by the mad crew of students, and her cleverly outwitting them so that they are all brought tipsy to her village, Mansilla, and forced to run for their lives. Justina's second wandering is to Leon, where she defrauds her hostess, changes a silver *agnus dei* for a gold one, blackmails a hermit, steals an ass to replace one stolen from her, disguises as a beggar in order to get funds, and after an irreverent pilgrimage to a neighboring shrine, befools a student with a pretended box of honey. She and a barber then trick an inn-mistress who falls ill, the barber passing as physician; and when the picara in turn has tricked the barber, she returns home to Mansilla a second time in triumph. Justina's third sallying forth is occasioned by the persecution of her brothers and sisters, who endeavor to disinherit her. She arranges, however, for a lover to steal for her the family jewels and plate, and so is allowed to depart unsuspected, going to Rioseco to enter a legal protest against her relatives. The lawyers get her money, and Justina is forced to take service with a wool-spinner, a *Morisca*. But the rich old hag dies, and Justina appropriates her property, pretending to be her heiress. With fresh funds and more discretion, the lawsuit ends satisfactorily, and for the third time Justina returns to Mansilla victorious. Each of these sallies has constituted a book, the first entitled *La pícara montañesa*, the second and longest, *La pícara romera*, and the third, *La pícara pleiteista*. The fourth and last book is *La pícara novia*. Here Justina is unsuccessfully courted by a maker of toys, by a foolish flagellant, and by lesser claimants; but finally she is wooed and won by a card-playing widower, an ancient man of arms, already appointed by the court the guardian of her estate, and therefore the wisest possible choice because the most profitable. The tale winds up with the marriage festival at the inn, where in the merriment even the *corregidor* dances, and Justina sounds her farewell, saying: "It is the wedding-night—good night!"

Each chapter was preceded by a versified gloss, fifty-one different measures being used in all, and among them the *versos de cabo roto*, found also in the *Quixote*. Poor as were these inventions for the most part, Pérez was undoubtedly proud of his talent, and the title-page said of the work, *Es juntamente Arte Poética.* Beginning thus with rhyme, each chapter closed with cold reason in an *aprovechamiento* containing the moral lesson to be conveyed, "which will show thee," says the title, "how to profit from this reading to flee the deceits current to-day." And in his prologue to the reader, the author, admitting that some few through his work might learn of devices undreamt of before, opposes to this the fact that every one must learn too to shun something of the world's naughtiness, while if the book had been all vanity it must have been wrong to print it, but if all holiness few would have read it. These moralizings, however, suggest that the volume to begin with lacked the holiness which the Inquisition as a condition of publication later insisted upon its appending to its vanity. But if the profitable remarks of the *Pícara Justina* are conveniently disposed for omission in reading, mere discursiveness is still as much as ever a feature, and the involved and eccentric style of Pérez renders his narrative fatiguing. He has been hailed as the first corruptor of Spanish prose, ever since Cervantes in the *Viage del Parnaso* condemned him,[1] and extravagant conceits, alliterations, plays on words, puns, and learned affectation are inseparable from

[1] Mayans y Siscar, preface to *Justina*, 1735, Madrid.

his writing. Like Juan Martí, his greatest lack was inventiveness, but in wit and satiric snap he was Martí's superior. The first to herald the brilliant burlesque of Quevedo's *Buscon*, he was the first also to seize upon a woman to be the rogue of his book, and in that respect he was the predecessor of Barbadillo and of Solórzano. From the mere fact of replacing the anti-hero by an anti-heroine, the element of the service of masters was almost eliminated. For women in those days were not admitted to many trades. Justina herself had but one mistress, the *Morisca ;* and thereafter, down to Moll Flanders, the women of the romances of roguery were treated rather according to their lovers and their personal exploits than according to their changes of service. The picara thus secured inevitably greater freedom of movement than the picaro, and through her was to come the evolution of the rogue novel to a higher stage, where the theme was not so much the classes in society as individual adventures and aspects of life. Justina herself was a distinct personality, as Lazarillo had not been, and Solórzano's Rufina proved more of a character still. The incidents of Pérez's novel were commonplace and deficient in ingenuity; Justina's wanderings were all within a narrow radius, of no real interest, and the action describing them was slow and circumscribed. Only the jocular handling of the story could have saved it from oblivion. No long tales, and few anecdotes, were introduced, mere rambling discourses taking their place. A good deal of travel description in a limited circuit was in evidence, as well as coarseness of the kind found in the German jest-books and in the *Buscon*. But the charge of lubricity often brought against Pérez is altogether unfounded. He knew nothing of the insinuating art of the French *conteur*, and his anti-heroine was chaste against odds. A *Segundo tomo*, to consist of four books like the first instalment, was promised, but spared the public, in spite of the moderate success of the original, which in 1608 was brought out in Brussels by Olivero Brunello, and in 1640 at Barcelona, where it was called *La pícara montañesa llamada Justina.*

In Italian the *Vita della picara Giustina Diez* was published at Venice by Barezzo Barezzi in 1624 in a first part, which, however, carried Justina only as far as her triumph over the students. The remainder of the two hundred odd pages of this redaction consisted of inserted anecdotes, and six love tàles cribbed from various sources and supposed to be told to the picara by the six chief gentlemen of Mansilla in honor of her return there. In 1629, Barezzi issued his *Volume secondo intitolato la dama vagante*, which got only as far in Justina's Leon journey as her stealing the ass. Two-thirds of this miserable piece of book-making was irrelevant interpolation consisting, in the words of Barezzi, of *molte vaghe historie, nouvellette, detti, sentenze, e facetie singolari.* The rest of the original, Barezzi was undoubtedly reserving as the framework for a third and fourth part which he threatened but failed to produce. The verses, although retained, he made no attempt to translate, speaking of them slightingly as serving *più a pompa che ad utile.* In Germany the Italian version was the basis for the book *Der Landstürtzerin Justinae Dietzin Picarae die frewdige Dama genannt*, printed at Frankfort by Caspar Röteln in 1627.[1] Barezzi was referred to on the title-page and his per-

[1] Gräsze gives 1618 for German *Justina*, whose translation, he states, forms the 2te Theil of Albertinus' *Guzman.*

formance exactly rendered. In France, an anonymous translation, the privilege for which dates from the first of May, 1635, was issued by Pierre Blaise, Pierre Bilaine, and Anthoine de Sommaville entitled *La narquoise Justine lecture pleine de recreatives aventures & de morales railleries contre plusieurs conditions humaines.* In the preface admission was made of Justina's superfluity of discourse being sloughed off, and restraint imposed upon her mingling of the sacred with the profane, but it was urged upon the reader to remember still *que ce n'est pas une vièrge de cloistre qui parle, mais une narquoise libertine.* In English, the work of Pérez led the list of similar fictions included in Captain John Stevens' *The Spanish Libertines*, printed at London by Samuel Bunchley in 1707. Here the *Pícara* was entitled, *Justina, the Country Jilt*, and Stevens said of his version, "it is not a translation, but rather an extract of all that is diverting and good in the original, which is swell'd up with so much cant and reflection as really renders it tedious and unpleasant." Whatever may be said of Stevens' novelistic rendering of the *Celestina*, his *Justina* in eight chapters was a vast improvement upon the

Spanish, whose jesting humor and chief incidents were retained, while the profitable remarks were dropped.

The *Lazarillo*, the *Guzman*, and the *Justina* were preëminently works of the first stage of picaresque fiction, not merely from chronology, but also from their general character. Formless in plan, and burlesque in style, they were crude, their satire fierce, their morality, if present, appended. To be ranged along with them as romances of roguery of the same primitive order were others, the *Desordenada codicia* of 1619, the *Lazarillo de Manzanares* of 1620, the *Alonso moço de muchos amos* of 1624 and 1626, and the *Vida i hechos de Estevanillo Gonzalez* of 1646. Between these there were wide differences, but in all, observation was paramount, the picaro but just emerging from his deeds, and a nearness to the origins of the romance of roguery apparent.

Estevanillo Gonzalez, although published so much later than the others, was cruder than any. It appeared at Antwerp with the widow of Juan Cnobbart, and, dedicated to Ottavio Piccolomini, it bore every mark of being the work of his buffoon, its professed author,

Estevanillo, *hombre de buen humor.*[1] Indeed, it contained commendatory verses from the picaro's companions in the Duke of Amalfi's service, and the prologue made apparent the literary ancestry of the book. "I warn you," says the rogue of his story, "that it is neither the pretended life of Guzman de Alfarache, nor the fabulous life of Lazarillo de Tormes, nor the supposed life of the Cavallero de la Tenaza, but a true relation," and the witnesses, he adds, are alive to verify its accuracy. In spite of this, it is probable that the autobiography, if such it really were, took as much from the romances of roguery and the author's invention as it did from fact, and distinct traces of picaresque influence are to be noted, especially from *Lazarillo*, *Guzman*, and the *Buscon.* Estevanillo, in telling his story, passes lightly over his parentage and his education, — his father a Spaniard in Italy, his mother dying there of eating mushrooms, and the picaro's best achieve-

[1] Nicolás Antonio believed in the apocryphal Brussels 1619 and Madrid 1620 editions, both of which are now generally discredited. The date, 1645, is specifically mentioned in the 13th *capítulo*, and Piccolomini himself was not born until 1599. Nor is there any ground for the occasional attribution of this work to the author of the *Diablo cojuelo.*

ment at school, the sale of powders to strengthen the memory. Apprenticed to a barber, he plies his trade so badly as to be obliged to flee from wrath, and between the shrine at Loretto and the haunt of rogues at Siena, he wanders about, cheating at dice and cards with the connivance of innkeepers. At Livorno he embarks in the fleet of the Duke of Tuscany, and constant mischief at the expense of the soldiers ensues. In Palermo he serves and tries to rob the secretary of Doña Juana de Austria, and in the kitchen of the archbishop he is a scullion. At Rome he is pledged to another barber, but decamps with his master's tools and sets up for a surgeon in Naples; and after a varied career in every capacity from alguazil to robber, he sails for Barcelona. Estevanillo, with two picaros for companions, travels over Spain as a pilgrim, living on what can be pilfered or received in charity, and turning his hand to all trades, from convent-building and goat-herding, to water-carrying and charlatanry. After having served in the army and navy successively, and as pedler, ballad-singer, and fisherman, he finally sails to Saint Malo and journeys through Normandy and Brittany.

He enlists against the English, but pockets his advance pay and escapes. He defrauds the Jewish colony at Rouen by distributing the feigned ashes of his father, a martyr to the Inquisition. He raises a blister on his leg at Paris after the fashion of Guzman at Rome and Gaeta, and returns down the Rhine to Italy, selling needles and making further profitable enlistments. From Naples he brings up in Spain and is condemned to death as author of a camp brawl, but being pardoned he is shortly back in Lombardy, and then in Bavaria, where as always his valor is conspicuous by its absence. He is *vivandero* in the Low Countries; and when Count Piccolomini, general of the imperial forces, receives him for page and jester, his day of glory has come. He stands head covered before the Empress of Austria; he is entertained by the viceroy at Prague. He arranges satiric shows for carnivals, carries important despatches from one end of Europe to the other, is hand and glove with all sovereigns, and shines in every waggery perpetrated in court or camp. In Flanders he steals from a commissary by tunnelling under his bed. In Poland he wins in a drinking-bout by means of sponges in his boot. In the Tyrol he is pressed into the service of a half-breed captain. On board an Italian felucca he taps a keg of wine, and lying down beside it at night pretends to be smoking when in reality he is drinking. At a village fiesta in Spain he carries off the prize for competitive verses to be hung on the church door, as nobody can understand what he writes, and he is accounted a second Góngora. At Falmouth, in England, he vends lemons and converses with the inhabitants in Latin; and in Brussels he discovers that a mistress he had left there has run off with another man. Disconsolate, and having the example of Charles Fifth before him, he too determines to abdicate. In retiring, his San Yuste is Naples, where he goes to take charge of a card house, a gift from the Spanish king. He writes verses to his mistress and an elegy upon the death of the Empress María. Then he takes leave of his master, the Duke of Amalfi, and the courtiers, composing a farewell poem to them without the use of the letter O.

This strange and hurried account, with its quips and satirical turns, its absolute lack of plan or development, was unique in some respects among the romances of roguery. Rude and merciless, it was a succession of practical jokes of a low order, perpetrated without malice and also without pity. True comedy never appeared, but coarse and ironic, with a devotion to fact not always entertaining, the narrative rattled on devoid of self-consciousness, meaning, or moral. The range of journeys undertaken was the largest in Spanish picaresque fiction, and travel description a considerable part of the story. But tricks, not observation, were always uppermost in the jesting anti-hero's mind. Estevanillo throughout was a merry rogue, a coward, and an inordinate guzzler. No other picaro could drink so much or so often as he. In more than one way resembling Falstaff, he, too, was a friend of those in high station, maintained by his distinguished patrons for his vices mellowed with wit, and yet, as compared with Falstaff, only a clown and not a man. The tradition of the service of masters Estevanillo preserved, but his pace was so rapid that he failed to secure the full benefit of the scheme. Often he did not stop to look about him, and his sketchy story gave nothing in detail save particular jests. Thus it did not possess the realistic merits of others of its class, and as a work of art it fell distinctly below them.

The English translation by Captain Stevens in *The Spanish Libertines* of 1707, dubbed Estevanillo "the most arch and comical of scoundrels"; and Stevens in his preface says, "In the opinion of many, he seems to have outdone Lazarillo de Tormes, Guzman de Alfarache, and all other rogues that have hitherto appear'd in print," adding that, "had the original come sooner to hand, it would have had first place in his book, but that wherever it is, the reader, it is hoped, will find his end here, which is diversion." The Englishing was done with spirit and practically in full, although all but two of the poems were suppressed, and new chapter divisions were made after the seventh of the Spanish. In France in 1734, Le Sage brought out his novel, the *Histoire d'Estevanille Gonzalès, surnommé le garçon de bonne humeur: tirée de l'Espagnol.* The title gave every reason to suppose the French work a translation of the other, and has led to repeated assertions to that effect, but it is nothing of the sort. As a matter of fact, the only borrowings from the Spanish

Estevanillo are to be found in Le Sage's first chapter, where the picaro's experiment as a barber, and his service as an hospital surgeon at Naples, are transferred from the first and third chapters of the original; but beyond that, there is no connection whatever with the Spanish tale. Ottavio Piccolomini is not mentioned, and the whole action revolves historically about the Conde de Lémos and more especially the Duque de Osuna, whom Estevanillo serves in his disgrace and up to the time of his death. The very opening of the misleading fiction of Le Sage is not from the Spanish *Estevanillo*, but from the *Vida de don Gregorio Guadaña* in the *Siglo Pitagórico*. Other passages were suggested by *Rinconete y Cortadillo*, by the *Alonso moço de muchos amos* and by *Marcos de Obregon*. From the latter at least one chapter was taken bodily,[1] and from the same source comes the account of Joachim's captivity at Algiers. The author of *Gil Blas*, who had improved *Guzman de Alfarache* by his omissions in doing it into French, may have felt that in *Estevanillo Gonzalez* he had something capable of improvement only by complete rewriting, thus retaining noth-

[1] *Estevanillo*, Chap. 20; *Marcos*, Rel. III., 4.

ing save the name of his original. Whatever it was that induced Le Sage to attempt to hoodwink the public with a pseudo-translation, he certainly succeeded. In his *Gil Blas*, however, the story of Scipion embodied the incident of Estevanillo's attempted flight from Palermo, after robbing his master, who in the French work was a gamester, and it also included Estevanillo's taking part in a play as the boy king of Leon, and running off from the stage Moors with his elegant costume. Le Sage said, too, of Scipion, "*on aurait pu le surnommer à juste titre le garçon de bonne humeur.*"[1] But if the Spanish novel were not flattered by general imitation, it had some influence, and chief among the fictions resembling and probably inspired by it was the *Avantures tragi-comiques du Chevalier de la Gaillardise* of the Sieur de Préfontaine, issued in 1662.

In 1620 at Madrid, the *Lazarillo de Manzanares, con otras cinco novelas*, by Juan Cortés de Tolosa, was published by the widow of Alonso Martin. All but one of the *novelas* had already appeared in Tolosa's *Discursos morales* three years earlier; two of them

[1] *Gil Blas*, X., 10; X., 8; and *Estevanillo*, 2.

were picaresque; but the *Lazarillo* was still more rigorously an imitation of the first romance of roguery. The anti-hero even begins his story as did the rogue of the Tormes, addressing the reader *Ansi que sabra vuessa merced.* He is born in Madrid, his father being a thief in jail for attempting to hang his mother, who is under suspicion of witchcraft. Lazarillo being sent to study at Alcalá, falls in love there with a pastry-cook and assists her in making pies from dead horses, but two misfortunes befall him, for his mistress presents him with a daughter, and his mother is seized by the Inquisition. Going to the Guadalaxara, Lazarillo secures a place with a one-eyed sacristan whose wife has a barber for gallant. In Madrid once more, the picaro serves a ruffian who badgers gentlemen that visit his clever spouse; but the lady who is left a widow being quickly consoled with another, Lazarillo is involved in domestic quarrels between the bride and her new husband, and for false swearing is stripped and whipped. Sadly he takes the road to Ciguença, but meeting a cheating hermit is admitted into partnership. For several years they wander over Spain together, Lazarillo finding his mother gracing an *auto da fé* at Toledo, and thankful to hear her confess him not really her son. After the hermit's death, Lazarillo conducts unfortunate intrigues for a young gentleman of Seville, becomes a beggar, and serves as tutor to the nephews of a canon. These pupils are rogues who make him think himself stabbed and bleed him with wine, and who rob their uncle by means of hired rascals clad in sheets, brought to his treasure room as statues. Lazarillo, resigning from this charge, is fleeced by a Portuguese, who pretends to be an alchemist, and dining unwittingly with a thief is taken to prison along with him. Released, he sets up a school, where all goes well until a matrimonial agent so hounds him concerning a marriage with a woman, beautiful in soul but in nothing else, that he has to resort to flight. But poetic justice is done, for the agent must wed his client himself, going to the galleys and the lady into exile, while Lazarillo returns and is engaged by an hidalgo in a matter of commerce to embark for Mexico, — "*donde me sucedio lo que a vuessa merced prometo en la segunda parte, prosiguendo hasta q̄ ya por mi mucha vejez no me pude contar entre los vivos.*"

No encouragement for the publication of this second part was merited or received, however, nor did it ever appear. And the first part does not seem to have reached a second edition or any translation.

The story was written in the usual jesting style, verging upon the burlesque, with anecdotes inserted, and a long dream of Lazarillo's, suggestive of the later *Diablo cojuelo* fantasy. It was coarse and crude, and even more than any of its forerunners the tale lacked unity, while most of the incidents were not worth reciting. Reminiscences of other picaresque novels were not wanting, and the title proclaimed its close relation to the *Lazarillo de Tormes;* but the almost certain prototype of this mediocre romance was the *Buscon* of Quevedo still in manuscript. There can be little question of the connection between these two fictions, and while Quevedo, whose work was not printed until 1626, might have borrowed from this, altering his own story composed more than a decade before, it is more probable that Tolosa was the plagiarist. Like Don Pablos, Lazarillo de Manzanares begins with student life and ends by hoisting sail for the Indies, and the passages relating to the witchcraft of the mothers of both anti-heroes, and to the pastry-trade, as well as the whole manner of the narrative, can leave no doubt of imitation. The *Marcos de Obregon*, published two years before, very likely suggested the amour of the barber with the sacristan's wife, but at all events the *Lazarillo de Manzanares* did not copy its predecessors closely enough to be redeemed through their virtues from its own mediocrity, and its only interest to-day, aside from its place in the picaresque development, is its rarity.

For Tolosa's *Discursos morales* of Saragossa, 1617, Lope de Vega, Barbadillo, and Vélez de Guevara wrote eulogistic verses, but the *novelas* printed there in the third book were, if anything, inferior to the *Lazarillo de Manzanares*. The first of them, the *Novela del licenciado Periquin* was picaresque, telling the story of the son of Pedro de la Oliva and María la Carga of Segovia. After a roguish youth he serves a farrier, a barber, and an innkeeper, thieving in each trade, and finally so injured, as the result of a quarrel, that he goes to a hospital. Beggary is his next resort, and then service with a curate, a lawyer, and a physician. He becomes a tutor at Ciudad Real and attempts a marriage cheat upon the daughter of an apothecary. Failing in this, he spends four years at Salamanca, studying and writing a book on the moral properties of animals. Forced to leave the university on account of an affray, he enlists as *alférez* for Sicily, becoming now Don Pedro. He has love complications with two ladies, who pursue him as he is endeavoring to elude them in a ship; one is drowned, he marries the other, and lives to be rich and happy, "dying full of days and not empty of merit." Of every picaro, as of this one, it might be said, "Periquin laughed with the happy, wept with the sad, gamed with the rogue . . . was in short a chameleon, which takes the color of the cloth on which it is placed." More vigorous, if less exactly picaresque, smoother in style and generally better, was the *Novela de la comadre*, the tale of a cheat put upon Beatriz, a midwife, and her pretty daughter, Felipa, of Jaen, by Molino, a lackey of Felipa's betrothed. The lover himself is absent in the Indies, but has left Molino to guard his interests. The picaro, however, associates with him another scoundrel, and the two playing a double rôle, first as religious ascetics, and then as wealthy Mexicans, manage very adroitly to ruin Beatriz, Felipa, and the latter's cousin, Isabel, escaping with their goods and leaving their ambitious victims each an heir. The humor of the story lay in the masquerade of the rogue lackeys as father confessors at one moment, and as gallants at the next, their holy disguise being used to aid and abet their rogueries.

Differing from any other of the picaresque novels of the first stage and embracing both the crude observation of rogue life and a distinct rogue fiction as well, the *Desordenada codicia de los bienes agenos* of 1619 was a curious accession to the series. Its author, Dr. Carlos García, of whom Nicolás Antonio says *Nescio quis, doctorem sese nuncpans*, had already printed at Paris in 1617 the more famous *Antipatía de los Franceses y Españoles*, his only work known to Antonio. Treating of the alliance between France and Spain through the marriage of Louis Thirteenth with Anne of Austria, this book was of sufficient general interest to be issued both in Spanish and French in 1622 and several times thereafter, in Italian in 1658, in German in 1676, and in English in 1704.[1] García himself must have been a refugee at the French court, where at that period the antechambers of the great were filled with Castilian adventurers, and it was from Paris and the press of Adrian Tiffaine that the *Desordenada* was published. In a bantering fashion the book compares the miseries of a prison to the pains of hell, and describes the life of the prisoners who live apostolically without scrip, staff, or shoes, having nothing superfluous or double. In eating they use their five fingers for spoons, and must drink from a pit in the top of their hats, getting more grease than wine. For napkins they have their skirts, "and for a tablecloth the wrong side of a poor old cloak, threadbare and fuller of beasts than the linen cloth which Saint Peter saw in Damascus." The author purchasing with silver the good-will of the rabble comes to be largely consulted by the gallants of hell, and by one thief in particular, Andrés, who expatiates upon the antiquity and nobility of his art. From nothing you

[1] For a fuller account of this and of García, see preface to the reprint of it together with the *Codicia de los bienes agenos* in Tomo VII. of *Libros de antaño*, Madrid, 1877.

make something in this trade, he says. All the monarchs of the earth practise it as well as the ecclesiastics and the merchants. Relating his own story, Andrés tells of the untimely end of his cheating parents, Pedro and Esperanza, who were hanged with others of the family for a little matter; the ceremony was performed by their dutiful son himself in order to save his own neck. He was apprenticed to a shoemaker, where it took him some time to learn to stitch, having been taught always to rip, but being detected in a notable cheat, he was scourged about the streets and banished. Entering the ranks of professional picaros after this, he lauds thieving anew as a liberal art practised by all, from the blind man who steals the half of every song he sings, to the physician applying plasters to feed the disease and swell his fee. Then the thirteen orders of Spanish rogues are described, with the functions of each. Personal reminiscences of the narrator in this or that order lead him finally to tell of being bound up in a bale and sent to a goldsmith whom he intended to rob. In cutting his way out to liberty he sliced an apprentice asleep on the bale, and so was sent to the galleys at Marseilles. But his wit did not forsake him there, for professing a knowledge of magic, he guaranteed to the galley captain and a steward to soften the hearts of their obdurate ladies by enchantment. At the full of the moon going to the fields with the picaro alone, the credulous captain was persuaded to strip and crawl into a sack, and the majordomo to be bound naked with a cord and his lady's hair, after which, knocking off his chain, and with the shivering lovers' horses, clothing, and money, Andrés rode blithely away. In Lyons he contracted an alliance with a lady of light virtue who pretended to love him for himself, and whom he loved for her pearl necklace. One night when he thought her sleeping, he arose, and on the point of being detected in stealing the necklace, had only time to swallow the pearls one by one. The police used an emetic to reveal the fraud, and Andrés again graced the cart's tail. At Paris when an accomplice in a bale had effected an entrance to a tradesman's warehouse and was throwing booty from the window to Andrés in the street, the watch came up and caught them both. The accomplice was sent to the galleys, and Andrés is in jail here expecting a like sentence. He confides the statutes and customs of the thieving fraternity to the author, with which this remarkable volume is brought to a close.

In Spanish this book's only predecessor as to a study of rogue language was the *Romances de germanía de varios autores, con el vocabulario por la orden del a. b. c.* of Juan Hidalgo, published in 1609. Christóval de Chaves, at the close of the second part of the *Relación de la cárcel de Sevilla* 1585–1597, had said, "*Pareciome poner aquí un breve discurso de algunos vocablos desta gente*," but his promise had not been fulfilled. Hidalgo, however, besides his canting verses, had given a dictionary of above twelve hundred words of thieves' slang which incidentally set forth orders of rogues, although without distinct gradations among them. The *Rinconete y Cortadillo* of Cervantes had been a still nearer approach; for, published with the *Novelas exemplares* in 1613, it depicted the notorious *hampa* assemblage of Seville and outlined what García gave in detail. Andrés, when pressed to divulge his true name and birthplace, makes the same reply as Rincon with Monipodio's approval, to the effect that the wise thief conceals such things, since then he can always plead to a first offence, and his relatives will be spared the pain of hearing their names coupled with his on the gallows. Jest-book lore furnished something toward this story too, and passages closely resembling several in *Til Eulenspiegel* are present. But the significance of the little fiction is its influence upon later works. The pretended magic practised upon the galley captain and the steward was repeated in the robber's spell upon Valentin in *La vraye histoire comique de Francion* of 1622. The incident of the swallowed pearls formed the tenth story of the third book of the *Histoire générale des larrons* of 1625.[1] This same episode appeared also in the *English Rogue* of Richard Head and Francis Kirkman, 1665–1671, as did the boot-stealing exploit of Andrés, and the account of his being discovered in hiding under a bed by a dog and a cat quarrelling there. The latter device cropped up in Spanish in

[1] The first book was issued at Paris, Martin Collet, 1623; the second and third books, Rolin Baragues, 1625; the three together, first at Rouen, M. du Souillet, ou J. de la Mare. The author was Sieur d'Aubrincourt or F. D. C. Lyonnois, pseudonymes probably of François de Calvi.

the *Novelas morales* of Agreda y Vargas of 1620, and in English in *The Complete History of the Lives and Robberies of the Most Notorious Highwaymen*, by Captain Alexander Smith, published from 1714 to 1720. This contained many other borrowings from the *Desordenada codicia*, including the pearl and boot incidents, verbatim descriptions of prison life, and the trick of having a crier proclaim articles just stolen as already found, so as to divert attention from the escaping thief.

And yet in Spain the *Desordenada codicia* had but one edition, although abroad its fortune was better. From its sub-title of *La antigüedad y nobleza de los ladrones* it was translated in French as *L'antiquité des larrons* by D'Audiguier in 1621, with later editions at Paris in 1623, and at Rouen in 1632. In English, it appeared as *The Sonne of the Rogue, or the Politick Theefe; With the Antiquitie of Theeves*, translated from the French by W. M., and noting the fact that a Dutch redaction had already come out. An English reprint in 1650 was the same in all respects except bearing the title, *Lavernae or the Spanish Gipsy; the whole Art, Mystery, Antiquity, Company, Noblenesse, and Excellency of Theeves and Theeving.* That the *Desordenada codicia* should have been appreciated in England was natural, for it came closer than any other Spanish work to following the course suggested in the rogue-pamphlets of Harman, Greene, and Dekker, and but for its humor and satire was not unlike its contemporaries there, the *Essayes and Characters of a Prison and Prisoners* by Geffray Mynshul of 1618, or more nearly still, *The Compter's Commonwealth* by William Fennor in 1617, reprinted in 1619 as *The Miseries of a Jaile.*

On the dividing line between the romances of roguery of the first and of the more cultivated kind stood the *Buscón* of Quevedo and the *Alonso moço de muchos amos* of the Dr. Gerónimo de Alcalá Yañez y Rivera. The latter resembled its predecessors in that it held fast to the service of masters, and was occupied rather with the rogue's observation of conditions of life than with his personal exploits; but the former accentuated the satire of the *Lazarillo* genre, and, passing lightly over the scheme of service, and observation of estates, it laid stress upon the rogue himself as a professional picaro, drawing out for him a more definite character as the chief interest in the story. It is therefore to be ranked as the first of the perfected picaresque novels, although still coarse and virulent, while the *Alonso*, if deficient in satire, was still of the primitive type and its last representative. This novel was published in two parts separately, the first at Madrid in 1624, and the second at Valladolid in 1626. Its author, signing himself *médico y cirujano, vezino, y natural de la ciudad de Segovia*, had studied the classics and theology at Alcalá, and medicine at Valencia. His lapse into fiction at the age of fifty-one proving more successful that his other literary ventures, the issue of a second edition of the original *Alonso moço de muchos amos* at Barcelona in 1625 must have spurred him on to compose his continuation, although in the prologue there he professes to have written it many years before, but to have feared putting it to press on account of the size of the volume. The story as to form was dialogued, although practically autobiographical; for, of the two personages who speak in the first part, a vicar and the anti-hero himself, the vicar's rôle is merely an excuse, Alonso recounting his life in response to an occasional perfunctory query. The picaro, when the scene opens, is employed as lay-brother in a convent, and tells his tale to the vicar of evenings as they walk abroad to take the air. He was early bereft of his parents, his father dying, and his mother leaving him with her brother, a miserly curate, by whom Alonso was so abused that he ran away to Salamanca. Hazed and faring ill at the university, he turned soldier, and with a rascally company foraged over Spain, until a brawl with peasants forced him to seek refuge with a sacristan. Rebukes administered to this master gained his dismissal, and going to Toledo he was engaged by a poor hidalgo, married to an ugly wife without a *real*. The miseries endured here and the poetizings of the bridegroom and ill-temper of the bride sent Alonzo questing once more, after advice administered to all concerned; and at Madrid he became secretary to a newly appointed judge for Córdova. Here he was successful until his fondness for counselling forced his departure for Seville. After adventures at an inn on the road, where matrimony was almost thrust upon him, he served a physician, praising the profession, but ousted from it for his unremitting talking. In Valencia he was employed as esquire by a poor widow, who, in defending her virtue, killed a mulatto, and Alonso, informing the authorities, was imprisoned for complicity. On his release he went to the Indies as servant to the chief alguazil of Mexico, and in that country, by clever commerce, grew rich. Losing everything, however, by shipwreck in trading with China, he returned to Seville to join a band of strolling players. All went well until a boy who tried to push past the doorkeeper at a performance was killed by a blow from the money-bag, whereupon Alonso, taking flight with the rest, found service with some nuns. Turned away by them after an illness, he came to the convent where already he has spent fourteen years as *donado*, whence the title, *El donado hablador*, the gossiping lay-brother, given to the book by its later publishers.

The sequel was conformable in plan and conduct to this original, arranged in dialogue as before, but Alonso having become a hermit, and the vicar giving place to the curate of San Zoles. The latter was a lay-figure as the vicar had been, although given more to say, and addicted to frequent moralizing on his own account. Alonso, picking up the thread of his narrative where he had left it, tells how he came to leave his position as *donado*, being discharged for much talking. He was kidnapped by gypsies, with whom he led a thieving life until, having escaped, he set up for a noble at Saragossa, attended social functions uninvited, and finally married a wealthy widow. Her sons, however, gave him no peace, and after two years and a half of purgatory, her death released him. As poor as ever, he wandered to Lisbon, serving a gentleman whose daughter he was at pains to guard from an obstreperous lover. The gallant he tricked and shut out in the rain as Guzman was served by the ambassador's lady, but the servants being leagued against Alonso for his prating, he left, and at Toro was employed by a bad painter, in whose pictures the sun and moon had to be labelled to be recognized. At Segovia, Alonso turned wool-carder, and embarking at Alicante for Barcelona he was driven in a storm with his old friends the comedians to Algiers and captured. Ransomed by the Santissima Trinidad, Alonso, in accordance with a vow, returned to Spain as a hermit, in which estate the curate of San Zoles now finds him.

Both parts of this novel were exceedingly discursive, containing together nearly fifty purely illustrative anecdotes, impeding the action, which but for them might have been fairly rapid and interesting. Besides these inserted fables, jests, and folklore tales, the moralizing was constant, and unrelieved by the keen satire that had distinguished *Guzman de Alfarache* or the *Pícara Justina.* Sometimes, indeed, satire was absent, although always included in the aggressively picaresque situations; but the anti-hero himself was less a picaro than his brothers, and often only an adventurer passing through society with eyes wide open. His character was inconsistent as Guzman's had been, for at one moment a rogue, at the next he would be declaring the purpose of his gossiping to be pious, the result of a "just zeal and being minded to bear some fruit in serving God with good counsel." This gratuitous distribution of advice figured as the Donado's principal trait, and brought him into all his difficulties. Perhaps the worthy author meant to have a fling at so common a failing, yet he was sadly subject to it himself. Ramblingly he dealt with everything, whether germane to his story or not, eulogizing at length his native city of Segovia, calling attention to himself as the writer of a pamphlet on the miracles of Nuestra Señora de la Fuenciscla, and entering into an extensive discussion with sacred citations to prove that the Virgin was a blonde. Apart from these digressions, the fiction itself was entertaining, and its view of life in the Peninsula graphic and exact. The anti-hero was still subject to events, and as always a fatalist. When ruined by the loss at sea of his merchandise, he exclaims, "I now have nothing to fear nor to lose; poor I was and poor I am; fortune has faced about, but if I thought myself a prince, being a picaro, I am still a picaro, come what will."

Although the *Alonso, Servant of Many Masters*, was frequently republished in Spain, it found no translators and was never influential abroad.[1]

[1] However, in the *Trutz-Simplex . . . Lebensbeschreibung der Erzbetrügerin und Landstörtzerin Courage* of Hans Christolph von Grimmelshausen, 1670, Kap. 19, there is some resemblance to the cheats of the *gitanas* in *Alonso*, and the general description of gypsy life, Kap. 27, is very similar.

For all that, it has not wanted admirers, from Georg Philipp Harsdörffer, the seventeenth-century translator of Gil Polo's *Diana* in Germany, to George Borrow in England, who said of it, "perhaps with the single exception of the grand work of Cervantes, there is no novel in existence which can compete with it for grave quiet humor, while for knowledge of the human mind and acute observation, we do not believe its equal is to be found." After such extravagant tribute, it was a matter of course that Borrow should add, with more fervor than wisdom, "*Gil Blas* sinks immeasurably below the *Alonso* of the Segovia Doctor."[1]

[1] *The Zincali, or An Account of the Gypsies in Spain,* London, 1843, I., p. 26.

CHAPTER V

THE EMERGENCE OF PERSONALITY

In the inevitable progression of fiction from events toward character, the picaresque novel in Spain was bound to show a change from its early to its later development, and the touchstone of this change was necessarily the emergence of the anti-hero as a person with a career of his own. The story of observation began to feel the need of personal interest, and of ordering events in accordance with some general idea, instead of describing merely impressions of external life pouring in pell-mell, confusedly. Therefore the romances of roguery of the second stage were tales in which less attention was paid to the classes of society, and more to the observer. Because he was a rogue, the eye was rather fixed now on his rogueries, not as mere tricks, but as expressing himself and contributing to a plot. Discursiveness and moralizing tended thus to dwindle, as the importance of the fiction itself was emphasized, and romantic elements began more and more to intrude for contrast, while the form of the narrative became less stereotyped and simple. The *Hyia de Celestina* and the *Necio bien afortunado* of Barbadillo, the *Lazarillo de Tormes* of Luna, the *Marcos de Obregon* of Espinel, and the *Teresa*, *Trapaza*, and *Garduña* of Solórzano were the principal works of this stage. The first of these in time and as to type, however, was the *Buscon* of Francisco Gómez de Quevedo y Villegas.

Issued at Saragossa in July, 1626, by Pedro Verges for Roberto Duport, the *Historia de la vida del buscon llamado Don Pablos, ejemplo de vagamundos y espejo de tacaños* was regarded as so marketable that Alonso Pérez, father of the poet, Pérez de Montalván, was condemned the following year for attempting to infringe Duport's rights with a Madrid reprint; legitimate editions appeared at Barcelona in 1627, at Rouen in 1629, and at Pamplona in 1631. Duport in his dedication to the friar Juan Agustín de Funes spoke of the story as *émulo de Guzman de Alfarache, . . . y tan agudo y gracioso como Don Quixote*, while less interested approbation was general. But the novel at the moment of its publication must have been well known already to Quevedo's intimates, if not to the reading public in general; for its composition is certainly to be assigned to the first decade of the seventeenth century, contemporary allusions contained in it ranging between 1602 and 1607, and the presence of the court at Madrid, and the mention of the hanged poet, Alonso Alvarez, drunk to by the *valientes* of Seville, suggesting the latter date or 1608 as the most likely for its completion. Quevedo was rarely in a hurry to print. His half-picaresque *Cartas del Cavallero de la Tenaza*, dating from the beginning of the century, were not published until 1627 with the *Sueños*, themselves written from 1607 to 1622. But in manuscript all of these works were popular from the first, and the author by so circulating them secured his fame without endangering his person, since the gauntlet of Church and State censorship had not to be run, and to disavow a troublesome piece was easy. Quevedo is called by Quintana "*el padre de la risa, el tesoro de los chistes, la fuente de las sales, el maestro de la jocositad*," and two talents he certainly possessed to an extraordinary degree, that of satire and that of observation, conspiring to make his presentations of low life inimitable. With the *Capitulaciones de la vida de corte y oficios entretenidos en ello*, composed in 1603 or 1604, he had given an early and careful study of the kingdom of rogues, including classifications of knaves and their functions, to have been acquired only by personal experience. There he passed in review the army of mendicants and swindlers, the real and pretended maimed, the ruffians, the gamblers, the courtesans, the complacent husbands, rascals of every shade and description from the jargoning crew of *germanía* to the sleekest of parasites. All that was needed was the thread of a story to bind such folk and such scenes together, and this was provided in the *Historia de la vida del gran tacaño*, as the *Buscon*, after its author's death, came to be called.

As rapidly told as the adventures of the first *Lazarillo de Tormes*, and with as little moralizing, the life of Pablos, the anti-hero of Segovia, is related by himself, from his birth as the son of a sharping father and an heretical mother, to his flight to the Indies after a drunken exploit in Seville. He learns from his parents that the trade of appropriating others' property is no base mechanic art, and at school, by toadying to a rich youth, Don Diego, prepares the way for attending him at a boarding establishment and the university as page. The drolleries of early student life are followed at the *pupilage* of the miserly Cabra by a losing fight against starvation, and at Alcalá by new rogueries to compensate for the torments of being hazed. When Pablos, not much the wiser for his dip into education, is recalled to Segovia to receive his inheritance, on the hanging of his father and the arrest by the Inquisition of his mother, he leaves one half of the town laughing at the other half's losses. A mad engineer, an eccentric fencing master, and a priestly poet enliven the journey to Madrid, beyond which a soldier, a gambling hermit, and a Genoese usurer are his travelling companions. Entering Segovia, Pablos spies his quartered sire adorning the city gate, and comes upon his uncle, the hangman, belaboring the backs of a train of culprits. This worthy relative entertains his nephew and a strange rogue company, but Pablos, who cannot think of adopting the hanging trade, runs away for Madrid when his portion is in hand, determined to see the world for himself. On the road he overtakes a mock hidalgo, the veriest rascal in Spain, by whom he is entertained with a minute account of the cheating fraternity of the capital, and the second book of the novel opens with the introduction of Pablos to these ornaments of society. They are skilled in infinite frauds and ruled by an old woman, who unfortunately gets them all into jail. But Pablos, bribing his way out and making love to his landlady's daughter, claims to be a noble and wealthy, and then to escape paying his board pretends to be seized by the Inquisition for magic. On commencing a cheat upon some fine ladies, hoping to secure a rich wife, the rare treat which he furnishes them goes for naught, as he is recognized by his old master and sorely beaten. The picaro, convalescing, turns beggar, hiring children to steal for him; he joins a strolling company of players and becomes their poet; he gallants with nuns, and having secured the best of his unattainable love's needlework on a pretence of its being raffled for, sets out for Seville. There he is brought into a gang of bullies, who in a wild carouse hunt alguazils about the streets, and having killed two by accident rather than by design, seek sanctuary in the cathedral. Fed there by all the courtesans in the town, Pablos escapes with one of them and embarks for the Indies, hoping to better his fortune. "But it proved worse, for they never mend their condition who only change places without mending their life and manners."

This was the anti-hero's last word, and the only moral reflection in the story. A second part, if not promised, was prepared for, much as had been the sequels of *Lazarillo de Tormes;* and the French version of La Geneste in 1633, to avoid the abruptness of Quevedo's ending, altered it by bringing Pablos to Seville with a comedian, and marrying him there after many ruses to the daughter of a rich merchant; and Restif de la Bretonne, in 1776, produced a more elaborate conclusion still. In its plan and its satire the *Buscon* was obviously attached to tales of the primitive class. The same mould that had served for them could serve for it, and no contribution in intrigue, nor originality in invention, was afforded, yet it went a step beyond what the primitive novels had taken. Just because the anti-hero was more the centre of the action than ever before, mere invention and intrigue were less important, and the satire on society not confined to a lackey's observations. Pablos, as page to Don Diego Coronel, was in service, it is true, but the boys were of the same age and the position of Pablos a free and easy one. Except for this and his part as player then, he was simply an adventurer. Attention was focussed always on him, not on his profession at the moment. Consequently, episodes and digressions which could only have diverted notice from the picaro, went by the board, and even the attack upon social conditions became more and more a personal matter. Here and there coarse to repugnance, and outdoing in this respect the *Pícara Justina*, the *Buscon* was never obscene. Its style was often frankly burlesque and characteristically careless, but the narrative's tireless vivacity, and the scintillation of verbal surprises corresponding to odd flashes of thought, gave it a certain distinction, indicating beyond doubt, that Quevedo, with patience, might have produced the masterpiece of the type.

In France, in addition to *L'avanturier Buscon, histoire facétieuse*, translated by La Geneste in 1633, with the *Lettres du Chevalier de l'Epargne*, and often reprinted, the Sieur Raclots in 1699 at Brussels included a new version in his *Œuvres de don Francisco de Quevedo*, borrowing La Geneste's conclusion, and in 1776, Restif de la Bretonne, aided by Vaquette d'Hermilly, brought out at the Hague *Le fin matois ou histoire du grand taquin*, with notes and a new ending, in eight supplementary chapters. This mediocre sequel, missing completely the spirit of its original, describes Pablos' marriage on shipboard to his Seville mistress, and their voyage to the Indies, the bride being appropriated by the captain, and finally killed by the pilot, while Pablos excites a mutiny. Becoming captain himself, but deposed through his old friend, the gambling hermit, the picaro is marooned on an island and succored by an Indian girl, whom he basely betrays to Spanish soldiers. Returning to Spain, Pablos encounters the hermit in jail, and the two, having been overheard confessing to each other their crimes, the hermit suffers death, and Pablos is condemned to the galleys, during a respite from which, in recovering from wounds from hard usage, he writes his memoirs. In 1793, the original was again translated at Lyons, by F. M. Mersan; and Germond de Lavigne, emending his own improvements upon Quevedo, first made in 1843, has given the standard modern French version. An Italian rendering appeared at Venice in 1634, bearing the title of *Historia della vita dell' astutissimo e sagacissimo buscone chiamato don Pablo*, transferred from the Castilian by Giovanni Pietro Franco; and in 1657 *The Life and Adventures of Buscon the witty Spaniard* was "put into English by a person of honour," and printed at London with the *Provident Knight*, a translation of the *Cartas del Cavallero de la Tenaza*. A fragmentary version in 1683 was issued with the *Auristella* of Gonzalo de Céspedes y Meneses, and in 1707 Captain John Stevens, editor of the *Spanish Libertines* and translator of many Spanish works from Avellaneda's *Quixote* to Mariana's history, included in his *Comical Works of Quevedo* the *Life of Paul, the Spanish Sharper*, still the best in English, although Pedro Pineda, a teacher of Spanish at London, in 1743, had a later redaction. A German and French edition was published at Frankfort in 1671, as *Der abenteurliche Buscon*, and a second translation into German was made in 1781 by Friedrich Bertuch, in his *Magazin der Spanischen und Portugeischen Litteratur* at Dessau. In Dutch, Jan ten Hoorn of Amsterdam printed an anonymous translation as the *Vermakelyke historie van den koddigen Buscon* in 1699, and at Amsterdam, without date, appeared also the *Hollebollige Buscon.* Except for the *Visions*, this novel was the most widely known of Quevedo's works, and after the *Lazarillo* and *Guzman de Alfarache* the most popular of Spanish romances of roguery.

As Dr. Carlos García published in Castilian during his Parisian exile, so his contemporary and fellow-refugee, Juan de Luna, an interpreter of Spanish at the French capital, brought out there in 1620 his *Vida de Lazarillo de Tormes, corregida y emendada*, adding to it *La segunda parte de la vida de Lazarillo de Tormes, sacada de las corónicas antiguas de Toledo.* Intending these as texts for the use of his pupils, Luna aimed to modernize and improve the diction of the original romance of roguery of 1554, and in his second part purposed to rationalize the fantastic, anonymous sequel of 1555. Although the first attempt achieved and deserved no particular success, the second was highly creditable; and it is for this new continuation of the *Lazarillo* that Luna is remembered. Confessing to have seen a foolish account of Lazarillo's adventures among the tunnies, Luna declared his intention of redeeming the anti-hero from such inappropriate exploits and environment, giving instead the true relation of the picaro's further deeds and misfortunes, as he had often heard them at the fireside of winter evenings from the lips of his great-grandmother, and as they were to be found preserved in the ancient chronicles of the begging fraternity of Toledo. The story, proceeding from the events of the first part, accordingly, followed the second in having Lazarillo embark against the Algerines from Cartagena and the ship founder in a storm; but Lazarillo remains only a brief time in the sea, discovering a treasure to which he ties a cord before rising to the surface. The other end of the cord is fastened to his foot, but in his rescue by fishermen they sever it, and then in chagrin on learning what they have lost, determine to exact some profit from the picaro, by showing him as a marine curiosity through Spain. Lazarillo is dressed as a merman forthwith and carried about the country until nearly drowned in one of his aquatic performances. Supposed to be dead, he is on the point of being thrown into the river, when, raising an opportune outcry, he escapes. Turning rogue in earnest, bringing a losing suit against his wife and the archpriest, he tricks and is tricked, carries a gallant to his mistress in a box, serves seven ladies at once as esquire, becomes a cheating hermit, the real one having died, and after being worsted by the daughter of the dead hermit, whom he had thought to marry, concludes his narrative, saying: "This, friend reader, is in sum the second part of the life of Lazarillo, without adding or abating anything, as I have heard it told by my great-grandmother. If it please you, that rejoices me, and so adieu."

The skill with which Luna joined this sequel to its original, echoing almost exactly the mocking laugh of the latter and maintaining its realistic spirit, was admirable. If the action was not as swift, nor the style as incisive as in the old sketch, the satire was fully as sharp, and the tale as free from the bane of moralization that came to haunt the intervening romances of roguery. Moreover here, as had not been the case in the first *Lazarillo*, the anti-hero, and not the society elbowed by him, was of prime importance; and faithful as the fiction proved as a sequel, it stood at a far remove in this respect from that of the jesting servant of seven consecutive masters, who presented in their professions estates of the world. The personal interest and personal satire were most marked, and the story, therefore, was no longer of the first crude stage of picaresque fiction. The Spanish edition of this *Lazarillo* in 1652, claiming to be printed at Saragossa by Pedro Destar, was probably a falsification and really a French reprint, since the most obvious errors of the *editio princeps* were blindly repeated. The initial of Luna's given name appeared as "H.," and his nationality, as in the first edition, was misspelled "Castellaño." In the year of its first appearance, this sequel was done into French at Paris by Vital d'Audiguier and issued with its original, and in the 1653 versified *Lazarillo* it was promised as a third part, with the 1555 Flanders continuation as a second. In the French redaction of George de Backer at Brussels in 1698, Luna was followed, and an epitaph given, dating Lazarillo's death as September 12, 1540, and his age at that time as thirty-nine years, five months, and eleven days. In English, the *Pursuit of the Historie of Lazarillo de Tormes by Jean de Luna* was published as early as 1622, with further editions in 1631 and 1655, purporting here, as well as in the joint editions with the first part, in 1624, 1639, 1653, and 1669, to be translated by Luna himself. James Blakeston, however, who in the last two of these joint editions professed to have corrected Rouland's version by comparison with the unexpurgated original during his "late abode in Toledo," probably had a hand in the Englishing of Luna's sequel. The 1688 London *rifacimento*, adopting Luna's second part, compressed and altered it, Lazarillo meeting shipwreck in returning from the Indies with the hidalgo of the first part.

In the steps of the *Pícara Justina*, but even more of a rogue than Pérez's anti-heroine, followed *La hyia de Celestina*,[1] whose story, written by Alonso Gerónimo de Salas Barbadillo, was first published at Saragossa in 1612. The fecundity and versatility of its author were demonstrated by a succession of plays, poems, and tales, interrupted only at his death in 1630, and closed by the posthumous *Coronas del Parnaso y platos de las musas* of 1635. From his early heroic poem on the Virgin of Atocha, *La Patrona de Madrid restituida* of 1608, to his prose burlesque, *El caballero puntual* in first and second parts of 1614 and 1619, or the *Estafeta del dios Momo* of 1627, Salas Barbadillo displayed the easy assurance of general if not distinguished talents. In 1620 with the *Escuela de Celestina* he dared emulate the notorious bawd of Fernando de Rojas, and in *El caballero perfeto* of 1620 turned to depict the ideal knight leading a life of honor in high offices. His *Don Diego de Noche* of 1623 presented nocturnal love adventures, his *Casa del plazer honesto* of 1620 amusing *novelas*, and the *Fiestas de la boda de la incasable mal casada* of

[1] Throughout in book-titles I have used the spellings that occur in first editions, thus employing *hyia* for *hija*, *passagero* for *pasajero*, etc.

1622 a *novela*, a comedy, and verse and prose dialogues. Such medleys bound together by an inconsequential fiction were his delight, and scattered through them occurred as many verses as were collected in his *Rimas Castellanas* of 1618. Even in his dramatic pieces, Salas Barbadillo's tendency to vary the performance with irrelative tales and rhymes was apparent, and if *El galan tramposo y pobre* and the *Victoria de España y Francia* proved fairly rigorous plays, the picaresque *Pedro de Urdemalas* and *Sabia Flora Malsabidilla* were merely dialogued stories. However, in *La hyia de Celestina*, or *La ingeniosa Elena*, as the edition of 1614 called it, was produced a novel possessing unusual unity, which was in matter a frank romance of roguery. Celestina, as a character, always appealed to Salas Barbadillo, and the literary influence of the *Tragi-comedia de Calisto y Melibea* he recognized more than once, notably in the preface to his prose comedy *El sagaz Estacio marido examinado* of 1620. His first and best picaresque novel therefore was not inappropriately entitled the Daughter of Celestina, although Elena, its picara, was the child of a Granada slave merely so nicknamed. The scene opens in Seville at a fiesta in celebration of the marriage of Don Sancho, whose rich old uncle is blackmailed by Elena and her pretended brother Montufar. During the rogues' flight to Madrid, Elena relates the story of her life to Montufar, her father having been killed in the bull-ring, and she and her mother supported by admirers. In a journey undertaken now by Elena, Montufar, and Mendez an old woman, all arrayed as pilgrims, Montufar falls ill of a fever, and the women, being wearied of him, sit on either side of the bed and administer mock counsel before departing with his goods. Convalescing after three days, he pursues his heartless accomplices, and overtaking them feigns not to be offended, but in a solitary place robs and binds them to trees, addressing them with grave humor in the very words they had used to him. He relents, however, a reconciliation is effected, and at Seville the three pose as saints, taking the town by religious storm. Mendez dying here from the lashes bestowed at the discovery of their fraud, Elena and Montufar escape to Madrid, where they marry on a convenient arrangement, providing for an income in the usual way. Montufar is so pleased that when eating any special delicacy he must always exclaim in gratitude, "Long health to him who sends me this;" but finding his wife infringing their contract, a quarrel ensues with fatal results. The gallant kills the devoted husband and is hanged, and Elena on the banks of the Manzanares is garroted. But before dying she makes a will which returns to Don Sancho all that was stolen from his uncle, and an admiring poet in Toledo writes her epitaph. In the edition of 1614 and that of 1737 four chapters of no value were added to the original, Elena reciting *romances*, and Montufar telling a long and unpicaresque *novela*, interspersed with songs from a muleteer celebrating famous thieves. In the prologue the usual moral purpose was professed,[1] but the story itself was happily free from moralizing and swift in action. Its divergence from the early picaresque type was marked, for it retained only the brief autobiography of the picara, and for the most part was told in the third person. No longer commenc-

[1] *Se pretende te muestra en la astucia y hermosura de Elena, y trato de su compañia lo que executa la malicia de este tiempo, y el fin que tiene la gente desalmada.*

ing with the birth of the rogue, and dispensing entirely with the service of masters, its observation of low life was only such as would contribute to the working of the plot, the intrigue standing out as supremely important. The incidents might have verged on the villanous had it not been for the jocose treatment they received and the satirical intent patent from beginning to end. Not meeting with foreign approbation, or the attention of translators generally, *La hyia de Celestina* was nevertheless transferred in part to French, where, masked under the title of *Les hypocrites*, the rogues Hélène, Mendez, and Montufar, figured in 1655 in a *Nouvelle de M. Scarron* published by Antoine de Sommaville, and reprinted as the second of the *Nouvelles tragi-comiques* of the author of the *Roman Comique* in 1661. Paul Scarron, who once signed himself Lazarillo de Tormes,[1] and who was ever a fancier of picaresque literature, appreciated for one the humor of the religious cheat of Seville; and through him it appealed to a greater, Molière himself, who did not disdain to use its suggestions for Tartuffe.[2]

[1] Scarron to Marigny, May 8, 1659.

[2] Molière may even have had access to the original. Such

Salas Barbadillo in his novel *El necio bien afortunado*, published at Madrid in 1621, took up again the picaresque tradition, but modified it according to his own notions, seeking satirically to show that prosperity and success in this world attend simplicity, thereby closely approaching the later scheme of Grimmelshausen in *Simplicissimus*, and the long list of German jests founded upon rogueries perpetrated through literal obedience. Doctor Ceñudo, a philosopher who pretends to be a fool, is consulted by Campazano, wishing through the Doctor's magic powers to ascertain the whereabouts of Doña Dorotea. Drawing a curtain, Ceñudo shows the missing lady to her swain, who believes it witchcraft, but Ceñudo, as a matter of fact, has merely kidnapped Dorotea out of revenge for ill words she has spoken of him. This slight framework is now filled in by Ceñudo's account of

at least is the conclusion of Eugène de Roberville in his brochure, *Molière, Scarron, et Barbadillo*, published in 1888 under the *nom de plume* of P. d'Anglosse. Sainte-Beuve's indication of a significant onomatopoetic connection between the names, Montufar, Panulphe, Onuphre, and Tartuffe, is discussed by Emile Roy, *La vie et les œuvres de Charles Sorel*, 1891, pp. 216, 217.

his own life, constituting the principal picaresque part of the fiction. Brought up by a miserly uncle, a curate, he was dubbed a fool from the first, the advantages of which were soon manifest, for no matter what mischief he played he was never suspected. Like the first Spanish rogue, he raided the larder, attributing losses of provisions to mice, and his reading embracing *El Pícaro, y Laçarillo y otros deste género.* Learning from comedians of the attractions of Madrid, he raised a cry of thieves in the house at night, and while the curate was rushing to the door, robbed his coffers, and shortly after set out for the capital unsuspected. He became a page at the court, but was relieved of most of his tasks by feigning simplicity. Assuming the rôle of a count, he snatched off a lady's rings on the pretext of having others made for her to match them, and as the seeming heir of Indian estates he was regaled by another lady until she discovered his true condition. Changing masters, he went to the University of Salamanca, and after a period of retirement due to his pranks but blamed on his master, he became chief alcalde. His simplicity was here his best title to success, and after strange tricks, feigning illness, cheating the physicians, and leaving a false will, which gained him the esteem of a lady who before had disdained him, he came into a great inheritance. Still careful to be thought a poor man, he enjoyed the advantages of riches, and knew none of their discomforts, appreciating that "all his fortune had befallen him for being a fool, and all his misfortune for being a wise man." At this point the autobiography is relinquished, and the story ends with Dorotea's release and the ineffectual lawsuit instituted by her lover against the Doctor for magic. The evidence, however, merely attests Ceñudo to be a fool, so he resolves to commit many more follies that he may not cease being happy, and promises a second part to appear within a few days.

In this novel, although so much was autobiography, and a trace of the service of masters remained, a still further step from the primitive picaresque fiction was taken, for the antihero proved something other than a rogue. Of the same family as the long line of popular idols of the Bertoldo type, his wit was of the cynical, sententious kind, assuring prosperity to its possessor and bidding in a naïve way for the reader's admiration of verbal quips. The mere picaros, on the other hand, were witty in action rather than in word, not riddle propounders like Bertoldo and his fellows, nor necessarily rising from a low estate to a higher, but actuated by avarice and adroit in thievery. To the new picaresque fashion, Salas Barbadillo adapted then the traditional character of the cynic or court fool, preparing unconsciously for the last of the Spanish rogues, the Periquillo of Francisco Santos. If inferior as a romance of roguery to the *Hyia de Celestina*, and of little direct influence anywhere, the *Necio bien afortunado* yet succeeded in coming into English at London in 1670, translated by Philip Ayres, as *The Fortunate Fool*, dedicated to "the most hopeful and most ingenious young gentleman, John Turnor," and spoken of as "a piece of innocent mirth." And ninety years afterward it was reissued in abridged form as *The Lucky Idiot*.

Vicente Espinel, the poet and chaplain of Ronda, inventor of *décimas* or *espinelas* in verse, of the fifth string of the guitar, and styled by

Lope de Vega *el padre de la música*,[1] gave the fruit of a long life of adventure and observation in his single fiction, the *Relaciones de la vida del escudero Marcos de Obregon*. This was first published at Madrid in 1618 by Juan de la Cuesta, and in the same year at Barcelona Sebastian de Cormellas issued a second edition and Gerónimo Margarit a third. The work was dedicated to the Archbishop of Toledo, Bernardo de Sandoval y Rojas, the patron also of Cervantes, and Espinel has been accused of seeking enviously to emulate the fame of his great contemporary. His words in the dedicatory, "*No sera Marcos de Obregon el primer escudero hablador que ha visto V. S. Ilma,*" have been taken as a jealous slur upon Sancho Panza, although the warrant for such a belief is wanting. Cervantes in the *Adjunta al Parnaso* spoke of Espinel as one of his oldest and truest friends, and Espinel in his *Casa de la memoria* did not fail to honor "the maimed one of Lepanto." Indeed, most of the poets

[1] Lope was not always so appreciative, and in the *Dorotea* occurs, *perdoneselo Dios á Vicente Espinel, que nos trujo esta novedad y las cinco cuerdas de la guitarra con que ya se van olvidando los instrumentos nobles.* Act. I., Sc. 8.

and musicians of the day were upon cordial terms with the Ronda chaplain, and Lope, besides judicious praise for him in the frequently injudicious *Laurel de Apolo*, composed like Argensola and others a laudatory sonnet for Espinel's *Diversas rimas* of 1591 in token of his own debt to his early friendly critic. The supposition that in the *Marcos de Obregon* the events of Espinel's life were paralleled had long been current when the researches of Juan Pérez Guzman placed it beyond question, and although the story is tempered with much of the merely fictitious, it is mainly an autobiography and a picture of the times. Espinel was no rogue, although objections to him from his townsmen of Ronda were frequent until in 1596 he lost his benefice of Santa María, and the next year his manner of life was complained of to the king. But the literary fashion moved him to include enough of the picaresque in his novel to class it as a romance of roguery; and his acquaintance with the type would be shown, if by nothing else, by the Latin epigram he wrote for the first edition of *Guzman de Alfarache*.

The novel of *Marcos de Obregon* is in three *Relaciones*, and differs from most of its predecessors, except the fictions of Barbadillo, by commencing *in medias res.* The anti-hero, after explaining that he is now an inmate of the Santa Catalina de los Donados at Madrid, and that his purpose, besides amusing, is 'to show in his misfortunes and adversities how poor esquires may overcome the difficulties of the world and breast the perils of time and fortune,' introduces himself as past fifty years of age, entering the service of Doctor Sagredo and his wife Doña Mergelina. Here Marcos saves the lady from discovery in a gallant adventure with a musical barber, a scene later to be made famous when transferred to *Gil Blas.* Marcos, leaving the physician's service, considers entering that of an hidalgo, as guardian of his children, but accompanying the gentleman to the house of a titled friend he sees enough of starveling hospitality to disgust him with high life. Refusing the proffered position, the next morning in a rain storm he takes refuge in an oratory by the Segovia bridge with a hermit who proves to be an old comrade of the wars, and to him, while it rains, the *escudero* tells his tale. He set forth in the world as a student bound for Salamanca, having learned something of Latin and music at home. In Córdova he was fleeced by flattery at an inn, an incident derived from the *Buscon* probably and reappearing in *Gil Blas.* But Marcos, taking a rogue's revenge on the flatterer, and after suffering at the hands of an insolent muleteer, arrived at Salamanca, to continue there three or four years. He secured a position in the Colegio de San Pelayo, but was called away from the university to receive an inheritance. Travelling south to Ronda, he met some merchants, whom he saved from robbery by a clever intrigue, had his own mule stolen, but regained it by a trick, and at an inn discovered for the proprietor the thief of some figs by means of a ruse, later employed in the *Alonso moço de muchos amos.* He was captured by gypsies in the mountains, but escaping, returned to Salamanca, securing an ensignship in the armada, then fitting out at Santander. The plague preventing its sailing, Marcos wandered through Vizcaya and fell in love, encountering dangerous opposition, however, even to the point of being thrust in the wheel-pit of a mill by bravos. At Saragossa, in playing third in a love affair for a friend, he made himself ridiculous, somewhat as Guzman de Alfarache before him had done, and at Valladolid he entered the service of the Conde de Lémos. Here ends the first *relación*, the hermit yawning, and he and Marcos supping together before going to sleep in the oratory.

The next morning Marcos continues his story, telling how in Seville in a love intrigue, a deceitful lady imprisoned him in a well-room, from which he escaped by setting fire to the house and springing out from the well-bucket to be mistaken for a demon when the fire-fighters came to draw water. Disguising as a beggar to evade the pursuit of justice for his incendiarism, and after a roguish career in Seville, Marcos embarked for Italy in the train of the Duque de Medina-Sidonia. On his being wrecked off the Balearics by a storm, Barbary corsairs surprised the picaro in a cave, and carried him to Algiers, where he was servant to a renegade, whose daughter fell in love with him. He was finally liberated for his ruse in exposing with a talking thrush the thief of the viceroy's treasure, and sailing back to the Balearics was mistaken for a Turk, and in captivity carried to Genoa; incidents recurring in the story of Don Raphael in *Gil Blas*. In the third *relación* Marcos describes his Italian rovings and his return to Spain. First journeying to Milan, he was jailed after a quarrel with peasants, but escaped by pretended alchemy, and later, on the way to Venice, he encountered a melancholy gentleman engaged in the cheerful pastime of starving his wife to death for a supposed infidelity. Procuring this lady's reconciliation to her husband, Marcos at Venice was defrauded by the sharping Doña Camila, whom he counter-tricked, an episode borrowed by Le Sage, and sailing from Genoa for Spain, he was forsaken on a desert island, but saved his life by swimming to the mainland. From Barcelona the *escudero* went to Madrid, where he entered the service of a great prince, a friend of poetry and music. Falsely imprisoned by alguazils, Marcos, when again free, departed for Andalusia, meeting at Córdova the son and daughter of his Algiers renegade, come to Spain to be Christians. Marcos himself was captured by corsairs once more, and no sooner got away than he fell into the clutches of robbers, who took him to their cave. There he found Doctor Sagredo, who related his own adventures met with in an expedition sent by Philip Second to the Straits of Magellan and culminating in a purely fantastic account of an island of one-armed, one-eyed, and one-eared giants whose message-bearers were relays of trained dogs, and whose great idol the Spaniards blew up with gunpowder. Doctor Sagredo's wife now appeared disguised as a page, having escaped from Turks, who had snatched her from her husband in a sea-fight off Gibraltar. She informed the robbers of plans on foot to arrest them, and the captives being loosed proceeded to Madrid. Here Marcos closes his narrative to the hermit, leaving the oratory and remarking the damage wrought by the storm. Wearied with so many turns of fortune, he determines to prepare for death, and concludes his third and last *relación*, justifying his use of simple language, and begging for corrections and the reader's indulgence.

While this fiction after its definite start was more interesting than most, its very complication in handling brought its author into difficulties that his less ambitious rivals had not to encounter. In the introduction of Sagredo a second time a glaring inconsistency emerged, for, at the commencement of Marcos' relation to the hermit, the picaro has but recently left the service of Sagredo, and practically his only intervening adventure has been a discussion upon education with an hidalgo, but in the latter part of this consecutive narrative he has met the same Sagredo in Andalusia after the doctor has spent between two and three years in travel, and when, according to the opening of the tale, the *escudero* has never left Madrid at all. Moreover, the autobiographical character of the work led Espinel into occasional inconsistencies, as when, confusing fact with fiction, he mentions being in Flanders at the siege of Maestricht, and yet, as far as his story is concerned, has travelled only in Spain and Italy. The identity of Espinel with his anti-hero was, however, obvious throughout. The *glosa* Obregon sings when retaken aboard the Italian ship is one of Espinel's best-known songs, "*unas octavas mias*," Marcos calls them, and, asked who he is, he replies "Marcos de Obregon," but another declaring his true name, the general marvels to behold in these humble circumstances one of whom he has heard so much. The unreal exploits of Sagredo on the Cyclops island suggested by Homer, and the incidents of the robbers' cave suggested by Apuleius, were added to Espinel's autobiography only when his actual life as adventurer had been exchanged for a quiet existence deemed too prosaic to serve as the theme for a picaresque novel. Except in its beginning, the narrative was no more than anecdotally discursive and the action rapid, with a sly if not aggressive satire maintained through most of it. The story was nowhere coarse or even questionable, and the style was pure and correct, Espinel declaring of the book, "I have written it in clear and easy language to give the reader no pains in its understanding." In spite of the inconsistency involved, a certain unity was attained by concluding with Sagredo as the account had begun with him, and this feeling for unity was further shown by the assimilation into the main plot of the Italian *novella* of the jealous Cornelio taking ingenious revenge on his innocent wife. Marcos himself was less a picaro than almost any other member of the Spanish rogues' gallery, and it is to be observed that his ruses were almost exclusively employed in self-defence, and not like those of Guzman, or Andrés, or Lazarillo de Manzanares, for the delight or gain of cheating. The reflection of Marcos after being outwitted at the inn at Córdova proves the theme of his whole career: "It is not to be wondered at that a youth without experience should be deceived by an old hand; but he would be worthy of punishment who should let himself be tricked a second time."

Voltaire's statement in 1775 in a new edition of his *Siècle de Louis XIV.*, to the effect that *Gil Blas* was entirely taken from this romance of roguery, if an exaggerated and hasty generalization, was effective as firing the first shot of a conflict that was to wage long and bitterly concerning the originality of Le Sage's masterpiece, and involving much more than the *Marcos de Obregon*. That the latter gave to Le Sage a good deal of what was best in itself is clear, but after the practical close of the controversy it is also apparent that beyond large pilferings from Espinel and other Spanish novelists and dramatists, *Gil Blas* contained sufficient original material and a sufficiently characteristic French treatment to withstand not only Voltaire's resentment toward its author, but the zeal of the Padre Isla and the plausible theories of Llorente.[1]

Long before the day of Voltaire or Le Sage, however, and in the very year of its issue in Spain, *Les relations de Marc d'Obregon* appeared at Paris, done into French by the Sieur d'Audiguier, who translated in that year as well six of the *novelas* of Cervantes and the *Persiles y Sigismunda*, and in 1621 the *Desordenada codicia*. D'Audiguier professed to think little enough of Espinel's novel, which he gave only in the first *relación*, declaring his excuse for printing it at all to be the desire to comply with requests urging him to the task. Of the Spaniards and Espinel he said, disparagingly, "*Je cherchois un autheur de ceste nation qui ne fut point discoureur, & j'ay trouvé un homme qui ne faict que babiller, & au mesmes lieux où il blasme les parleurs, se monstre plus impertinent que ceux qu'il propose pour exemple d'impertinence.*" Yet he added that in this novel

[1] For a concise list of parallel passages in *Marcos de Obregon* and *Gil Blas* see Gustav Haack, *Untersuchungen zur Quellenkunde von Lesages 'Gil Blas de Santillane,'* Kiel, 1896, and for a view of the whole controversy, E. Veckenstedt, *Die Geschichte der Gil Blas-Frage*, 1879.

he had found some good things, though badly arranged. But Obregon was never popular in France or anywhere out of Spain. In England it did not come out until 1816, when Major Algernon Langton translated it in two volumes, the original having been given him at Ronda by a priest. In Germany, as the *Leben und Begebenheiten des Escudero Marcos de Obregon*, it was spiritedly rendered by Ludwig Tieck, at Breslau in 1827, with notes and a preface.

As prolific and as versatile as Salas Barbadillo, Alonso de Castillo Solórzano was a master of the comic and the serious in fiction, surpassing Barbadillo in the realm of the picaresque novel, and his equal certainly in that of the *novela*. The *Jornadas alegres* of 1626, the *Tardes entretenidas* of 1625, the *Noches de placer* and the *Fiestas del jardín* of 1631 and 1634, with the *Quinta de Laura* and the *Alivios de Cassandra*, were all in Barbadillo's manner, collections of short stories intermingled with comedies and verse; while still lighter works, such as the *Donaires del Parnaso* of 1624 and 1625, the *Tiempo de regocijo y carnestolendas de Madrid* of 1627, and *Los amantes andaluces* of 1633 were balanced by the grave in the *Sagrario de Valencia* of 1635, or the *Historia de la vida y hechos del rey don Pedro de Aragon* of 1639. But Solórzano's essentially realistic ventures were made in the four *novelas* of *Las harpías en Madrid* of 1631; and more particularly in his three recognized romances of roguery, the *Niña de los embustes*, *Teresa de Manzanares*, the *Aventuras del bachiller Trapaza*, and the *Garduña de Sevilla*.

Although *Las harpías en Madrid y coche de las estafas* went through two editions, the second being issued in 1633, it is one of the rarest of Castillo Solórzano's works, as well as one of the most curious. A poor widow with two pretty daughters on her hands leaves Seville for Madrid, determined to make her fortune. Quarters are found in the capital with another widow blessed with two daughters also, and a rich gallant becomes attentive to the ladies. On one occasion he even loans them his superb coach and four to attend a bull-fight at Alcalá. During their absence he is killed by stealth by an old enemy, his servants make off with everything, and so the coach as a godsend falls into the possession of the astute maidens. With this common stock-in-trade, it is agreed that each of these Harpies shall perpetrate a fraud, and the four frauds or *estafas* constitute the body of the story. Feliciana as the eldest is allowed the first chance, practising her wiles upon a wealthy Milanese. Riding forth in the coach at evening, she has a disturbance raised by her pretended servants before her victim's door, and of course she is rescued by him, and explains that a distasteful match is being forced upon her. The Milanese becomes infatuated, presents her with a ring to replace the one she feigns to have lost, and is about to marry her and depart for Italy, when she contrives to elude him, appropriating a chest of jewels and making it appear that her relatives had seized upon her in his absence. The second trick with the Coach of the Frauds is assigned to Luysa, who befools a rich Genoese, pretending to be a wealthy widow of Saragossa come to court as the prospective heiress of an uncle in the Indies. A forged money-order from a banker in Seville is cashed by the admiring Genoese, who carries on his courtship with poetic fiestas. An *entremés* is even acted, but Luysa, in the rich garments provided for her, suddenly disappears, and the coach which had gained her credit is turned over to Constancia. She too becomes for the nonce a widow, but sets her trap for a miserly curate. Her husband has died, she says, bequeathing his goods to build a memorial chapel, and she has determined to present this chapel to the curate's church, and to install him as chaplain. Delight is his portion until the architect, an esquire in disguise, demands advance payment. The lady cannot disburse at once, and the curate is persuaded to make her a loan on certain jewels. But a duplicate casket filled with pebbles is substituted at the last moment, and Constancia comes off in triumph. The youngest of the Harpies, Dorotea, inspired by these signal successes, drives in the magic coach to the Guadalaxara Gate, examining there at leisure rich stuffs from a shop. An extravagant gallant, perceiving all this magnificence, insists upon presenting the lady with the goods she admires, and commences forthwith an ardent wooing. An old flame appears, however, and when the gallant thinks to crown his desires, Dorotea and her first love by means of a sleeping-potion relieve him of his large winnings at play, and leave the dormant suitor exposed at a door as a foundling, in burlesque attire, and with verses pinned on his breast. Then the four Harpies with their *coche de las estafas* set out rejoicing for Granada, where for a time they live in peace, and where, says Castillo Solórzano, "the author of this book leaves them for the present, promising, if it meet the reader's approval, to write that of *los vengadores de las estafas plaziendo á Dios, y la niña de los embustes.*" The *Niña de los embustes* did appear in 1632; but the story of the *Revengers of the frauds* was never issued.

If the picaresque form was not attempted in this amusing book, the picaresque spirit was sufficiently manifest, and it is interesting as paving the way for Castillo Solórzano's more typical novels. The same kind of cheats occur in both, the device of the sleeping-potion and the gaining admission to a household by pretending distress proving the favorite machinery of this author, here and elsewhere. But comparatively little inventiveness was displayed in *Las harpías en Madrid*, the charm lying rather in the graceful working out of a simple plot. The inevitable lugging in of extraneous matter in *romances* sung to the guitar, in *entremeses*, and in poetical *academias* alone marred the unity here, superior to that attained by most preceding writers. In the *estafa* of Dorotea was introduced a tale admitted to be from "*vn libro de Nouelas de vn Italiano, llamado Francisco Sansouino*," and in the *estafa* of Constancia was included as a piece in a long academy, a *Romance contra los que toman tabaco*, not unlike some of the early English tobacco invectives. The moralizing which Castillo Solórzano later learned to dispense with altogether, he here retained in appended *aprovechamientos*, precisely in the manner and no doubt upon the model of those in the *Pícara Justina*, saying of the trick on the curate, for example, "To deceive ecclesiastics is terrible audacity, since they are persons to whom is due the same respect as to God."

The novel of *Teresa, the Child of Frauds*, appeared at Barcelona in 1632, Solórzano returning to the autobiographical, straightforward narrative of the earlier romances of roguery, and abandoning in this and his later picaresque fictions the more difficult device of the framework employed by Barbadillo. Teresa's grandmother was a shepherdess of reality, not of the pastorals, and her mother a maid at an inn, who fell in love with a canon's servant, and robbing her aunt, ran away with him. Teresa, born of a new alliance with a Gascon, is left an orphan at ten, and enters service with two sisters, becoming the go-between for Theodora, the daughter of one of them, and her lovers. After this Teresa is a hairdresser, the wife of a jealous widower, and a duenna. Sarabia, a student lover, pretending to be pursued, gains entrance to the house and outwits the widower, who dies regretting his harsh treatment of Teresa, and as duenna the picara is dismissed for letting one of her charges elope. Seeking refuge from robbers in the Sierra Morena with a hermit, from the story of his life she takes a cue which enables her later at Málaga to counterfeit the long-lost daughter of a wealthy captain, stolen in infancy by the Moors. At Granada, finding her old love, Sarabia, in a company of comedians, she marries him, turns actress, and receives the plaudits of the people and the adulation of a prince. Sarabia is killed by physicians, however, for ridiculing them in an *entremés*, the company breaks up in debt, and

Teresa, changing her name, puts a cheat upon a Peruvian of fortune, who becomes her third husband. After a season of well-founded jealousy he dies, and Teresa, discovered for the sharper she is, flees to Toledo. There with two girl slaves she passes off one of them as her niece, an heiress, and fleeces two gallants who vie with each other in their gifts. But when the time is ripe to be rid of them, they are treated to a ghostly apparition, and the honest household removes to Madrid. The offended gallants induce the pretended niece to rob Teresa, who, in chagrin, retires to Alcalá, where her old friend, Theodora, is married to a merchant. And here with the miserly cousin of this merchant, the picara contracts her fourth alliance, promising a new volume to treat of the avarice of his and her family, to be entitled *La congregación de la miseria.* Included in this story were *romances*, a serenade, and two *entremeses*. Except for them and an occasional lagging chapter, it was well and swiftly told in the same satirical vein as the *Hyia de Celestina*, although fuller of incident and less detailed. Teresa was a great rogue, never weary in ill-doing, but an amusing one in her inexhaustible wit and determination to surmount all difficulties. Undiscouraged by failure, and not overelated by success, she took life as she found it, making, however, little real progress in the world.

In place of the promised sequel to these adventures, Solórzano, probably in 1634, and certainly by 1637,[1] published his *Aventuras del bachiller Trapaza, quinta essencia de embusteros y maestro de embelecadores.* The antihero receives his name Trapaza, or deceit, as a phonetic combination of those of his parents, his mother being called Tramoya, intrigue, and his father Trampa, or snare. Light-fingered from infancy, Trapaza begins his career by leaving Segovia for Salamanca, winning a small fortune at cards and purchasing an outfit with which to play the fine gentleman. At the university he is more successful in gaming than in love, for his false pretension to be the son of a wealthy noble of the Grand Canary,

[1] The latter edition in the British Museum is of Saragossa, with an *Aprobacion* there of 1635. Barrera y Leirado gives Valencia 1634 as the date of the first edition, but the Madrid 1733 edition expressly declares itself *Segunda impression.* Nicolás Antonio does not so much as mention the work.

and his serenading by proxy are exposed by a rival. But robbed by students of most of his profits at play, and detected in a theft when acting as third in a love affair, he departs for Andalusia with a domestic, Estefanía, also implicated; and after cheats and misfortunes on the way, at Córdova she deserts him, running off with his goods and his lackey. Selling his own horse, and trying vainly to steal another, Trapaza proceeds to Seville with Pernia, a youth who, pretending to be the Monja Alférez, a famous amazon returned from the Indies, is exhibited from town to town as a curiosity.[1] Trapaza engages as servant to a poor and eccentric hidalgo, but is dismissed for tricking him, and at Jaen, being robbed, enters the service of a physician whose wife presently causes his discharge. Meeting Pernia again, a marriage

[1] The first account of the actual Monja Alférez appeared in 1618 in the *Capítulo de una de las cartas que diversas personas embiaron de los Indios*, etc., and in 1625, at Seville, was issued the *Relación verdadera de las grandes hazañas, y valerosos hechos que una muger hizo en veynte y quatro años que siruió en el Reyno de Chile y otras partes al Rey nuestro Señor en abito de soldado*, etc. A *Segunda relación* came out the same year, published at Seville by Cabrera, and also by Faxardo, the latter misdating his edition 1615.

cheat is arranged upon a lady whose miniature he has captured, but discovery of the fraud and a scourging ensue, and Trapaza leaves for Madrid. There he encounters his first flame, Estefanía, making her believe in wonderful exploits performed by him in Africa and his adoption by a rich Portuguese whose life he saved there, but Estefanía growing jealous of the picaro contrives to send him to the galleys, for which she is soon enough sorry, as she bears him a daughter. With the assurance of the immediate appearance of the adventures of this new anti-heroine, "*La hija de Trapaza, y polilla de la corte*," the novel ends. On the whole it was inferior to the *Niña de los embustes*, although very similar in style and satire. The introduction of unpicaresque tales and verses was rendered more systematic by their being recited ostensibly to while away three long journeys undertaken by the picaro. Thus a *novela* with its scene in ancient Rome is told by a physician; another of a shipwrecked prince by a student, and a poet gives an *entremés* of his own composition on a girl chestnut vender, who went to Seville and returned such a lady nobody knew her. The invention was of less account than in the *Teresa*, for reminiscences of other picaresque works were not wanting. The hidalgo, Don Tomé, for example, was a composite souvenir of the master of Lazarillo de Tormes and of the rhyming gentleman served by *Alonso moço de muchos amos.* The game of disguising as statues had already been tried in Barbadillo's *Pedro de Urdemalas*, and in Tolosa's *Lazarillo de Manzanares*, while a story in the latter of a rogue obliged to give a mule wine to avoid being exposed in stealing, and thus sharing the profits with its pretended healer, reappeared here. The old trick of filling a bladder with blood to be stabbed was repeated, and the intrigue of a casket containing jewels and a miniature being handed to the anti-hero from a doorway through mistake was in the *Varia fortuna del soldado Píndaro* of Céspedes y Meneses.

Neither the *Teresa* nor the *Trapaza* proved especially successful; but *La garduña de Sevilla y anzuelo de las bolsas* was more fortunate.[1]

[1] Nicolás Antonio states the date of the *Garduña's* issue as Logroño, 1634. An edition of Valencia of 1634 is mentioned by Barrera y Leirado, but the earliest I have seen is of Madrid, 1642, in the Bibliothèque Nationale at Paris.

Whether first printed in 1634 or in 1642, it at all events fulfilled the promise contained in the conclusion of the *Trapaza*, describing the sharping adventures of that rogue's daughter, Rufina. Estefanía having procured Trapaza's release from the galleys, they are married when Rufina has already seen five summers. After several years the girl is left to show her beauty at the window, for her father, whose gambling has impoverished the family and brought the mother to her grave, thinks of nothing but a profitable match. Wedded to the agent of a *perulero*, Rufina is soon tired of him, and falls in love with a rake in quarrelling with whom her father succumbs. The picara's sharping career begins after her lord's death from mere choler at discovering her unfaithfulness. She secures entrance to the *quinta* of a miser near Seville, and Garay, her accomplice, makes an uproar at the door by night, whereupon the miser after due warnings shoots the supposed robber, a straw man operated by Garay. The miser is terror-struck at the murder he has committed, and on Rufina's advice, before fleeing to a monastery for sanctuary, buries all his treasure in the garden lest alguazils confiscate it. Of course the rogues dig it up, and are soon on the way to Córdova. There, after release by an error of justice, they enjoy the hospitality of a rich Genoese, a student of alchemy, upon whom they contrive a cheat, Garay seeming to produce gold, and promising to devote himself to the discovery of the philosopher's stone. Extensive purchases are made, and the delighted Genoese, the better to ally himself with so marvellous a man, begs Rufina's hand in marriage. But left in charge of the victim's goods, the rogues decamp, and the Genoese in order to elude his creditors is obliged to return to Italy. In the meantime, Rufina and Garay, near Málaga, overhear enough of the plotting of robbers in a wood, to learn of Crispin, a thieving hermit, who is their receiver. Rufina gains access to the hermitage, and with Garay drugs, robs, and informs on the hypocrite, who, however, escapes from jail and pursues the rascal pair to Toledo. There, planning revenge, he introduces into their house a servant as a pretended fugitive from justice; but unexpectedly Rufina and this Don Jaime fall in love, the latter confessing the hermit's schemes, and both fleeing from Toledo in Garay's absence. Crispin, who has been informed on again, is hanged, and Garay, taken in a robbery, is sent to the galleys, while Jaime disguised as a poet, having stolen from a company of players at Madrid, goes with his bride to Saragossa, where the happy pair open a silk-shop, the remainder of their days being spent in "dedicating themselves to acts of virtue to amend in part their past extravagances."

In every way this was the best picaresque fiction produced by Solórzano, and one of the most entertaining in the whole range of the romances of roguery. Free from the discursiveness of early specimens of the type, neither coarse nor moralized, its relentless satire made the low-life adventures interesting, and scenes of real comedy were frequent. The autobiographical form employed in the *Teresa*, but rejected in the *Trapaza*, did not appear here, the author having gained sufficient courage to attempt the third person narrative, the exception and not the rule in romances of roguery. The care with which the pictures were drawn showed what the novel of observation had accomplished for fiction before again becoming subject to the story for the story's sake. And the stride forward in art from the first picaresque tales with their lack of arrangement and crude digressions was remarkable, even if no study of character as such was present, nor any strong unity of plot. At the same time, the intrigue was as compact as the Spanish type of picaresque fiction could produce, and the inclusion of the three *novelas* comporting with the fashion of the time did not affect the main action. The first, entitled *Quien todo lo quiere todo lo pierde*, was supposed to be read from a volume a priest was taking to print at Madrid; the second, and best, *El conde de las legumbres*, was related by a robber in the hermit's hut with a humor not unworthy of Cervantes; and the third, *A lo que obliga el honor*, Jaime told Rufina during his courtship. These episodes were even translated separately in English as *Three Ingenious Spanish Novels*, published in a second edition at London in 1712, without disclosing whence they came, while from the *Conde de las legumbres* Willem Vander Hoeven took his comedy in Dutch, *De vermomde minnar*. The third *novela* of *La garduña de Sevilla* was also the second of Solórzano's *Alivios de Cassandra*, there entitled *A un engaño otro mayor*, and Paul Scarron, toward the close of the first part of the *Roman Comique* of 1651, had his Doña Inezilla read it aloud to the comedians at a wedding. The entire novel of *La garduña* was translated to French by the Sieur d'Ouville, brother-in-law of Boisrobert, and published at Paris in 1661, after his death, as *La fouyne de Seville ou l'hameçon des bourses*, although registered as early as 1653. Aside from its division into four books and ending with the promise of a second part, it was a fairly faithful transcription,[1] and from it, as the work of "one of the most refin'd wits of France," John Davies of Kidwelly took his version of the *Garduña* printed at London in 1665, and entitled *La Picara, or the Triumph of Female Subtilty*. Toward 1770 appeared a compression of Davies' production in three parts as *The Life of Donna Rosina*, "by the ingenious Mr. E. W., a known, celebrated author;" but here Rosina and Jaimo, in accord with English

[1] H. Koerting (*Gesch. des fr. Romans im 17 Jahrh.*, II., 267) speaks of it on the contrary as "*ein ausgelassener pikaresker Roman aber im Vergleich zu dem Spanischen Vorbild stark erweitert durch launige Ausfälle 'contre les pures infantes, les chastes vièrges du roman heroïque.'*"

moral notions, were hanged at the close. In 1717, a really new version was called *The Spanish Pole-Cat: or the Adventures of Seniora Rufina*, "begun to be translated by Sir Roger L'Estrange, and finish'd by Mr. Ozell;" and a second edition ten years later bore the name *Spanish Amusements*. In Dutch *Het leven van Ruffine of het weseltje van Sivilien* was published at Amsterdam by Gerrit Bos in 1725.

Castillo Solórzano, whether consciously or not, had obeyed the tendency in the air as fiction commenced to recover from the excess of realism into which by a recoil from pure idealism it plunged. Preserving all the incisive wit of the picaresque novel, he softened only its method, and so produced some of the most entertaining tales of the kind. The story of *Don Pablos* was perhaps more truly picaresque, but the *Teresa*, *Trapaza*, and *Garduña* were better organized, heralding the further development of the type already begun across the Pyrenees. In Solórzano, then, the Spanish romance of roguery reached its high-water mark, and after him in Spain the tide turned rapidly.

CHAPTER VI

IMPERFECT AND ALLIED FORMS

Besides the romances of roguery which have been treated in detail and which constitute the flourishing period of the type in Spain, a series of works appeared there, accompanying the general development and subject to its influence, although differing from it in form, or else picaresque only in part. Chief among these, after occasional prison pamphlets or invectives against gaming, were the *Viage entretenido* of 1603, the *Novelas exemplares* of Cervantes of 1613, the *Engaños deste siglo* of 1615, *El passagero* of 1617, the *novelas* in the collection of Agreda y Vargas, and in the *Guia y avisos de forasteros*, both of 1620, and the two dialogued pieces of Salas Barbadillo, the *Pedro de Urdemalas* of 1620, and the *Sabia Flora Malsabidilla* of 1621. Not to be classed as romances of roguery in the strict sense, these were all too intimately connected with picaresque fiction to be overlooked in a study of the genre.

As early as 1528, Diego del Castillo at Valladolid issued a *Tratado muy útil y provechoso en reprobación de los juegos*, intended to expose the frauds of card-playing, and reprinted at Seville, in 1557, as *Satyra y invectiva contra los tahures*. Adrian de Castro in his *Libro de los daños que resultan del juego* of 1599 at Granada was inspired by a similar motive, and Quevedo in the *Flores de corte* gave minute studies of tricks at play which were continued by others down to the *Casa de juego* of 1644 by Francisco de Navarrete y Rivera. Of the same class as the *Mihil Mumchance*, printed in 1597 in England, and attributed to Robert Greene, or the *Art of Jugling or Legerdemaine, . . . Cautions to beware of Cheating at Cardes and Dice* of 1612, all these essays were at least in line with the more ambitious tales of rogues, furnishing material for the picaresque novels as the English pamphlets did for their fictional descendants, the *Compleat Gamester* by Cotton of 1674, and Theophilus Lucas' *Memoirs of Gamesters* of 1714.

Criminal low life was observed, too, with some humor, the prison of Seville offering the theme for a noteworthy sketch in three parts, the first and second by Christóval de Chaves, the last assigned to Cervantes, and the whole bearing the title, *Relación de la cárcel de Sevilla.* It was begun after 1585, and the final section and additions were completed by 1597. Chaves as an advocate of the *Real audiencia Sevillana*, or Cervantes as a prisoner in that very *cárcel*, must have had ample opportunities for observing what was so graphically described. The manners of this curious community of eighteen hundred souls were reviewed with genuine zest, and life in the courtyards and various sections of the jail made a little less dismal, whether in the vaults, in the old or new galley, or in the chamber of iron. The three gateways, nicknamed the gold, the silver, and the copper, with their avaricious keepers, draining unfortunates of those metals in passing, were faithfully pictured, and the threefold warning cry before the final closing of the doors at night seems to echo yet above the clamors of the confined. *Valientes* assembling in mourning garments about the death-bed of a comrade in durance; the judge, preparing to make a requisition, and passing at night with a flaring torch through the great apartment of the women, lighting up fantastically the dishevelled, mocking company; prisoners ekeing out a livelihood by inscribing love-letters, or painting hearts and cupids for the amorous in liberty,—such scenes as these the *Relación de la cárcel de Sevilla* presented in striking colors. The tricks of the citizens of this republic to move compassion, the duties and profits of the governor and under-governor, and the ruses and escapes put in practice from time to time, were all detailed, and anecdotes of famous rogues related. One picaro writes a letter to a bravo from his chains in the good ship, "Eagle," declaring, "The news of the galleys amounts to this, that of thirty-two ounces of hard-tack allowed to each convict heretofore, there now is given no more than twenty-six," signing himself with a flourish, "Yours till death; the name you know, and I say no more." Another prisoner, Don Gómez de Tarán, grows so attached to the jail that he refuses to leave when discharged, a story frequently cropping up elsewhere in picaresque fiction.[1] From the account of the escape, by

[1] For example, in the *Histoire d'Estevanille Gonzalès* of Le Sage, 1734, Chap. 37.

way of the roof, of one condemned to death, a Spanish Jack Sheppard, there was taken an incident in Juan Ruiz Alarcón's play, *El texedor de Segovia;* and from the story of the tunnel made by the prisoners, and used for unexpected egress during a fiesta performance on the eve of San Juan, came the more elaborate episode recounted of the prison at Córdova in the *Varia fortuna del soldado Píndaro.*[1] Indeed, the *Relación* was at no far remove from the romances of roguery, and Christóval de Chaves, had he but chosen to celebrate a picaro instead of a place, might have anticipated Aleman and been the first to follow in the steps of the *Lazarillo.* Some fear of reproach haunted him, however, even as it was, and he said here, "If the wise reprove me for having occupied myself with affairs of so little moment, foundation, and fruit, I can defend me in that at least I have written the truth in appropriate language concerning what passes in this inferno or prison where are met together folk of such strange manners." But he did not give what he half promised, a vocabulary of rogue-slang, which

[1] *Píndaro*, Lib. I., ii.

would have made him the forerunner of Juan Hidalgo and his dictionary of *germanía*. As to Cervantes, whether he really composed the brief third part or not, he was certainly acquainted with all three, and the *Entremés famoso de la cárcel de Sevilla* has been attributed to him, although included in the *Séptima parte* of the comedies of Lope de Vega, printed at Madrid in 1617. This *Entremés* was related to the elder work, the Paisano of the *Relación* reappearing in it; and in 1627 the Licenciado Martin Pérez brought out at Madrid with Diego Flamenco a new *Relación verdadera, que trata de todos los successos y tratos de la Cárcel Real de la ciudad de Sevilla*, the author proclaiming himself "prisoner in the said jail." So famous indeed had these descriptions of prisons become that Castillo Solórzano in the *Garduña de Sevilla* when about to touch upon the same theme, checked himself, exclaiming, "I would paint that insufferable life had not others of genius so employed the pen with much ostentation and erudition."

A work unique in Spanish literature, valuable as containing the most complete account of the early Peninsular stage, was *El viage entre-*

tenido composed by Agustín de Rojas and published at Madrid, in 1603, by Juan Flamenco. Rojas in the four books, written in haphazard dialogue frequently interrupted with verses, describes the wanderings of strolling actors, Rios, Ramirez, Solano, and himself, as they plod from town to town. Although it was apparently deficient in plan, analysis discloses a scheme according to which the *Amusing Journey* was ordered. For first, the dialogue presented reminiscences of the comedians' trade and of actual occurrences in their adventurous careers; second, a series of *loas* or prologues, nearly all in verse, in honor of each of the principal cities visited, supplemented with more detailed descriptions and praises in prose; third, a story of love intrigue entirely romantic and even subject to the *cultismo*, told by Rojas in three disconnected sections, one in each book except the first; fourth a series of *loas* and prose passages describing the actor's profession, its history and its hardships, which with the personal reminiscences of the players constitutes the freshest and most entertaining portion of the work; and fifth, miscellaneous anecdotes and *loas* meant to display the author's erudition in the fashion then prevalent in Spain, and later exemplified in the *Alonso moço de muchos amos*. To this final category belong especially the *loas* of the last two books, such as those to the letters A and R, to days of the week, and to the ages of the world, making these books less interesting and less characteristic than either the first or the second, while in them the trace of picaresque influence discernible earlier in the fiction almost disappears. Rojas, who was born in 1577, and as he tells us, neither in the *potro* of Córdova, nor the *zocodover* of Toledo, nor the *corrillo* of Valladolid, nor the *azoguejo* of Segovia, all notorious picaresque haunts, but instead in the good city of Madrid, announces himself to the reader complacently: "Know that for four years I was student, then page, then soldier, then picaro, then captive, that I drew the nets, labored at the oar, became a merchant, a gentleman, and a clerk, and finally an actor. . . . What Guzman de Alfarache or Lazarillo de Tormes had more masters, or played more tricks, or what Plautus gained more offices than I in the same space? Behold me now in comedy, where I am known to you for the *loas* that I say, and the little that

I act." And according to his own confession it was the having in stock these *loas* that first suggested to him the idea of building a book around them, where, indeed, no less than forty were included. Apart from the autobiography of the author, to be pieced together rather more from his verse than his prose, the most picaresque adventures are those related by Rios in the first book, while the strollers are making their way from Seville toward Carmona. According to this narrative Rios and Solano had been picaros forced to every expedient of thievery to keep soul and body together as they roamed about giving bad performances in inns, picking up odd jobs, skipping their lodging accounts, and fleecing the public; and later Rios tells of similar roguish experiences in company with Ramirez. As for Rojas, the mere mention of Málaga brings to mind his taking sanctuary there for a murder and nearly starving. Venturing forth one night from his hiding-place, he gave his clothes to an old woman to sell, in the hope of getting something to eat, but she ran off with them, and he was obliged to turn beggar. A friar finally hired him to copy sermons, and this employment failing, he snatched capes in the dark, ravaged vineyards and gardens, took to fishing, and being caught in a storm was captured. Imprisoned at La Rochelle in France, rowing in the galleys, setting up a shop, tricked by an old woman, his adventures throughout smacked of the purely fictional picaro's, and like Barbadillo's Fortunate Fool he played the philosopher, prescribing satirically for those who visited him, flattering the old, being eloquent with the Tullys, and a lamb with the humble. On one occasion he has a *loa* in praise of thieving, a forecast of *La antigüedad y nobleza de los ladrones*, suggested here by a boy, who, coming after the performance to flatter Rojas, steals from his pocket while doing it. In the second book occurs the anecdote, that is Shakspere's *Induction* to the *Taming of the Shrew*, to prove the world a dream, but this had been known in England as early as 1570, in Richard Edwards' collection of comic stories.[1] It is in the descriptive catalogue of the eight orders of comedians, in the historical account of dramatic presentations in Spain, and in the lists of

[1] Warton. *History of English Poetry*, edition of 1824, Vol. IV., 117.

authors and actors responsible for the development of the art there, that the *Viage entretenido* is peculiarly rich and of most worth. It was picaresque incidentally, simply because the life of the stroller then was bound to be more or less roguish. The supposition of Nicolás Antonio that the book dated from 1583 has long been disproved, and on internal evidence its composition can be definitely ascribed to 1602. The Inquisition did not treat it any too lightly, and the famous 1667 *Index*, which renewed the ban upon the first *Lazarillo* and objected to passages in *Marcos de Obregon* and in the *Buscon*, suppressed passages in the first and fourth books of this edition. A continuation was not promised at the end of the *Viage* proper, although at the close of the intrigue story it was said: "What succeeded further in the discourse of the life of these two mirrors of honor and love will be told in new books in which will be prosecuted this sweet, pleasing, and agreeable history."

The extent of the debt to the *Viage entretenido* of Scarron's *Roman comique* has been frequently debated, but comparison of the two fails to disclose more than a borrowing of the general conception, and Scarron was certainly far more indebted to his own observations, whether of the troop of Filandre or of another, than to Agustín de Rojas. Nevertheless, while the Frenchman did away with dialogue and brought order out of chaos, there is a certain resemblance still between his account of the comedians of Mans, and this of the Spanish wanderers, for in both the low-life adventures are balanced by romantic incidents dispersed in separate sections as a relief through the work. The method as well as the conception, therefore, may have been derived from Rojas, although the matter was Scarron's own.

A book whose outline may have been suggested by the *Viage entretenido*, was Dr. Christóval Suarez de Figueroa's *El passagero, advertencias utilissimas á la vida humana*, published at Madrid in 1617, and reissued the following year at Barcelona. In his dedication to the republic of Lucca, the author spoke of seven other books of his already published, the best known of which, the *Constante Amarilis*, appeared in 1609. Of his other productions a translation of the *Pastor Fido* in 1602, an epic poem, *La España defendida* in

1612, a biography of the Marquis of Cañete in 1613, the encyclopædic *Plaza universal de las ciencias* in 1615, and the score of essays of 1621, *Varias noticias importantes á la humana comunicacion*, indicate sufficiently the author's range. He was an envious, ungenerous man, who railed at his rivals from Ruiz de Alarcón to Cervantes, but his *Passagero* was interesting, if for nothing else, because of the side-lights it cast upon contemporary men and events. As in the *Viage entretenido*, the piece was in dialogue with four interlocutors who relieved the tedium of travel by conversation. One was a master of arts bound for Rome, another a soldier with a commission for Naples, the third a jeweller seeking a bequest at Milan, and the fourth the author himself with the title of Doctor, but rather a Doctor in experience than in science. Journeying from Madrid to Barcelona to embark for Italy, the four sleep through the heat of the day and discourse at night in ten *alivios*. No regular story is carried on, although each of the characters relates something of his own life, and the account of Figueroa's is more or less picaresque. Born in Valladolid, he began his vagabond career by making for Italy, but being recalled by the death of his father, he vowed a pilgrimage in the midst of a storm on the way home. Discouraged in performing this by a roguish pass with a muleteer, and rescued at last from prison, he abandoned his enterprise only to get into fresh trouble by stabbing one who insulted the profession of the law. Fleeing from pursuit, the Doctor, on the road to Andalusia, met a hermit who entertained him with his private history, and at an inn he encountered a veritable picaro in the host, an old soldier friend of Italy. This fellow, Juan, then gave an account of his life since his embarking from Genoa that constituted a romance of roguery in miniature. On his falling in love, aboard the galley bound for Cartagena, with a Spanish adventuress, the captain became his rival, and abandoned him on shore at Toulon. Here Juan was robbed, cheated, and forced by grave-despoilers to enter a tomb and dismantle a corpse. He retained a fine ring for himself, hiding it in his mouth, but the robbers ran off and left him immured until his cries, disturbing monks at their matins, procured his release. Next day a bishop let him ride behind his coach to Marseilles, where, selling the ring, Juan embarked for Barcelona. Vagabond adventures followed. At Alcalá and Madrid, with the tale of being a poor soldier, and begging and doing errands, he managed to live until admitted to the brotherhood of a hospital. But dissatisfied with attendance on the sick, he turned to love, and the intrigue being discovered, he was dismissed by the superior with penance inflicted on his shoulders. He became a bully on familiar terms with all the nobles of the capital, until, obliged to absent himself after an affray, he left the scene of his triumphs with La Melendez, his mistress. As she was adroit at making a little go a long way, this *venta* on the road from Jaen to Granada was rented, and maintained with such tricks as the Picara Justina's parents best knew. The Doctor, proceeding with his own story, recounted his unfortunate gallantries in Granada and his after-wanderings, matters of fact gradually obscuring the fictional interest of what, at all events, ceases to be a picaresque narrative. The account of Juan, however, was excellent, although probably a pure invention inspired by the romances of roguery. Its fictional character is shown by the single incident of the tomb-robbing which figured as far back as a *fabliau* of Boivin de Provins, and in the fifth story of the second day of the *Decameron.* Later, too, it was taken into French in the *Histoire générale des larrons* of 1623, and somewhat altered it appeared in *L'infortuné Napolitain, ou les aventures du Seigneur Rozelli* of 1708, and in the German, Italian, and several English redactions of that work. The remainder of *El passagero*, notable for its attack upon the old drama, and its view of Spanish conditions, was unpicaresque.

In the *Engaños deste siglo, y historia sucecida en nuestros tiempos*, published in 1615 at Paris, Francisco Loubayssin de la Marca included several picaresque adventures that were taken over into French in the translation of 1618 by François de Rosset, entitled *Les abus du monde*, in that of 1639 by the Sieur de Ganes called *Les tromperies de ce siècle*, and in the still more successful although anonymous *Histoire des cocus* of 1746. Here the old familiar farce-complication of the "night at the inn," in which everybody mistakes everybody else, was prominent, and Don Rodrigo, the innkeeper, like Juan, was a thorough rogue, outwitted nevertheless by his wife Doña Catalina, and eventually hanged after having been fought over by the civil and religious authorities in seeking sanctuary.

Among the burlesque writings of Quevedo aside from the *Buscon*, alone qualified to claim full citizenship in the republic of picaros, were others not so privileged yet almost picaresque. His *Prematicas*, his *Origen y definiciones de la necedad*, his *Libro de todas las cosas*, the *Capitulaciones de la vida de corte*, and the *Cartas del Cavallero de la Tenaza*, caught at least the manner of the romances of roguery if lacking the form, and the readiness with which these essays could be absorbed into the novels is instanced by the fact the *Arancel de necedades* which the Saragossa innkeeper reads to Guzman de Alfarache on his return from Italy, in Aleman's sequel of 1605, was simply the beginning of Quevedo's *Prematicas y aranceles generales*, used once more from its reworking as the *Prematica del tiempo* in Salas Barbadillo's *Sagaz Estacio*; while in the *Buscon* Quevedo inserted his own *Prematicas del desengaño contra los poetas gueros*, later imitated by Vélez Guevara in the *Diablo cojuelo*. An unfinished dramatic piece, the *Pero Bazquez de Escamilla*, bade fair to rival the *Rinconete y Cortadillo*,[1] and the *Cartas del Cavallero de la Tenaza*, the Provident Knight of the English version, presented the obverse side of picaresque avarice. All but one of the seventeen letters are written by the saving hero himself, addressed to different people, mostly courtesans, refusing demands made upon him, and the whole preceded by a sketch of the Cavallero who vows neither to give, loan, nor promise anything in thoughts, words, or works. This retentiveness, pushed to acquisitiveness, would have produced a rogue where the passivity of avarice gave only a miser. Belonging to a more advanced class of satire, the *Sueños* employed the old device of the vision, hitherto often used for purposes of edification, but now turned to a stinging critique upon the follies of the day, attacking the minions of justice in *El alguacil alguacilado*, and the cheats of all trades in *El juicio final*. Endowed with

[1] Barrera y Leirado says of it (*Catálogo bibl. y biográfico del teatro Antiguo Español*, etc., p. 313): "*El genio é ingenio de Quevedo se retratan á maravilla en tan picarescos rasgos, siendo lástima quedara sin concluir este cuadro de costumbres populares cuando parecia que iba á hombrear con Rinconete y Cortadillo.*"

greater freedom than picaresque fiction, but less effective except in the hands of a master like Quevedo, the *Sueños* attained immense popularity, and at home inspired unworthy imitators from Jacinto Polo to Francisco Santos. Translated into French by La Geneste in 1633, into German by Moscherosh in 1639, with additions of his own in 1642 and 1650, into Dutch by Haring van Harinxma in 1641, into English by Roger l'Estrange in 1667, with a Latin redaction in 1642, and into Italian at the beginning of the eighteenth century, Quevedo in this one genre had incalculable influence.[1]

[1] In rogue verse, too, Quevedo was prolific at a time when *Romances de germanía* were the vogue. See *Poesias picarescas inéditas de D. Fr. de Q. V. entresacadas de varios manuscritos . . . por un Bibliófilo*, Madrid, 1871, and 1884. Here, too, may be mentioned a curious publication sometimes attributed to Diego Hurtado Mendoza, although not appearing until 1601 with the title *La vida del picaro compuesto por gallardo estilo en tercia rima por el dichosissimo y bienafortunado Capitã Longares de Angulo, Regidor perpetuo de la hermandad picaril en la ciudad de Mira de la Prouincia del Ocio: sacada á luz por el mesmo autor, a peticion de los cortesanos de la dicha ciudad. Van al fin las ordenanzas picariles por el mesmo Autor* ·:· Valencia junto al molino de la Rouella, 1601, 8°, 8 ff. The Ordenanzas were in prose, but the verses reappeared in the Spanish edition of the *Lazarillo de Tormes*, Paris, 1827, 32°.

But the author of the *Buscon*, if he excelled in satire, had not that broad view of life and intimate feeling for nature that distinguished Cervantes. Both of them were students of society, knowing the under crust as well as the upper, and bitterly cynical at times. But Quevedo, in his portraiture of the other half conveyed primarily an impression of *esprit* in the artist, where Cervantes carried only the conviction of absolute fidelity in the picture. Cervantes reflected truth directly; Quevedo caricatured it. So marked was the affection of Cervantes for the rout of rogues in his day overrunning the Peninsula, and so uniformly successful was his presentation of them on paper or the boards, that it is not a little noteworthy that he should never have ventured to compete with the regular romances of roguery. It is true that at the appearance of the *Guzman de Alfarache* he was already past the half-century mark, and the height of the picaresque fashion was to be attained only after his death; content to follow the lead of the pastoral novel, in all else that he did Cervantes' originality refused to be curbed by custom or law, and for this reason, if for no other, he could not have seen sufficient inducement to conform to the picaresque type. In individual rogues, and scenes of consummate roguery, however, his works were by no means deficient. Ginés de Pasamonte in *Don Quixote* had shown himself of the family of all picaros, and his relationship to Lazarillo de Tormes was openly proclaimed. It has been held indeed that the parallelism between this rascal and Guzman de Alfarache is more than casual, and that in the supposed autobiography of Pasamonte, Aleman's novel is directly designated. Whether this be so or not, Ginés writes his life from the galleys, as did Guzman, declaring his familiarity with hard-tack and the convict lash, and his affair with a *comisario* at an inn is similar to Guzman's theft on his way to the galleys where the profits were shared by the guard. As in the *Orlando Furioso*, Brunello steals Sacripante's horse and Marfisa's sword, so here, "thanks to Ginés de Pasamonte," Don Quixote himself loses his trusty blade, and Sancho Panza, his no less trusty ass. Ginés with his ruses and his disguise as a gypsy, had he but been given a larger rôle to fill, might have rivalled any of the picaros. Cervantes in his pieces for the theatre, and particularly in his

Ocho comedias, y ocho entremeses nuevos, published in 1615, showed the influence of picaresque fiction from *El gallardo Español*, with its rogue soldier practising a religious cheat similar to that of Salas Barbadillo's Elena, to the *Rufian Dichoso* and *Pedro de Urdemalas*, where low life was dissected even more carefully. Christóval de Lugo, the happy ruffian, servant to an inquisitor by day, president of the Seville *hampa* by night, is a strange picaro, pious and quarrelsome, contemplating highway robbery, and suddenly inspired by success at cards to turn monk. In Spain a rogue, in Mexico he becomes a saint, voluntarily assuming the sins of a dying penitent, and defying the demons who claim his soul. Calderon himself could have sounded the mystic note scarcely better. But Pedro de Urdemalas, the victim of fate, takes no stock in mysticism or reform. He is taught fasting and prayer by the whip and dry bread. As cabin boy he voyages to the Indies, and at home again, figures in the conclaves of the *hampa*, turns boasting soldier, sells brandy and pastry, serves a blind man, and becomes at Urde a farm-hand. A band of gypsies honor him by an invitation to cast in his lot with theirs, and his first exploit is defrauding an avaricious widow, by assuming the contract to pray her relatives out of purgatory. Then he is hermit, student, beggar, and finally comedian, though never more than picaro, while Bélica, the gypsy, becomes Isabel, the fine lady, all by a different toss of the dice. Pedro who once had said, "I learned thievery to eat, and lying for defence," to the last must retain his weapons.

But it was in the *Novelas exemplares*, dedicated to the Conde de Lémos and first published at Madrid in 1613, that Cervantes best traced the traits of picaresque Spain. Inspired by his six years in Italy with the ambition of rivalling Boccaccio, the Spaniard called these twelve short sketches exemplary, in contradistinction to those of his Tuscan master, and claimed to be the first to give such original fictions in Castilian. They differed from the Italian *novelle* in being more essentially based upon observation of manners and national methods and moods, thus approaching the modern short story, and, after the *Hidalgo of La Mancha*, no other work of Cervantes was so popular or influential. The more serious tales of the collection were the least meritorious, since in them the machinery to excite surprise and satisfy curiosity became perhaps too apparent; but in the stories of low life, the wealth of familiar detail and the scrutiny of actualities took precedence of the intrigue. *La gitanilla* showed the little gypsy girl, Preciosa, dancing for the nobles of Madrid and bewitching a cavalier to turn Bohemian for love of her. But Preciosa proved to be only a gypsy by adoption, and the romanticism of her story, which recommended her to Victor Hugo as the model for his Esmeralda, operated to obscure the faithfulness of the tale as a view of *gitano* conditions. Still her adventures were dramatized by Montalván and Antonio de Solís in Spain, as the *Spanish Gypsy* by Middleton and Rowley in England, and by Mœller and by Wolf in Germany as *Die Zigeuner*, of 1778, and *Preciosa*, printed in 1823. The complement of this *novela* was that of *La ilustre fregona*. There Don Diego Carriazo, pretending to set out for Salamanca and the university, runs off to fish for tunnies at Zahara with his equally rich and noble comrade, Don Tomás de Avendaño. While they are in the guise of picaros, rejoicing in their freedom, the *fregona*, the maid at the inn, dawns upon them. Avendaño for her sake becomes servant in the hostelry and marries his mistress; but it is not his fault if, after all, like La Gitanilla, she turns out to be better born than she seemed. The suddenness of social metamorphoses is struck at, and the restlessness of the adventurer driving him to become the rogue. In *El casamiento engañoso*, presenting the counter-cheats of a knave and a picara marrying on false pretensions and each deceived in the other, the laugh at the expense of both was a trifle cynical; and in the *Coloquio de los perros Cipion y Berganza* it was almost bitter. The former work became the basis for Beaumont and Fletcher's *Rule a Wife and Have a Wife* of 1624, and appeared rewritten in *The Wits, or Sport upon Sport*, a collection of drolls and farces, compiled in 1673 by that inveterate book-maker, Francis Kirkman, author of the second part of the *English Rogue* and collaborator in the third and fourth parts. At Copenhagen in 1724 the *Casamiento* was dramatized in three acts by Ludwig af Holberg as *Henrich og Pernille*, printed in 1731; and adaptations from

Beaumont and Fletcher resulted in Tobin's *Honey-moon* and Schröder's four-act comedy, *Stille Wasser sind tief.* As for the *Coloquio de los perros*, granting the fable of the dogs endowed for one night with speech, the realism, the satire, and, above all, the method were analogous to the romances of roguery; and Cipion in his gravity, and Berganza with his ruses, proverbs, and common sense, resembled that more illustrious pair, Quixote and Sancho Panza. In old age, in the Hospital de la Resurreccion at Valladolid, Berganza, looking back upon his life, describes to his companion, Cipion, the shifts of condition and the many masters he has served, from the thieving butchers of Seville to the shepherds of the fields, so different from the piping swains of Montemayor. Wherever he has gone, honesty has got him into disgrace and disillusionment has been his portion. As a watch-dog, vigilance merely deprived him of liberty, and as aid to an alguazil, he has found his master in league with the king of the rogues, Monipodio. Suggesting reforms to a corregidor, he has been saluted with missiles; and students, soldiers, *Moriscos*, and actors have been served only to call down his derision. The classes of society defiled in procession and were satirized, not by a rogue, it is true, but by an humble and honest dog informed through a witch, he declares, that dogs shall yet be men.. A masterful plea for the third estate, the *Coloquio de los perros*, borrowing in Berganza's relation the form of the romance of roguery, was Cervantes' protest against the maladministration of Spain and the fate of would-be reformers, a complaint of the neglect his own untiring efforts had encountered. The most picaresque of his dozen *novelas*, however, was the *Rinconete y Cortadillo*, mentioned already in the forty-seventh chapter of *Don Quixote.* With the country thieves, Rinconete and Cortadillo, the reader is introduced to the city thieves assembled in solemn conclave under the watchful eye of Monipodio. The ragged boys who have met at an inn on the edge of Andalusia, — the one a cut-purse, the other a card-cheat, — and have travelled to Seville, exercising their noble profession, find a welcome from the masters of their trade in the *hampa;* but they learn that independent foraging must give way to organized roguery. The purse which Cortadillo has secured from a sacristan is returned because the alguazil demanding it happens to be a friend of the band; and districts for the transaction of further business are assigned to each. In the laws of this fraternity and the piety of its members was offered an opportunity for satire that Cervantes did not neglect, while the *hampa* scene is one of the most picaresque in his whole gallery. *La tia fingida*, although not included in the original collection, and only printed in 1814 in castigated form by Arrieta in his *Espíritu de Miguel de Cervantes*, was one of the earliest *novelas* by the master, presenting the ruses of the false aunt banking upon the charms of her pretended niece, whose virtuous exterior fascinates the student world of Salamanca. The traits of these students — the Valencians, Catalans, Aragonese, Castilians, Asturians, Galicians, Andalusians, and the rest — are remarked by the wily old aunt for her charge's benefit; and the story, if merely an intrigue tale, approaches the manner of the picaresque narratives, and, in the scheming duenna, reproduces a familiar picaresque figure.

In 1616 at Venice the *Novelas exemplares*

were published in Italian by Barezzi, and in 1629 Donato Fontana gave a Milanese redaction. In France in 1618 François de Rosset and Vital D'Audiguier produced a translation, and Pierre Hessein a new one at Amsterdam in 1700. In 1640 six of the *novelas* were Englished by Mabbe under his pseudonym of Don Diego Puede-Ser, although it is noteworthy, considering Mabbe's affinity for realistic work, that in this selection he should have omitted just those most picaresque. In 1694 William Pope, the astronomer, printed six in his *Select Novels*, adding a story attributed to Petrarch. Richard Codrington's *The Troublesome and Hard Adventures in Love* of 1652 had included tales falsely pretending to have been written by "that excellent and famous gentleman, Michael Cervantes," although in the epistle dedicatory it was stated with pleasing accuracy that the Spanish author was "the same gentleman that composed Guzman de Alfarache, and the second part of Don Quixote." In 1728 Harry Bridges, who had accompanied the Earl of Sandwich in his embassy to Spain in 1666, issued seven in his *Collection of Select Novels*; and Samuel Croxall the next year introduced them in his *Select Collection of Novels and Histories.* Some appeared in Dutch in 1731 at Amsterdam as the *Vermakelyke Minneyren;* and some in Danish at Copenhagen in 1780 as the *Laererige Fortaellinger.* In Germany with *Rinconete y Cortadillo* printed in Niclas Ulenhart's translation of 1617, and several others by Harsdörffer in *Der grosse Schauplatz jämmerlicher Mord-Geschichte* — published in two parts at Frankfort in 1650 and 1651, and enlarged the subsequent year, — the *Casamiento* and the *Fregona* appeared in 1700, and Conradi in 1752 brought out at Frankfort and Leipzig the *Satyrische und lehrreiche Erzählungen*, followed by Julius von Soden's *Moralische Novellen* of 1779 at Leipzig, *zum ersten Mal aus dem Original übersetzt.*

A late echo of *Rinconete y Cortadillo* was the *Ardid de la pobreza y astucias de Vireno* in the collection of Andrés de Prado, the *Meriendas del ingenio y entretenimientos del gusto* published at Saragossa in 1663. Four rogues were pictured meeting on the banks of the Ebro to establish a mendicant fraternity: one, a sergeant returned from the Flanders wars minus a leg;

another, a student devoted to charlatanry; the third, an ex-coachman arrayed in remnants; and the fourth, a decayed man of letters. The sergeant having been elected arch-mendicant, and the poet secretary, districts for begging are assigned to each, and rules made to govern the professors of this royal art. The student, Vireno, falling in love with a soft-hearted lady of whom he asks charity, is employed to teach her to read, and becomes so infatuated that, in order to secure money to bestow upon her, he plays a trick whereby he sells for a great price a watch he has found. His triumph is shortlived, however; for, encountered walking in the sergeant's begging territory, he is fined for trespass; and then going to reclaim his loan, he discovers his lady's household broken up, and that seeming pattern of virtue arrested by alguazils. On a plea at his lodgings of stepping out to dine with a friend, Vireno steps away for good and all, forgetting to discharge his reckoning, and qualified to say *omnia mea mecum porto.*

In the *Novelas morales útiles por sus documentos* of 1620, written by Diego Agreda y Vargas and done into French the subsequent year by Baudoin, the twelve tales, followed by profitable remarks pointing out the lesson to be learned from each character, were occasionally picaresque, as in the second story where a young man coming to Madrid is victimized by a rogue with *valientes* at his command who tries the badger trick on the stranger. Again, in the fifth *novela*, a jealous husband, worsted by his wife and her gallant in endless ways, is outwitted on the same plan employed by Guzman de Alfarache's father in gaining possession of the ecclesiastic's mistress; and in the eighth *novela*, two rogues, a maidservant and her lover, put up a cheat on a merchant and his bride, involving a scene borrowed from the *Codicia de los bienes agenos;* but falling out among themselves they are detected and punished. In the last story of all, Pedro de Salzedo, sent to Madrid on business, meets a cunning courtesan who professes to have come out to buy a hat for a small boy, but to lack sufficient money. Pedro complacently purchases the hat, with which the boy departs, and the lady, contriving then to elude her admirer, is boasting of the trick to her bully, when the boy returns, having been met again and relieved of his prize by the wary Pedro on the pretence of changing it for a better one.

Slight as were these plots, they were wrought out with a humor and attention to detail that affiliated them with the romances of roguery, although in the same collection romantic elements and a flowery style were not lacking, as in the first tale, *Aurelio y Alexandro*, a rewriting of Bandello's *Romeo and Juliet*, which had already appeared in Spanish as early as 1589 at Salamanca.

Superior to these and more picaresque in tone than any *novelas* save those of Cervantes were most of the fourteen included in the *Guia y avisos de forasteros que vienen á la corte* composed by Antonio Liñan y Verdugo, and first published at Madrid in 1620. Don Diego, a young gentleman coming to court to dispute at law an inheritance, is met by an old courtier and a master of arts and theology, who propose that he lodge with them, offering to advise him how to live at Madrid and avoid its perils. Accordingly, the book is arranged in eight *avisos*, all but the last illustrated with a story or stories to prove concretely the wisdom of the advice already given in the abstract. Warnings as to the choice of a neighborhood, of friends, of streets to frequent, of those in whom to confide, and of amusements, cautions against courtiers in general, and suggestions for getting on at court and bringing up children in safety, are the excuses for relating some excellent stories, evidently based upon the observation of actual life, graphically told, and free from moralization. In all these tales there was the touch of the romance of roguery, although some conclude tragically, as when Filarco, sent to Madrid as an agent, forsakes his business for a mistress, who finally has him stabbed, or when Doña Juana, kept at the window to draw custom, forces a young hidalgo to marry her, and then really falling in love with him, dies of grief at his abandoning her. The humor of others was delicate, as in the marriage fraud put upon a rich countryman and his daughter by a rogue playing on their ambition, or in the unprofitable loan made by a trusting peasant to a crazy engineer, a companion character to the mad *ingeniero* of the *Buscon*, who had invented a mill to operate like clockwork, by weights. The cheat practised at the expense of a lieutenant by two gentlemen of industry, begging in his name at a gaming-house; the proposed marriage of two adventurers, a vague souvenir perhaps of Cervantes' *Casamiento Engañoso;* or the surprise of a stranger who, having made friends with a seeming fine gentleman, is arrested as receiver of a gang of thieves, of which this fellow was the chief, — were equally comic in spirit. Perhaps the most successful of the *novelas* was that recounting the cheats of a picara and her gallant, half student, half bully. She is the widow of a soldier killed in Peru, and he, although never having injured anybody, is so adroit in talking the *valiente* jargon that he is approved by the doctors of the stabbing faculty. Inclined rather to sharpness than to force, this rogue leaves Seville for the capital, pretending to be the lady's esquire, and having hired a train of servants at Córdova, the reservoir of discharged pages, lackeys, cooks, and duennas, the two set up on credit a fashionable establishment at Madrid. There the picaro commences his frauds, "than which those of Pedro de Urdemalas were no greater," it is said. With a memorandum book he goes about jotting down what from simple servants he can learn of the business of their masters, and transcribes his complete information to a ledger. He frequents the comedy, the gaming-houses, and the Prado, pulls papers from his bosom ostentatiously, and by his air of consequence and his omniscience comes to have several negotiations committed to his charge. In the meantime the anti-heroine so worms herself into the fine society of the town that she is overwhelmed with paying and receiving visits, regaled by all because she knows the knack of deceiving all. The shopkeepers are blinded by her elegance, as are the nobles, but a young soldier paying court to the lady, her rogue esquire becomes uneasy. He finds himself forgotten, and, what is worse for a picaro, robbed, since presents are sent to the soldier. A duel ensues, the watch appears, the soldier confesses from spite, and the rogue upon the rack. Condemned to the galleys, the ambitious picaro and the fine lady are whipped through the streets, while windows are hired along the route for all Madrid to witness their dolorous exit.

The Pedro de Urdemalas referred to in the above *novela* was probably the knave of Cervantes' comedy of the same name, although in the early part of 1620, the very year of the appearance of the *Guia y avisos de forasteros*, Salas Barbadillo issued at Madrid his *El subtil*

Cordovés Pedro de Urdemalas, a dialogued fiction, a considerable portion of which was in verse.[1] Pedro, the picaro, is discovered entering an inn at Granada, having stolen a mule, but so disguising himself with the aid of the maid, Marina, that he deceives the muleteer and alguazil sent after him, he plays the astrologer, and makes the officer believe the muleteer to be the thief. The latter is put to torture and confesses what he never did, while Pedro persuades Marina to accompany him toward Málaga. On the road another rascal is met, whom Pedro, appearing to assist in a theft, really defrauds, sailing with Marina and his booty for Italy. A priest, convinced that the storms which beset the ship are caused by Marina's sins, prevails upon the captain to set the two rascals ashore at Valencia, and nothing loath, they settle down there under new names and with great pretensions. Fine acquaintances are made, with whom the time is passed pleasantly in playing

[1] Pedro was a popular figure, however, and by the last third of the sixteenth century he was already in evidence as in the *Diálogo de Pedro de Hurdimalas y Juan de Voto-á-Dios y Máta-las-callando, que trata de las costumbres y secta de los Turcos, y de otras cosas de aquellas partes,* noted in Gallardo, *Ensayo*, numero 592.

tricks and enjoying poetical academies. But the plot after this goes to pieces, for the wiles of the picaro are all to no purpose. He cheats a miser by pretending to perform a spell for buried treasure, has a quarrel with a Valencian gambler, and tells stories of his past exploits that are neither interesting nor original, while the narrative method is an exasperating one, since every mediocre episode is given in sections, separated by pages of irrelative verse. At the close of all is printed the text of a comedy, *El gallardo Escarraman*, said to have been played by these *academicos*.

More romantic and less picaresque than the *Pedro de Urdemalas* of Salas Barbadillo, his *Sabia Flora Malsabidilla*, published at Madrid in 1621, proved a better performance, even if written in the same loose dramatic form. Flora, a gypsy and picara of Cantillana, having had her first love affair with Teodoro, a youth since emigrated to the Indies, has passed through various dishonorable vicissitudes, allying herself with a Sevillian, and finally with a minister of the court at Madrid. Learning, however, of the return to Spain of Teodoro, rich and prosperous, she changes her name and residence, and pretending to be a relative, determines to captivate him. He still remembers his gypsy love, and declares he would not scruple to marry her could she be found, but doubting this, and fearing her identity to be suspected, Flora circulates a report of the death of the gypsy. The gallant, becoming more and more infatuated with the adroit lady, hires two *valientes* to dispose of a supposed rival, and when his own lackey, putting them to flight, proves to have been their mistaken victim, Teodoro, gains sufficient courage to ask Flora's hand, and she, knowing the marriage will not be legal unless she confesses her real identity, and moved, too, by remorse, admits to being no other than the gypsy girl of Cantillana. Teodoro half believes her jesting, but to humor her has the ceremony performed under that name, and the piece ends with Flora's friends wishing her joy. "*No te llamen la Malsabidilla pues con esto te apartas de todo mal, sino la sabia y prudente Flora.*" Although the plot was no more roguish than that of many another comedy, the handling was essentially picaresque, and the burlesque style, especially in the portions referring to Flora's past and to the bullies, quite in line with that of the *Buscon.* The touch of cheap morality here, such as Cervantes had too much taste ever to administer, had appeared even more noticeably the year previous in the same author's *El sagaz Estacio marido examinado*, translated to French in 1634, as *Le matois mary, ou la courtezanne attrapée.* There, a courtesan in search of a complacent husband finds one through a marriage agent, but he proves after all to be less of a dupe than he has seemed, for after the wedding he explains that when shipwrecked he made a vow to draw a sinful woman from depravity by marrying her, a somewhat doubtful expedient, which, however, succeeds in this instance, since he now is redeemed from poverty by his wife's riches, and she from her evil courses by love for him. Other works of Barbadillo were roguish in character too, the *Cortesano descortés* of 1621, a comedy resembling the *Sabia Flora*, and the still earlier *Correcion de vicios en boca de todas verdades* of 1615, a prose satire on decayed poets, musicians, and courtiers in the mouth of a fool, intermingled with *novelas* in verse. Six satiric portraits had been presented in the *Curioso y sabio Alexandro fiscal y juez de vidas agenas*, and among the sixty-four scathing epistles of the *Estafeta del dios Momo* of 1627 occurred a *novela jocosa*, entitled, *The Thief Converted to Innkeeper*, describing the marriage of the rogue, Galbarro, with Rufina la Tempestuosa, the daughter of a merry landlord.

The taste for picaresque literature for a while was too general not to affect other fictions, and among them some that may since have dropped from view. Collections of short stories were innumerable in Spain in the seventeenth century. Many of the tales, like those of Cervantes, were the result of immediate observation of life, and a number, therefore, were sure to satirize society through the person of so popular a figure as the picaro. With the advance of the century, however, more and more the *cultismo* prevailed. The subjects best adapted to such a style were love and extravagant adventure, — whatever is opposed to the picaresque. The romance of roguery, therefore, could attain little scope in the *novela* collections as a whole, although from the first successful here and there. The *Escarmientos de Jacinto*, by the Marqués de Osera, in their illustrative warnings to the hero, might betray the rogue's influence, or an occasional *novela* among a sentimental set suggest it, like the *Miseria castigado* of María de Zayas y Soto Mayor; but even those who in longer compositions employed the picaro freely, thought it wise, with Bardadillo and Solórzano, to exclude him from the shorter forms.

At certain angles, moreover, the regular drama reflected the *gusto picaresco*, as in the *comedias de enredo* and *de costumbres*, and in the *sainetes.* Picturing the manners and disorders of the time, Lope de Vega's *La bella mal maridada*, *Santiago el verde*, or *Los melindres de Belisa*, were not far removed from the romances of roguery. Agustín de Moreto in his *gracioso* pieces like the *Trampa adelante*, and more closely still in *Defuera vendrá quien de casa nos echará*, approached the picaresque; as did Antonio de Solís in *El amor al uso*, and Francisco de Roxas in the comedies destined to give to the French their Crispin and their Jodelet. The entire relation of the *gracioso* of the Spanish stage to the other characters had in it much in common with the picaro's relation to society. Heir of the old comedy rogue and buffoon of Plautus, the *gracioso* was a dramatic anti-hero, as the picaro was a novelistic one. The *bobo* or fool of Lope de Rueda and the *simple* of Juan de l'Encina were immediate antecedents of this stage-rogue, perfected by Lope de Vega, who urged for his *Francesilla* the honor of first presenting the full-fledged *gracioso.* But to whomever belongs the credit of the invention, it is a significant fact that the dramatic development destined to lead through the Scapin of Molière to the Figaro of Beaumarchais, should have taken its rise in Spain synchronously with the fictional development destined to lead through *Francion* and *Gil Blas* to *Colonel Jack* and *Ferdinand Count Fathom.* The *gracioso* and the picaro were brothers, reared in the same environment at the same time; and the descendants of each, however differentiated from one another, carry still the traits of cousinship.

CHAPTER VII

THE DECADENCE OF THE PICARESQUE NOVEL

WHILE the romance of roguery admitted considerable latitude of invention and observation, and in this respect far transcended the novel of chivalry and the pastoral, its scope, after all, had a limit, which the vogue of the genre, and the frequent and repeated experiments made in it could not but early overpass. The fundamental conception of a rascal serving, defrauding, and satirizing masters, traversing all society to describe its faults and foibles, if excellent, was too eccentric to endure when the zest of novelty had worn away. The picaro in himself had no greater resources of entertainment than had the shepherd or the knight, although he lived in a world sure to be supremely interesting because so genuine. But the rogue was popular less on his own account than as the antithesis to impossible, unfailingly virtuous heroes, between whose exploits and those of the folk of every day the incongruity had become more and more apparent. If, however, the public had wearied of the heroic in fiction, there was no guarantee that the anti-heroic would not fatigue, and indeed the reversion to some sort of idealism was certain to occur. A literature of villains, or even of merry rogues, can never be more than a negative, transient literature. Before the adventures of very many picaros had been celebrated, the recurrence of the romantic element began to be manifest in rogue tales, strongly marked in most of those of the second stage, and reaching its climax in the *Soldado Píndaro.* Of the fictions which did not succumb to this romantic influence, some employed the picaresque tradition fantastically, as in the *Diablo cojuelo*, the *Siglo Pitagórico*, or the *Historia moral del dios Momo;* others used it merely to sketch scenes of real life, suppressing the unit of the rogue himself, as in the *Dia y noche de Madrid;* while still others, like the *Vida del conde de Matisio*, neglecting the study of reality, laid so much stress upon the picaro that he became a sheer villain. In all of these is seen the disintegration of the picaresque novel, a process that was nearly complete by the middle of the seventeenth century, and which in 1668, in the *Periquillo, el de las gallineras*, employing the same old tradition and with reminiscences of the picaros of yore, included a moralizing hero more of a philosopher than a rogue. Stories of knaves might yet have been written in Spain, but there was no demand for them. What was best in the vein had been mined already, and the workings there were fairly abandoned.

The *Varia Fortuna del Soldado Píndaro*, dedicated to the Duke of Medina-Sidonia, appeared at Lisbon in 1626; its author was Gonzalo de Céspedes y Menses, whose *Poema trágico del Español Gerardo y desengaño del amor lascivo* of 1615 and 1617 had sufficiently indicated his romantic tendencies. In 1622 at Madrid he published an *Historia apologética de los sucesos de Aragon en los años 1591 y 1592*, and at Saragossa in 1628 he gave a series of six *novelas* as *Historias peregrinas*, each one praising a different city of Spain. A life of Philip Fourth was issued in 1631, and his *Francia engañada y Francia respondida* appeared in 1635; but it was the *Gerardo* for which he was chiefly known, done into

English as early as 1622 by Leonard Digges, and used by Beaumont and Fletcher in the *Spanish Curate* and the *Maid of the Mill.* Retaining many features of this prose romance, and the same system of interlaced tales and complicated intrigue, the novel of the *Soldado Píndaro* was a better performance from the stylistic point of view, exemplifying the fiction of adventure in the picaresque mould grown into the novel of manners and sentiment. In the introduction, the author told how waiting at a port in the winter of 1623 and 1624 for an opportunity to embark, and being disturbed one night in the monastery where he lodged by the advent of a wounded soldier seeking sanctuary, he received from the intruder on convalescing two volumes of autobiography in manuscript. One is published in this book and the second is shortly to appear. With so much of a setting, then, the history of Pindaro, the Soldier, begins. He was the son of a gentleman of family reduced to poverty through an affair of honor. Sent to school to the Jesuits, and fearing punishment for a boyish scrape, at the age of twelve he with a companion, Figueroa, ran away with two *reales*, a Virgil, and a Tully between them. In a vineyard they found a sword, and Figueroa girding it on was apprehended for a thief, while Pindaro escaped by claiming stoutly that the owner tried to steal it from them. After seeing an old man reprieved who had been about to be executed at Toledo, and hearing his tragic story told by a priest, Pindaro at Tembleque was mistaken by friars for another runaway, and to secure the money they promised him, made a false confession. Leaving them in the lurch and going to Extremadura, he entered the service of Don Gutierre, the nephew of a prince. Here he was employed in a romantic intrigue for his master which ended unhappily, and enlisting as a soldier, he became the recipient of a mysterious casket while acting as watcher for a friend, Francisco, during a night-wooing. Later at San Lucar the owner of the casket was happened upon in a disconsolate lady to whom, after hearing her story, Pindaro and Francisco returned the treasure. A military voyage to the Indies, the disappearance of Francisco at Seville, spirited away by his crafty mistress, another voyage for consolation's sake by Pindaro, and the death of his father and the departure for the court at Valladolid of the adventurer and his brother, brought to a close the first part of the novel. The second opens describing the gay life led by the soldier at the court and the remarkable intrigue he had with a fair unknown whom he always visited blind-folded, but who turned out to live just above him in the same house. Forced to fly to escape this lady's jealous resentment, he was assaulted in the mountains by a rogue innkeeper, and at Madrid was persecuted by the attentions of a foolish girl enamored of him. At Toledo he rescued Francisco from jail, where his false mistress had brought him, and at Ocaña was given a casket containing a new-born infant, whose history was later related by its father and a priest. After saving once more the recaptured Francisco, Pindaro, sailing for Italy, was wrecked off Iviza and did battle with the Turks, one of whom he took for slave, and in Flanders discovered him to be the long-lost Figueroa who, after melancholy adventures in Spain, having been captured by corsairs, became one of them. With the repentance and death of Figueroa the book concludes, promising a second half to treat of the pure love of Isabel and the further adventures of the faithful Pindaro.

Manifestly, this novel was not picaresque in the sense that *Guzman de Alfarache* or even *La garduña de Sevilla* had been so. The hero was not a rogue although he was an adventurer. Capable of generous action and of some real emotion, he had not even experienced the changes of condition that were prerequisites of the picaro's programme. With being a runaway, a page, and a soldier, his whole range of exploit was exhausted. The satire of the novel, moreover, was neither aggressive nor continuous, and it lodged in the incidents rather than in the whole story, where whatever was picaresque found place as well. But in these incidents there was much worthy of the romances of roguery and inspired by them. The early history of Pindaro, his descriptions of prison life, the roguish tricks of Pero Vasquez, the passes with a witch, the flings at innkeepers, at alguazils, and gypsies, and the realistic treatment maintained throughout, gave the fiction, in spite of its very romantic intrigue, an air of naturalism akin to that in the picaresque tales and which but for them it could never have acquired. Autobiographical but less discursive than most of its predecessors, the *Soldado*

Píndaro included a number of anecdotes and notably seven long episodes, the first of which alone had no direct connection with the story. The second and fourth were embedded in the plot itself, and the other four ingeniously related to it. In the narratives of Francisco and of Figueroa there were picaresque traits, but the remaining episodes were love adventures verging on the tragic, the best being that celebrating Don Gutierre's devotion to Doña Hortensia, Pindaro's own account of his almost fatal fascination by his mysterious neighbor, and the story of Anselmo and Estela. In these and in the history of Don Quevedo, far from there being anything picaresque, the manner was passionately serious and the influence of the Italian *novelle* frequently strong.[1] The entire work was pervaded by an evident attempt to attain unity by completing the circle of events artistically, bringing back the threads of the story to their beginning and so improving immeasurably upon such formless fictions as *Estevanillo Gonzalez.* The author had come to a consciousness of the real business of the

[1] Indeed, Pindaro's adventure with the unknown lady is simply Massuccio's 26th novella enlarged and improved.

story-teller, omitting moralization, and wherever he made a digression feeling the need of apologizing for it, and in style and in the control of the action, his novel was one of the most polished and careful. Rather a mingling of the picaresque and the romantic types than either singly, it stood for the outgrowing of narrow conditions prescribed by the romances of roguery.

Similarly, *El siglo Pitagórico y vida de Don Gregorio Guadaña* stepped without the picaresque circle although into the realm of fantasy instead of that of sentiment. Its author, Antonio Enriquez Gómez, born in Segovia of Jewish Portuguese stock, but a refugee in France in 1638 and later burnt in effigy by the Inquisition, wrote several other works, including *La culpa del primer peregrino* of 1644, *Luis dado de Dios* the year following, *La politica angélica* and *La torre de Babilonia* in 1647, as well as a religious narrative poem *Sanson Nazareno*, and a miscellany *Las academias morales de las Musas*. The *Siglo Pitagórico*, published at Rouen in 1644 by Laurens Maurry, was a curious fiction, the object of which, according to Gómez's own statement, was to draw from a false theory a true doctrine. In other words, adopting the scheme of the Pythagorian metempsychosis, it was proposed to show, in place of a picaro passing through service, a soul variously incarnated. Thus to the conception of an unaltering rogue handed from master to master was added that of a soul which in a like round of transformations should gradually develop until finally attaining to virtue. The entire work was supposedly a vision, for the narrator during sleep is visited by Pythagoras, who bids him forsake his present body and seek another: —

Tu vida busca, tu valor reforma,
Libre del cuerpo estàs, no del pecado,
Busco otro nuevo, y purga lo passado.

Thirteen detailed transmigrations and a number of lesser ones follow, described in essays in verse and in prose, some of them not unlike the English Books of Characters, although more animated in style. Each incarnation was closed with a *décima* or a *soneto* explaining the transition to the next; and the last short stanza of all, after the sleeper had seen himself become a righteous man, pictured him awaking and bidden by Pythagoras to search out virtue and live within himself. In its relation to the romance of roguery this work had a double significance, showing a fantastic phase of the Spanish scheme of the service of masters, and presenting besides in the fifth transmigration a fragmentary picaresque tale in prose, occupying more than a third of the book and entitled *La vida de Don Gregorio Guadaña.* The name of the anti-hero, Guadaña, or Falsehood, sufficiently indicates his character, and his direct dependence upon the romances of roguery was confessed in the flattering references made in the introduction to the *Buscon*, *Pícara Justina*, and *Guzman de Alfarache;* but the account of the life of Gregorio was exceedingly poor and absolutely without unity. The picaro relates the story of his birth in Triana, his mother a midwife, and his father a physician. His start in the world is made when he sets forth for Salamanca and the university. At Carmona he meets a judge attended by his notary and alguazil; a lawyer bound for Madrid to reform legislation joins the party, which is presently reënforced by a coach-load of travellers, a friar, a sick soldier, a politician, a philosopher, and a lady with her charming niece. With the latter,

Doña Beatriz, they all fall in love, and after Gregorio has doubtfully assisted the judge in rounding up two gentlemen sought for by justice, and a philosophical academy has been held, the company leaves Carmona. In the Sierra Morena, joined by a poet, they are all robbed at an inn, but reach Madrid, where a relative of Gregorio induces him to dispense large sums in paying suit to a lady, Doña Angelica. Quarreling with an alguazil who steals his guitars, the adventurer takes summary vengeance upon him; and discovering the judge in an intrigue with Beatriz, he perplexes the community by stopping up their doorway with masonry over night. He gallants with the wife of an alguazil, and innocently tells the husband all about it, only to be jailed. He is concerned in a plot to waylay the mid-wife of the Queen; he is wounded, and in continual difficulties, bribing off from prison, tricking a physician and the city authorities, until being pressed to fulfil his promise to wed Doña Angelica, he refuses, and his soul is happily released to pass into a hypocrite. The tedious, trifling, discursive style, the lack of plan or invention, the coarseness, and the glaring faults of construction, are by no means compensated for in the Scarronic skill with which a number of characters are handled together, or in the philosophizing.

Somewhat allied in plan to the *Siglo Pitagórico*, if not picaresque in matter, was the *Historia moral del dios Momo* of Benito Remigio Noydens, published at Madrid in 1666, and describing the transmigrations of the mischief-working god Momus through different classes of society during his exile from heaven, each of his eighteen changes being accompanied by moralized illustrations. Noyden's aim, however, was to attack romance writing, and his book in this connection is of interest therefore only as an echo of the old method popularized by the romance of roguery.

In Luis Vélez de Guevara's *El diablo cojuelo, novela de la otra vida traduzida á esta*, published in 1641 at Madrid, a satirical view of society was afforded by a different device still further removed from the picaresque procedure. Guevara's four hundred dramas, although they brought him fame as an early follower of Lope de Vega, scarcely secured the vogue of this single piece, slight by comparison, but bequeathed to general literature through the *rifacimento* of LeSage. Don Cleofas, the student who, in eluding the pursuit of emissaries of the wily Doña Tomasa, takes refuge in the garret chamber of an astrologer and there releases from a phial the lame devil, has no need of serving various masters in order to view the interior workings of the households of Madrid. Instead, the grateful *diablo cojuelo* becomes his cicerone, magically unveiling the deceits of society in the ten *trancos*, or strides through space, taken by the pair. The human comedy is laid bare with the devil for showman and interpreter; it is Mephistopheles and Faust with the tragedy left out. From the shop for providing ancestors at Madrid to the inn and its mad poet at Toledo, from the *venta* in the Sierra Morena where foreigners wrangle to the fencing exhibition at Córdova recalling to Cleofas the *Buscon* of Quevedo, from Carmona to Seville, flit the devil and his disciple. Rufina María, the roguish hostess of the latter town, born in gypsy Triana, and therefore to be suspected of magic, aids the devil in showing to Cleofas in a mirror all that is happening at that moment in the *Calle Mayor* at Madrid, the King and the court passing in review. A poetical academy is attended at Seville, and a sitting of the rogues' parliament, an obvious souvenir of Cervantes' *hampa* of Monipodio. There, with a porter at the door to give warning of the approach of the enemy, are assembled the mendicants, — Pié de palo the courteous, Moricélago who begs of nights crying in the streets, Sopa en vino the drunkard, Faraon the rascal who sits at church-doors with painted sores, Paulina who curses those who refuse her, Galeona who hires children to demand charity, and all the rest, even to the so-called Duke with his rags and ridiculous airs. But when Cleofas as president of the poetical Academia Sevillana has delivered his set of satirical rules to be observed by the members, forbidding, for example, any poet to speak ill of another oftener than twice a week, and demanding that comedies concerning Moors be baptized within forty days or leave the kingdom, Doña Tomasa and her bully appear in pursuit. The lame devil bribes their agent, the alguazil, so saving Cleofas, although himself summoned back to hell; and Tomasa and the bully depart for the Indies, while Cleofas, undeceived with the world, returns to complete his studies at Alcalá.

When LeSage, in 1707, published his *Diable boiteux*, there was little in common between it and this work beyond the introduction and the general conceit. The 1726 additions from Francisco Santos, and the masked scandals of the French court, made a volume still more widely divergent from the Spanish original, with all the paraphernalia of incorporated *novelas*, yet the fundamental idea was so much the most noteworthy part of the fiction that Vélez de Guevara's share in the composition has never been forgotten.

Related to the other allegoric satires, and directly patterned upon the *Sueños*, was *La flema de Pedro Hernandez*, printed in 1657 at Madrid, and written by Marcos García, a surgeon there. In a vision vouchsafed to the author in reading Quevedo, "*nuestro grande sin imitación, y discreto sin lisonja*," he sees soldiers, students, and physicians, the folk of all classes scrambling to get on in the world, willing in their haste to employ fraud, but not content to travel the slow and sure road to success. The mythological Pedro Hernandez, a Spanish proverbial figure, noted for his listlessness, is called upon disdainfully by all the short-cut pretenders, the poetic aspirant, for instance, when told that in order to succeed he must spend ten years in study, crying out, "To Pedro Hernandez with that phlegm, I expect to be a poet from this moment." So the lover who has had to wait a whole week before seeing his lady, exclaims, "*Fuego de Dios* upon this phlegm and whoever invented it." Thus in satirizing the little patience of the Spanish people and the consequent cheats and ruses resorted to in different professions, García reviewed society somewhat after the picaresque scheme, and frequently regarded picaresque scenes. At the same time he struck at the very root of the picaresque in peninsular life, the ingrained contempt for toil and the readiness to seize prizes without having won them, — "A contagion," he has the cheating physician exclaim, "which has spread to many." The text of the whole book was "make haste slowly," — "*Conoscas los daños de la priesa, y los provechos de la flema bien usada.*"[1]

[1] With the *Flema* and the *Siglo Pitagórico* Llorente associates the story, *Don Raimundo el entremetido*, printed at Alcalá by Antonio Duplastre, without date, but in 1627. Its author was Diego Tovar y Valderrama, who wrote also the

Juan de Zavaleta, who in his *Dia de fiesta por la mañana* gave character sketches of the miser, the gallant, the glutton, the coquette, the poet, the hypocrite, and the rest, as found by the morning of the fiesta, and then in his *Dia de fiesta por la tarde*, as left at its close, did not attempt in his *Vida del conde de Matisio* of 1652 satiric observation, but turned to writing a novel, the hero of which was a sort of Robert the Devil. The scene is laid in France, near Lyons, and Ludovico, the only child of indulgent parents, grows up with two pages, the good Mauricio and the bad Leonardo. Ludovico's earliest amusement consists in watching teeth pulled one by one from a fellow hired for the purpose; and when his father dies he cashiers all the old servants, retaining, however, the pages and his tutor, against the virtue of

Instituciones politicas of 1645. The former three works, according to Llorente, were aimed against the *gusto picaresco.* Don Raimundo seems to have been such a rogue and busy-body as the later Bigand, anti-hero of *La Mouche*, of 1736, by the Chevalier de Mouhy. The Spanish novel is short, and to-day rare, not being contained in any of the Paris libraries, nor in the British Museum, although a MS. copy of it is in the Bib. Nacional at Madrid. An extract from the preface, by Quevedo, is given in Ernest Merimée's *Quevedo*, etc., Paris, 1886, p. 168.

whose daughter he has designs. Leonardo, the wicked page, given the task of winning for his master this lady's favor, and failing, pretends to Ludovico that she will consent to anything, provided he first furnish her with a husband, who is promptly provided in the unconscious Mauricio. After Ludovico and Leonardo in Paris have led a dissolute life, the count returns to his estate, robs a church of its treasure, and attempting to put into execution his plot with regard to the bride of Mauricio, discovers the perfidy of Leonardo, whom he kills. Then, kidnapping both Mauricio and the lady, he binds the husband where he can overlook the entertainment prepared for his bride; but, heaven fortunately interfering, the villain hears himself irresistibly summoned, and on the very spot where Mauricio had demanded justice, Ludovico is enveloped in a black cloud and vanishes. This mystical climax and the entire story were unpicaresque enough, and the book was in the spirit of an expanded Italian *novella*, lacking humor and imagination; yet it indicated an endeavor to overpass the bounds of the romance of roguery, although by insisting so violently upon the moral obliquity of the anti-hero it made him a monster unreal and repugnant. In English fiction precisely the same step was taken in Dr. John Moore's *Zeluco* of 1786, and in that case, on the author's own confession, the moral aim was responsible for the exclusion of comedy and the central figure's consequent transformation from a rogue to a villain. "If the hero of a romance," said Dr. Moore, referring to his own novel and to Smollett's *Ferdinand Count Fathom*, "is described devoid of principle, and perfidious, the more detestable he is made in all other respects, the better will the work serve the purpose of morality,"[1]—a plan fruitful perhaps in edification, but barren certainly for art.

At all events, through the intrusion of romantic, fantastic, or moral motives, the picaresque novel in Spain lost its original character. Of the later tale-writers, Francisco Santos alone was endowed with satirical power and observation sufficient to continue the type had it seemed worth while. Though he attempted in most of his works the ironic allegory, as in

[1] *A View of the Commencement and Progress of Romance* in Vol. I. of *The Works of T. Smollett* . . . Edited by John Moore . . . 8 vols., London, 1797.

El diablo anda suelto of 1677, and *El verdad en el potro y el Cid resuscitado* of two years later, it was only in his early *Dia y noche de Madrid*, and in the *Periquillo* that the traditional picaresque manner was at all retained.[1] Even the *Day and Night in Madrid* of 1663 was a fiction not unlike the *Limping Devil* in construction, although shorn of the fantastic element. Onofre, a Neapolitan, arriving in Spain after having been freed from Algerine captivity, and desirous of viewing the Spanish capital, is led about by Juanillo, a child of the people, well qualified by his roguish experience to explain the mysteries of the town. A mere panorama succeeds, with Juanillo as expositor, until Onofre in his wanderings chances upon a burning house, from which he rescues a lady whose rich father in gratitude bestows her, together with an

[1] Santos' other works, *El sastre del campillo*, *El escandalo del mundo y piedra de la justicia*, *El rey gallo y discursos de la hormiga*, *El vivo y el defunto*, and *El arca de Noe y campana de Belilla*, etc., may best be consulted in his *Obras en prosa y verso*, Madrid, 1723, 4 vols. His influence was slight abroad, although his *Descripcion breve del monasterio de S. Lorenzo el real del Escorial*, of 1657, was Englished by "A Servant of the Earl of Sandwich" in 1671, and reappeared in 1760 as translated by G. Thompson.

adequate dowry, upon the gallant adventurer. Narrated in eighteen *discursos*, this fiction embraced the story of Onofre himself, related at the end of the book on the eve of his marriage, and the story of Juanillo told at its beginning on his meeting Onofre. Here and in the main body of the work, devoted to satire and observation, the picaresque influence was strong. Juanillo was born in Madrid in poverty, and commenced life by begging. Left to his own devices at ten, he learned reading from a kind clerk, and took to collecting wax from burnt candles on altars. A water-carrier frightened him off from this lucrative employment, wishing to appropriate it himself, and Juanillo passed to the service of a priest. Running away and roving the fields, a mendicant on crutches introduced him to others of the fraternity, and he became the boon comrade of another boy, stolen in infancy. Developing some scruples as to the begging trade, to get on in which he must feign lameness, Juanillo finally declared his preference for seeming what he really was, — simple, — and so turned poor philosopher. In the shifting street-scenes through which he leads Onofre, a rapid study of manners in the spirit of the romances of roguery was given, from the cheats of coquettes at the bull-fight, an incident borrowed in the *Diable boiteux*, to the old *Eulenspiegel* trick of a boy being defrauded out of his mule by a picaro who takes it and pretends that a surgeon will pay for it as soon as he is at leisure, the surgeon having been previously informed that the boy wishes to speak to him regarding a malady.[1] Blind men praying at the foot of the gallows, rogues with bloody rags crouching at the church-door, *valentones de mentira* making a show of fighting, the gossiping crowd about a fountain where *aguadores* are drawing water, a midwife called out on a false summons only to be robbed, — all these and more were presented in lifelike vignettes.

Five years after this essay, when Santos had given in the interval his allegoric satires, — *Las tarascas de Madrid y tribunal espantoso*, and *Los gigantones de Madrid por defuera*, as well as the poems of *Cardeno Liro, alma sin crepusculo, y Madrid llorando*, — he brought

[1] One of the most frequent jests in picaresque fiction, the 1st of Sozzini, the 2d of the 13th Night of Straparola, and in most of the English jest-books and every conny-catching pamphlet.

out the novel, *Periquillo of the Poultry-yard.* Periquillo is a foundling cared for by a pious pair, and diligent in his studies until forced to enter service with a woman of the neighborhood, a dealer in poultry, whence his nickname. After another servant from envy has sought to injure him with his mistress, who discovers the cheat, she falls in love with him, but, at his rejection of her proposals, pretends that he is the offender, — a passage closely parallel to Joseph Andrew's adventure with Lady Booby. Periquillo is next accommodated as servant to a kindly man who wishes to make the boy his son rather than his lackey; but the design is opposed by the gentleman's wife, who suspects Periquillo to be her lord's son already. A third master for the adventurer is found in a blind man, to whom satirically he explains all that he sees. "And as I have heard that it is a great life to be a picaro, I have become one," Periquillo declares, although presently he determines to leave the guiding of the blind to Lazarillos and Alfaraches, and installs himself with a new master. Well treated, but obliged to assist in systematic thieving from houses into which agents are hired as domestics, Periquillo decamps, and in his roaming is beset in the mountains by three outlaws, each of whom relates the story of his life. Periquillo having been persuaded to join them, all are captured after a robbery, from which, however, he is exculpated by the others, and sets out afoot for his own country disillusionized. Greeted by crowds of children crying, "*Al loco! al loco!*" he is regarded half as fool, half as sage, and, supported by charity, goes about rebuking everybody fearlessly from the stable-boy, anxious to be called hidalgo, to his own rich patron, addressing whom he says: "You adorn my body, who do not adorn your soul." Periquillo, dispensing allegories and sermons, comes to his end surrounded by admirers and praying devoutly. "And thus," concludes the author, "expired he who gave me material to write this book, this example of the world, this man who knew himself, rich in poverty,—*Periquillo, El de las gallineras.*"

While the merit of the fiction was slight enough, yet as the last expression of a once popular type it was significant. The roguishness in the central character had disappeared, but the cycle of events and the service of masters remained. The three *novelas*, included as related by the outlaws, were merely tragic and romantic episodes, and digressions in anecdotes were frequent throughout, after the manner of the *Alonso moço de muchos amos.* From the latter, indeed, was taken direct the fable of the lion whose breath was complained of by the lioness seeking a divorce.[1] That the story of Periquillo had a shadow of historical basis, the address to the reader confessed, referring to a rogue well known in Madrid between the years 1636 and 1640, called *Alonsillo El de las gallineras;* but Periquillo had need of no such parentage. He was of the same literary family as the Ceñudo of Salas Barbadillo, or Santos' own Juanillo, a popular hero dowered with worldly wisdom and a sharp tongue, all the more effective because of their possessor's masquerade as a fool. Bahalul or Al Megnum, the jester of Haroun Alraschid, was his distant ancestor, while Heinrich Steinhöwel's German *Life of Æsop* in the fifteenth century had celebrated a similar character, and the translation there in 1490 of Diogenes Laertius farther ex-

[1] *Periquillo*, 5, and *Alonso*, I., 9.

tended the vogue of this type of plodding, satiric philosopher. Diogenes, indeed, seems all along to have been regarded as a kind of elder brother to the picaro, and Boileau even proclaimed his intention of writing a life of him to rival the picaresque novels and to be "of the most perfect roguery, much more pleasing, and much more original than that of Lazarillo de Tormes and Guzman de Alfarache."[1] Such a cynic was Periquillo, heir of the picaros of old, but rather tedious than amusing. He went through the same vicissitudes as they, but only mechanically. All the vitality was gone out of him, for in Spain the romance of roguery had lived its day and fulfilled its mission.

Beginning as a collection of jests, and in its restriction to actuality opposed to idealistic fiction, the picaresque novel had come to absorb the talent for observation of a people gifted in satire, and striving manfully against social and political decadence. As a literary form it had been refined from its first crude, haphazard detailing of manners to a study of roguery in an anti-hero gradually emerging from his

[1] *Bolæana*, Amsterdam, 1742, 12°, p. 41.

deeds; and if it failed to attain to an actual study of character, at least it made manifest the importance of the personal interest on the one hand, and inaugurated the careful scrutiny of common conditions on the other. Then, when all that was fresh, picturesque, and original in national scenes of low life had found presentation, and the picaro himself, from the frequency of his appearance, had lost charm, the decline of the romance of roguery was immediate and inevitable.

Its possibilities, however, transcended those that were realized in the Peninsula. By adopting the same procedure, the literary artist in France, in Germany, in Holland, or in England, could satirize the manners of his own country, pouring new wine into old bottles. Moreover, beyond differences in the mere subject-matter, the general evolution of fiction as an art was bound later and elsewhere to modify this genre. The rogue of eighteenth-century England could not be dealt with as had been the rogue of sixteenth or seventeenth century Spain, for the slow but sure individualization of the central figure developed for him finally a definite character of more moment than any of his actions.

And if in France was best exemplified the subordination of observation and intrigue to the personal interest, in England occurred the supplanting of the personal by the deeper interest of morals and of character. The cheats by degrees cut less and less of a figure, and the cheater a larger, their ingenuity ceasing to be an essential feature. Not the cleverness but the emotional and moral quality of the action predominated, and with the unfolding of the interest in character, the scene of conflict was shifted to the conscience. The old expedient of making the anti-hero conscienceless because young was partially exhausted, and less regularly could indulgence be urged for him on that score. Instead, the fatalism consequent upon his genesis from events became more marked, necessity was his plea, and the force of environment and up-bringing his principal excuse for roguery, although the enlistment of sympathy with him as a child was often yet retained to advantage. Finally, his life, closing hitherto without inward condemnation, could no longer end in prosperous reform, or the restraint brought by lack of opportunity. The awakened ethical sense demanded positive repentance, and the rogue stood forth at last transformed from a witty, humorous creature to a sinner, truer to all the laws of life, if less entertaining.

Such was the picaro's destiny, and Spain, long after the coming of sterility for herself, could witness the multiplication of her literary descendants abroad. In a right line they led through the perfected novel of manners to the modern novel of character, and the talent for observation that at the Renaissance had been the inheritance of anti-heroes alone, came at length to be shared by heroes as well, proving, with the attention bestowed upon character, their best title to reforming fiction. Rogues in letters could and did arise independent of Spanish influence, suggested by the rogues of actuality always present and always interesting; but with very few exceptions, those that count for anything in the development of romance bear unmistakable token of kinship to the picaros of Spain.

A BIBLIOGRAPHY OF SPANISH ROMANCES OF ROGUERY

1554–1668

AND THEIR TRANSLATIONS

[This bibliography does not pretend to be exhaustive, but it does seek to note all significant and most early editions of the works considered. Modern editions find a place here only when for some particular reason it seemed best to name them. Capitals, italics, and the alignment are indicated, vignettes are shown by the sign ∴, and libraries by obvious abbreviations.]

1554. *Editio Princeps.* (So far as known)

La vida de Lazarillo | de Tormes: y de sus | fortunas y aduer|sidades.| 1554. (Page enclosed in scrolls and adorned with figures.) The colophon reads: Impresso en Burgos en | casa de Juan de Junta. Año de | mil y quinientos y cinquen- | ta y quatro Años.| 48 ff. Sm. 8vo.

Unique exemplar at Chatsworth House; but see reprint in 1897, by H. Butler Clarke (250 copies), as *Lazarillo de Tormes conforme á la edición de 1554.* Oxford, B. H. Blackwell, 16mo.

1554. Alcalá

La vida de Lazarillo de | Tormes : y de sus fortunas : y | aduersidades. Nuevamente impressa, : corregida, y de nuevo añadi-|da en esta segũda im-|pression.| Vendense en Alcala de Henares, en | casa d̄ Salzedo Librero. Año | de M.D. LIIII. | 46 ff. Colophon reads: Fue Impressa esta presente | obra en Alcala de Henares en casa | de Salzedo Librero ı a veynte | y seis de Febrero ı de Mil | y Quinientos ı y Cin- | quanta ı y quatro Años. | (Figures and motto, Pacientia vincit malicia.) B. Letter. (Butler Clarke.)

1554. Antwerp

LA VIDA DE | *LAZARILLO DE* | *Tormes, y de sus for-|tunas y aduer-|sidades.* | ∴ (Pietas Homini Tutissima Virtus) (Scroll and storks.) | EN ANVERS, | *En casa de Martin Nucio.* | 1554. | *Con Preuilegio Imperial.* | 48 ff. Privilege for five years signed Facuwes. (Br. Mus., and Ticknor Coll.)

1555. Anonymous Sequel. *Editio Princeps*

LA SEGVN-|DA PARTE DE LAZA-|RILLO DE TORMES: Y | de sus fortunas y ad-|uersidades | ∴ (As above.) EN ANVERS | En casa de Martin Nucio, a la en-|seña de las dos Cigueñas. | M.D. LV. | *Con Preuilegio Imperial.* | 69 ff. (misnumbered). Privilege for four years.

1555. Second Antwerp Edition of Part One

La vida de Laza-|RILLO DE TOR-|MES, Y DE SVS FOR-|tunas, y aduersi-|dades. | ∴ | EN ANVERS, En el Vnicornio dorado, en ca-|sa de Guillermo Simon. | M.D.L.V. | 94 ff. (72d duplicated). 12mo.

1555. Second Edition of Part Two

LA SEGVN-|DA PARTE DE LAZA-|RILLO DE TORMES, Y | de sus fortunas, y ad-|uersidades. | ∴ EN

ANVERS,| and as above, adding *Con Priuilegio Imperial.* 12mo. 83 ff. (Salvá.)

1573. Expurgation

LAZARILLO | DE TORMES | Castigado. | ⁖ (con descuydo — Mercury's rod). IMPRESSO CON LICEN| cia, del Consejo de la santa In-|quisicion, | *Y con preuilegio de su Magestad, para los | reynos de Castilla y Aragon.* This is included in the *Propoladia* of Bartolome de Torres Naharro "Impresso CON LICEN | cia, etc. . . . | En Madrid, por Pierres Cosin. | M.D.LXXIII." The Lazarillo begins on f. 373, extending through f. 417. Approvals Aug. 21 and 5, 1573.

The *Castigado*, or expurgated version, is also printed with Gracian Dantisco's *Galateo Español* and the *Destierro de la ignorancia*, Madrid, 1599, 12mo, Luis Sanchez; Medina del Campo, Christoval Lasso Vaca, 1603; Madrid, Andrés García de Iglesia, 1664. Out of Spain it appeared at Rome, Antonio Facchetto, 1600, published by Pedro de Robles, dedicated to the Duque de Sesa, Spanish ambassador at the Pontifical Court; and in Spain it was published as late as 1831, Madrid, 12mo.

Other early editions of *Lazarillo* in Spanish are 1586, Tarragona; 1587, Milan, the 1st and 2d parts (ad instanza de Antono (*sic*) de Antoni — Por Iacobo Maria Meda. Dedication dated Dec. 20, 1586); 1595, Antwerp, 1st part with chap. on Germans — En la oficina Plantiniana, and there again in 1602; 1597, Bergemo (dedication Apr. 29, 1597), a reprint of Milan edition and by Antoni; 1599, Çaragoça, Iuan Perez de Valdiuielso, 1st part, omitting chap. on Germans; 1607, Alcalá; 1615, Milan; 1626,

Lisboa, Antonio Alvarez, 1st part omitting chap. on Germans; etc., etc.

"Valladolid, 1603; Lerida, 1612," are cited by Brunet. In 1722, 1728, 1746 at Madrid; 1769, Valencia; and 1796 in Barcelona, *Lazarillo* was printed with the *Galateo Español.*

[To avoid confusion in dealing with translations of the *Lazarillo* the 1620 sequel is treated here, and not in its chronological place.]

1620. Luna's Emendation and Sequel

"Vida de Lazarillo de Tormes," etc., as below. En Paris, Rolet Bovtonne, MDXX (1620). 5 ff. + 120 pp. Then, Segvnda parte, de la vida de Lazarillo de Tormes. Sacada de las Coronicas antiguas de Toledo. Por I. de Lvna, Paris, Rolet Bovtonne, M.DC.XX. 12mo. 5 ff. + 168 pp. (Br. Mus.)

The same, 1620, Zaragoça, por Pedro, Destar; and there again as VIDA DE | LAZARILLO | DE TORMES. | CORREGIDA, Y EMENDADA | Por H. DE LVNA Castellaño (*sic*), | Interprete de la lengua | Española. | ⁘ *En Zaragoça*, | POR PEDRO DESTAR, a los Señales | del Feniz. | M.DC.LII. | 6 ff. + 120 pp. 12mo. And the 2d part with 6 ff. + 168 pp., presumably a French forgery. (Bibl. Nat.)

Modern editions in Spanish of one or another of the parts: Vida de L. de T., Cotejada con los mejores exemplares y corregida por J. J. Keil, Gotha, C. Stendel, 1810. 8vo. (1st part + chap. on Germans.) So also La vida de L. de T. . . . Burdeos, P. Beaume, 1816. 12mo. La vida de L. de T., nueva edicion de lujo, aumentada con dos segundas partes. . . . Madrid, P. Mora y Soler,

1844–5. 8vo. (The 3 parts.) At Paris, Baudry, 1847, 8vo, the three parts appeared together. A modern Portuguese version, made through the French, reads, Aventuras maravilhosas de Lazarilho de Tormes, extrahidas das antigas chronicas de Toledo, por G. F. Grandmaison y Bruno. Traduzidas da lingua franceza. Paris, J. P. Aillaud, 1838. 18mo. (1st and Luna's 2d part.)

FRENCH

1561. Saugrain's Version of Part One

L'HISTOIRE | **PLAISANTE ET** | FACETIEVSE DV | Lazare de Tormes | **Espagnol.** | *EN LAQVELLE ON PEVLT* | *Recongnoistre bonne partie des meurs, vie* | *&* *conditions des Espagnolz.* | ∴ (motto — BENEDICES | CORONAE ANNI | BENIGNITATIS| TVÆ | PSALM. 64. |) *A PARIS,* | *Pour Ian Longis & Robert le Mangnier Libraires, en* | *leur boutique au Palais, en la gallerie par ou* | *on va à la Chancellerie.* | *AVEC PRIVILEGE.* | 60 pp. Sm. 8vo. Privilege to Vincent Sertenas for six years, from April 24, 1561. Dedication AV VERTVEVX, ET TRES Honorable Seigneur, le Seigneur Sebastiẽ de Honoratis, Iean Saugrain salut & felicité perpetuelle. Story printed with occasional rubrics in 31 chapters, the last, "De l'amitie que Lazare eut a Tolette auec certains Allemans, & de ce que luy aduint auec eux." (Bibl. de l'Arsenal.)

1594. Second Edition in French of Part One

"Histoire plaisante, facetieuse, et recreative ; du Lazare de Tormes Espagnol," etc. Anvers, Guislain Jansens, 1594. 16mo. Licensed, Sept. 30, 1593. (1st part only.)

HISTOIRE | PLAISANTE, | FACETIEVSE, ET RE- | CREATIVE; DV LAZA- | re de Tormes Espagnol : | *En laquelle l'esprit melancolique se peut re- | creer & prendre plaisir :* | Augmentée de la seconde partie, nou- | vellement traduite de l'Espagnol | en François. | A ANVERS, | Chez Guislain Iansens. | 1598 | 126 pp. 16mo. (Bodleian.) Separate title for second part:

1598. First French of 1555 Sequel

LA II. Partie | DES FAICTS | MERVEILLEVX | DV LAZARE DE | Tormes : | Et de ses fortunes & aduersitez. *Nouvellement traduite de l'Espagnol | en François :* | Par Iean vander meeren, d'Anvers. | EN ANVERS, | Chez Guislain Iansens. | 1598. pp. 126–308 + 4 pp. 16mo. Approvals May 4, 1598, and Sept. 22, 1598. (Bodleian.)

1601. Spanish and French Versions

LA | VIDA DE LAZARIL- | LO DE TORMES. | Y de sus fortunas y aduersidades. | LA | VIE DE LAZARILLE | DE TORMES, | Et de ses fortunes & aduersitez. | *TRADVCTION NOVVELLE,* | *Raportée & conferée avec l'espagnol,* | Par P. B. Parisien. | A PARIS, | Par NICOLAS & PIERRE BON- | FONS, en leur boutique, au quatries- | me pillier de la grand' Salle du Palais. | 1601 | *Auec Priuilege du Roy.* | 238 pp. 12mo. Double columns; French on left, Spanish on right. Translator states that he has been served occasionally by the "ancien traducteur de cette mesme œuvre." (Bibl. Nat.)

The same. Par M. P. B. P. A PARIS, Par Nicolas Bonfons, 1609. 12mo.

The same. Par M. P. B. P. ∴ | A PARIS, | Chez IEAN CORROZET, dans la | Cour du Palais, au pied des degrez | de la saincte Chappelle. | M.DC.XV. | 12mo.

The same. | Chez ADRIAN TIFFAINE, ruë des | deux portes à l'Image nostre Dame. | M.DC.XVI. | 12mo.

1620. *The same* with Luna's Part Two in French

The same. Chez ROLET BOVTONNÉ, au Pa- | lais, en la gallerie des prisonniers, | pres la Chancellerie. | M.D.XX (*sic*, 1620), *Avec Priuilege du Roy.*| 12mo. Together with the SECONDE PARTIE | DE LA VIE DE | LAZARILLE | DE TORMES. | *TIREE DES VIELLES* | *Chroniques de Tolede.* | Traduicte nouuellement d'Espagnol|en François, par L. S. D. | etc. 6 ff. + 288 pp. (Reprinted in 1623.) The initials, L. S. D., stand for Le Sieur D'Audigiuer. The translator of the first part is usually supposed to be Pierre D'Audiguier, Vital's nephew, with whom Vital himself is often confused. (See Brunet; Michaud, *Biographie universelle;* etc.)

1657. French Verse

LA VIE | DE | LAZARILLE | DE TORMES, | SES FORTVNES, ET SES | ADVERSITEZ, | TRADVITE EN VERS FRANCOIS | *PAR LE SIEVR DE B**** ∴ | A PARIS, | chez LOVIS CHAMHOVDRY, au Palais, vis à vis | la Sainte Chappelle, à l'Image Saint Louis.| M.DC.LIII.| *AVEC PRIVILEGE DU ROY.*| 3 ff.+ 170 pp. 4to. Priv., Sept. 22, 1653; achevé d'imprimer Sept. 25, 1653. (Bibl. Nationale.) A rare book. In 8 syllabled couplets and in 8 chants; the 1st pt. of Lazarillo with the chapter on the Germans, promising a second and a third part "Si ces Rimes se vendent."

Other early editions of Lazarillo in French, 1649, Lyon, Bachelu (Luna's); 1660, Paris, Cotinet (Luna's); 1678, Paris, Barbin (trans. by l'abbé de Charnes); 1697, Lyon, Viret; 1698, Bruxelles, Geo. de Backer, reprinted in 1701 and after. The Abbé de Charnes' unfaithful version reappeared at Paris, 1817, 12mo, with the old title *Aventures et espiègleries de Lazarillo de Tormes.* See new translation, *Vie de L. de T. Traduction nouvelle et préface de A. Morel Fatio.* Paris, H. Launette & Cie. 1886, 8vo. (1st Pt. + Chap. on Germans.)

ENGLISH

1568. Licensed

"The marvelus Dedes and the lyf of Lazaro de Tormes," licensed in the Stationers' Registers to Thomas Colwell for viij d, the 4th entry of year, 22 July 1568–22 July 1569.

1576

"The Pleasant History, etc. (as below). Imprinted at London by Henrie Binneman, dwellyng in Knyght-rider Streete, at the sygne of the Marmayde. 1576. 8vo." Bagford Collections (Harl. MS. 5910), and Harleian Cat. Sought in vain by bibliographers, according to Hazlitt. But Bagford's description makes it tally with following:

1586

The Pleasaunt | Historie of Lazarillo de | *Tormes a Spaniarde, where-*| in is conteined his mar-| *veilous deedes and life.*| With the straunge ad-| *uentures happened to him* | in the seruice of sun-| *drie Masters.*| Drawen out of Spanish by Da-| *uid Rouland of Anglesey.*| *Accuerdo,*

Oluid. | ¶ Imprinted at London | *by Abell Ieffes, dwelling in the* | fore streete without Crepell | gate nere Groube streete | at the signe of the Bell. | 1586. | 64 ff. A to H_8 in 8 s. 8vo. Ends with the birth of Lazarillo's daughter, after his friendship with "certain high Dutchmen." Dedication to the "right Worshipfull Sir Thomas Gressam *Knight.*" At end, verses by G. Turbeuile, gent. (Bodleian and Br. Mus.)

The same. LONDON | Printed by Abell Ieffes, dwelling in the Blacke | Fryers neere Puddle Wharfe. | 1596. | A to H_4 in 4 s.

1596. First English of 1555 Sequel

The most Pleasant and delectable Historie of Lazarillo de Tormes, a Spanyard; And of his marvellous Fortunes and Aduersities. The second part translated out of Spanish by W. P. (histon). Printed at London, by T. C. (Thomas Churchyard) for Iohn Oxenbridge, dwelling in Paules Church-yard at the Signe of the Parrot. 1596. A to J_4 in 4 s, 4to. A dedication by Oxenbridge to "my verie good friend, Maister Ionas Tirill of Burstow." (Bodleian, lacking title-leaf, and Br. Mus. — Grenville.)

It is noteworthy that Thomas Middleton's "Blurt, Master Constable," printed for Henry Rockytt, 1602, 4to, contains a character Lazarillo de Tormes, who, however, bears no resemblance to his Spanish prototype.

1622. First English of Luna's Sequel

"The Pursuit of the Historie of Lazarillo de Tormes. By Jean de Luna, London, 1622. 8vo." (Watt, Hazlitt, and Lowndes.) Editions of 1631 and 1655, both London, 8vo, are noted by Hazlitt. I have been unable to see any of these, but the "Pursuit" was undoubtedly that published with the first part in 1624, 1639, 1653, and in 1669–70, as noted below. Luna, in 1622, had "Dialogues in Spanish, with the English Version, by J. W." 8vo. And in 1623, a "Short and Compendious Art for to learn to Read, Write, Pronounce, and Speak the Spanish Tongue." 4to.

1639

"The Pleasant History of Lazarillo de Tormes. . . . Drawne out of Spanish by David Rowland of Anglesey. . . . Printed by E. G. for William Leake 1639, with the Pursuit of the Historie of Lazarillo de Tormes . . . by Jean de Luna. . . . 2 vols. in 1, 12mo." (Noted in Bernard Quaritch's *Bibliotheca hispana*, 1895, p. 76.) Quaritch says that Luna's dedication in Spanish "contains an assertion that it was he who had caused the book to be translated into English. This dedication is addressed to Robert Car, Earl of Ancram. The translator (?) J. W. dedicated the second part to Lord Strange, Albert Stanley, and Anne Carre."

The edition of both parts, in 1624, 8vo, was doubtless like the above, which Collier calls the third. The 1653 edition, by William Leake, resembled it except that the dedication was to George Lord Chandos, Baron of Sudeley, and signed by James Blakeston, the supposed translator, as below (A to Y in 8 s). There was also a 1655 edition of both parts, London, R. Hodgkins, 12mo.

1669–70. Blakeston's Version with Luna's Part Two.

LAZARILLO, | OR, | The Excellent History | OF | LAZARILLO de TORMES, | The witty Spaniard. | *Both Parts.* | The first translated by | *David Rowland,*

and the second ga-| ther'd out of the Chronicles| of *Toledo,* by *Iean de Luna* a Ca-|stilian, and done into | *English* by the Same Author.| *Accuerdo, Oluido.*| *London.* Printed by *B. G.* for *William* | *Leake,* at the Crown in *Fleet street,* be-|twixt the two Temple-gates, 1669.| B_2 to K_8 in 8 s.

The Dedication to George Lord Chandos, Baron of Sudeley, is signed by James Blakeston, who claims to have found the unexpurgated original during his "late abode in Toledo," and to have sought now "to help Lazaro out of worse hands than any of his seven masters."

Part Two has separate title page thus:

THE | PURSUIT | OF THE | HISTORY | OF | *Lazarillo De Tormes.*| Gathered out of the anci-| ent Chronicles of TOLEDO.| By *Jean de Luna,* a Castilian: | and now done into *English,* and set | forth by the same Authour.| *LONDON,* | printed for *William Leake,* 1670.| L to Y_8 in 8 s. (Br. Mus.)

Carta dedicatoria in both is the same and in Spanish. Nine quatrains in conclusion "To the Publishers," etc., signed T. P., and a certificate in Spanish from Jean de Luna attesting genuineness of the version. The Death and Testament of Lazarillo promised in all of these failed to appear, but instead an account of Lazarillo's son was issued in the following:

1688. *Rifacimento*

THE | Pleasant Adventures | OF THE | WITTY *SPANIARD,* | *Lazarillo de Tormes.*| Of his Birth and Education: Of | his arch Tricks in the Service of the| Blind Man, the Priest, the Squire, and | several others; Of his dining with Duke Humphrey, &c. Of his Voyage | to the *Indies,* | his Shipwrack, and of his | being taken out of the Sea, and shown | for a Monstrous Fish: And lastly,

Of his turning Hermit, and writing these | Memoirs. | *Being all the true Remains of that so much | admired Author.* | To which is added, | The Life and Death of *Young Lazarillo,* | Heir Apparent to Old Lazarillo de Tormes: By which it plainly appears, that the Son | would have far exceeded the Father in Inge- | nuity, had he not come to an untimely End | in a *House-of-Office.* | LONDON, Printed by J. Leake, and sold by | most Booksellers in *London* and *Westminster,* | *MDCLXXXVIII.* | front. + 6 ff. + 204 pp. 12mo. (Bodleian.)

Part One of the original is fairly followed, though compressed. Luna's sequel is used and altered, but the Life and Death of Young Lazarillo is merely a steal from other picaresque works, mostly English, "All the Gusmanick, Busconick, Scarronick Writers agree," says the author, "that Lazarillo had a son."—He kills geese with a string and bullet, glues the eyelids of a sleeping girl, and ties a pot to a jack-weight as in the *English Rogue.* The Buscon's playing King of the Schoolboys is repeated here,—etc., etc.; but the story is without merit.

Among the many other English editions may be mentioned those of 1672 and 1677, 8vo; that of 1708, 8vo; and the Life and adventures of Lazarillo de Tormes (2nd edit.) London, 1726, 12mo, J. Bonwick and R. Wilkin; the 19th corrected edition from the French of Abbé de Charnes, London, 1777, 12mo, S. Bladon; Life, etc., London, 1789, 12mo, J. Bell—etc., etc., and of modern English versions that of Thomas Roscoe in his Spanish Novelists, 1832 (1st Pt. and chap. on Germans) reappearing as the Life and Adventures of Lazarillo de Tormes, tr. from the Spanish by Thomas Roscoe (with Life and adventures of Guzman d'Alfarache, or the Spanish rogue, by Mateo Aleman. From the French ed. of Le Sage, by J. H. Brady). London, 1881 (1880), 8vo, 2 vols.

DUTCH

1579. Anonymous

"De ghenuechlijke ende cluchtighe historie van Lazarus van Tormes wt Spaingen; in de welcke ghij eensdeels meucht sien ende leeren kennen de manieren, condiciën, zeden ende schalckheyt der Spaingnaerden. Nu eerst nieuwelijcx int licht brocht ende overgheset in onse taele. Te Delft bij Niclaes Pieterssen, ende men vintse te coope t'Antwerpen bij Heyndrick Heydricsen in de Leliebloeme." 1579. 12mo. [Noted by Ten Brink — *Eene studie over den Hollandschen schelmenroman, etc.*, Rotterdam, 1885, 8vo.]

't WONDERLYK | Leben ı klugtige Daden ı en dap- | pre Schimp-ernst. | *VAN* | LAZARUS van TORMES. | *Nieuwelijcks uit het Spaans in beknopt Duits,* | Door D. D. HARVY vertaalt. | ∴ (QVOS ASPICET FOVET.) | Tot VTRECHT, | Dit de Boek-winkel van Simon de Vries, | ANNO M.DC.LIII. | 12mo. 312 pp. (Br. Mus.)

Het leven, de lotgevallen en guitenstukken van den kleinen Lazarus van Tormes. . . . Uit het Spaansch vertaald door I. P. Arend. Amsterdam, J. J. Abbink, 1824. 12mo. Etc., etc. (Br. Mus.)

GERMAN

1617. Vlenhurt's Version

"Zwo Kurtzweilige, lustige, vnd lächerliche Historien, Die Erste, von Lazarillo de Tormes, einem Spanier, was für

Herkomens er gewesen, wo vnd was für abenthewrliche Possen, er in seinen Herrendiensten getriben, wie es jme auch darbey, bisz er geheyrat, ergangen, vnnd wie er letstlich zu etlichen Teutschen in Kundschafft gerathen. Ausz Spanischer Sprach ins Teutsche gantz trewlich transferirt. Die ander . . . . etc. (Cervantes' Rinconete y Cortadillo) Durch Niclas Vlenhart beschriben. Gedruckt zu Augspurg, durch Andream Aperger, In verlegung Niclas Hainrichs. M.DC.XVII. | 8 ff. + 389 pp. + 3 pp. 8vo." (Goedeke, *Grundriss*, etc.)

An edition, Nürnberg, bey Mich. Endter, 1656. 8vo, etc.

1624

"Historien von L. de T. einem Spanier, was für wunderliche bossen er in seinem Leben verübet, vnd wie es jhm dabey ergangen. Leiptzig bey Mich. Wachsman, 1624. 8vo. Draudius 1625 — 3, 623."

1627

Historien | Von Lazarillo | *de Tormes*, einem stolzen | Spanier: was fůr wunderliche ı sel- | tzame vnd abenthewrliche Ding ı er in seinem | Leben vnd Herrendiensten verůbet ı Vnd wie es ihme | darbey bisz er geheyrathet ergangen ı Auch wie er letzt- | lichen mit etlichen Teutschen in Kundschaft ge- | rahten ı vnd was sich nach abscheid dersel- | ben mit ihme zugetragen. | Zu mancherley bericht sehr lustig | zu lesen. | Ausz Spanisch in Teutsch vbersetzt. | Mehr etliche auszerleszne schǒne | Gleichnussen ı vnd Reden grosser | Potentaten vnd Herzen. | ∴ Erstlich gedruckt zu Augspurg ı durch | Andream Aperger ı | 1627. | 6 ff. + 130 pp. 8vo. (Br. Mus.) A pleasant gossiping preface; and the main work in 28 chapters, quite faithfully rendered.

Lebens-Beschreibung des Lazarillo . . . aus dem Italiänischen (of Barezzo Barezzi) ubersetzt von Araldo. Freyburg, 1701, 12mo, etc., etc.; and so recently as Der erste Schelmenroman, Lazarillo de Tormes. Herausgegeben von Wilhelm Laufer, 1889, Stuttgart, J. G. Cotta, 16mo.

ITALIAN

1622. Barezzi's Second Edition of Part One

IL | PICARIGLIO | CASTIGLIANO, | Cioè | LA VITA DI | LAZARIGLIO di TORMES | *Nell' Academia Picaresca lo Ingegnoso Sfortunato*, Composta, & hora accresciuta dallo stesso LAZARIGLIO, | & trasportata dalla Spagnuola nell' Italiana fauella | da BAREZZO BAREZZI. | *Nella quale con viuace Discorsi, e gratiosi Trattenimenti si* | *celebrano le Virtù e si manifestano le di lui, & le altrui* | *miserie, & infelicitadi: e leggiadramente si spiegano*

Ammaestramenti saggi,	Sentenze graui,
Auenimenti mirabili,	Fatti egregi,
Capricci curiosi,	Detti piaceuoli, &
Facetie singolari,	Proverbi sententiosi.

Ornata di due copiosissime Tauole. | DEDICATA | Al Molto Magnifico Signor PIETRO ZERBINA. | SECONDA ⁘ (*Dios pro nobis, quis contra nos.*) IMPRESSIONE | IN VENETIA, Presso il Barezzi. MDCXXII. *Con Licenza de' Superiori, e Priuilegi.* 20 ff. + 263 pp. + 1 p. 8vo. (Bibl. de Ste. Geneviève, Br. Mus.)

Approval: IX. Kal. Decemb. MDCXXI. Dedication dated January 17, 1622. First edition could not much have preceded this, judging from privilege. Navarrete in *Bib. de aut. esp.* vol. 33, gives 1622 as first edition. First part of Lazarillo only, but much altered, introducing Cervantes' *La gitanilla* in 90 pp.

The same. Venetia, Barezzi, 1626. 8 ff. + 263 pp. + 39 pp. (Bodleian.)

The same. Venetia, Barezzi, 1635. 26 ff. + 368 pp. (Br. Mus.) with a second volume as below.

1635. Barrezzi's Version of Part Two of 1555

IL PICARIGLIO | CASTIGLIANO, | SECONDA PARTE, | che continua la Narratione della VITA del Cattiuello | LAZARIGLIO di TORMES|etc. . . . 20 ff.+ 400 pp. 8vo. (Br. Mus.)

Based on 1555 *Lazarillo*, it is swelled up with an immense amount of extraneous matter. 235 pp. of irrelevant discourse is given to Lazarillo before the story really opens, 55 chaps. in all. As an example of Barezzi's method see 13th chap., entitled, "*Don Diego di Mendozza discorre della Ingratitudine, vito abbominabili, & che distrugge le virtudi; & à questo proposito narra vn' Auenimento di uno ingrato seruo; caso veramente molto singolare,*" etc., etc.

1599. Aleman's Part One. *Editio Princeps*

PRIMERA PARTE|DE GVZMAN DE AL-| farache, por Mateo Aleman, criado del | Rey don Felipe. III. nuestro señor, y natural vezino de Seuilla.| *Dirigida à D. Francisco de Rojas, Mar-|ques de Poza, Señor de la Casa de Monçon.| Presidente del Consejo de la hazien-| da de su Magestad, y Tribu-|nales della.|* Con licencia y priuilegio.| *En casa del Licenciado Varez de Castro,*|En Madrid, Año de 1599.| (LEGENDO SIMVL Q̄ PERAGRANDO)| 16 ff. + 256 ff. 4to. (Br. Mus.)

Aprobacion January 13, 1598, signed Fray Diego

Dauila. Tassa, March 4, 1599, and Royal approval February 16, 1599.

The same. 1599 Barcelona, privilege April 27, 1599 (rare, probably corresponding to Sebastian de Cormellas' 1600 Barcelona edition of 8 ff. + 207 ff. + 1 f.)

The same. |En Çarogoça, por Iuan Perez de Valdiuielso.| M.D.XCIX.| 8 ff. + 208 ff. 8vo. Licenses June 21 and 22, 1599. (Bodleian.)

1602. Sayavedra's (Martí's) Part Two

"Segunda parte de la vida del picaro Guzman de Alfarache." Mateo Luxan de Sayavedra, probably Valencia, 1601, or 1602. An Aprobacion dated Çaragoça, November 8, 1602, speaks of it as already printed in Valencia.

SEGVNDA PARTE|DE LA VIDA|DEL PICARO| Guzman de Alfarache.| *Compuesta por Mateo Luxan de*| *Sayauedra, natural vezino* | *de Seuilla.*| *Con licencia,* | EN MADRID, | En la Imprenta Real.| M. DC. III.| *Vendese en casa de Francisco Lopez librero.*| 12 ff. + 438 pp. Colophon,—EN MADRID.|Por Iuan Flamenco.| Año 1603.| Aprobacion Valencia, August 8, 1602, and May 31, 1603. Licencia, Valladolid, July 1, 1603; and Tassa, September 3, 1603. The Al Lector signed by Francisco Lopez is dated Madrid, September 23, 1603. (Br. Mus.) Catalogo de Sora mentions Zaragoza edit. 1603. 8vo; probably by Angelo Tavano.

The same. DIRIGIDO A DON GASPAR|*Mercader y Carroz, heredero legitimo de las*|*Baronias de Bunyol, y Siete Aguas.*| EN BRVCELLAS, | Por Roger Velpius, en el Aguila de oro, çerca | del Palacio, Año 1604|*Con*

Licencia| 7 ff. + 382 pp. 8vo. Aprobacion, Çaragoça, November 8, 1602; and royal permission Çarogoça, November 12, 1602; and Brucellas, January 15, 1604.

Fúster in Bibl. Valenciana, p. 198, t. 1, speaks of "muchos impresiones," but they cannot now be traced.

1605. Aleman's Part Two

SEGVNDA PARTE | DE LA VIDA | DE GVZMAN DE ALFA- | RACHE, ATALAYA DE | la vida humana. | *Por Matheo Aleman su verda-|dero Autor.*| Y aduierta el Letor que la segunda parte que salio| antes desta no era mia, solo esta lo es.| DIRIGIDA A DON MIGVEL | de Caldes Señor de las Baronias de| Segur, &c.| Año 1605.| CON LICENCIA.| Impressa en Barcelona en casa Sebastian de|Cormellas, al Call.| *Vendese en la mesma Emprenta.*| 16 ff. + 264 ff. 8vo. Aprobaciones, Lisboa, Sept. 7, 1604, and Sept. 9, 1604; Barcelona, Oct. 5, 1605, and Oct. 27, 1605. Nicolás Antonio speaks of Bruselas 1605, 8vo edition, without specifying the part.

The same. Valencia, 1605

The title reads as above, but instead of saying "la segunda parte que salio antes desta no era mia, solo esta lo es," this has, "solo esta reconozco por tal," and the dedication is different, reading:

Dirigida a don Iuan de Mendoça Marques de San| German, Comendador del Cãpo de Montiel, Gentilhom-| bre de la Camara del Rey nuestro Señor, Teniente General de las Guardas y Caualleria de España,|Capitan General de los Reynos|de Portugal,|Año ∴ 1605.| CON PRIVILEGIO.| Impressa en Valencia, en casa de Pedro Patricio|Mey junto a S. Martin.| A costa de Roche Sonzonio mercader de libros.| 12 ff. + 585 pp. + 7 pp. (Ticknor Coll.)

Royal permission, Valencia, Sept. 22, 1605, church permission, Valencia, Oct. 17, 1605. This may then have slightly preceded the Barcelona edition, although there is no mention of a privilege as early as the "Lisboa, 1604" date given in the Barcelona print. Ticknor thought this the first, though he had not seen the other. Quaritch and most others believe in a Lisboa edition as the first of this genuine second part, basing their opinion on the Lisboa privilege.

Other early editions of Guzman are, 1600 Madrid, Varez de Castro, 12mo; 1600 Barcelona, Seb. Cormellas; 1600 Coimbra, Na officina de Antonio de Mariz, 8vo; 1600 Bruxellas, Iuan Mommarte, 8vo; 1600 Paris, Nicolas Bonfons, 8vo; 1601 Madrid, Iuan Martinez, 8vo; 1603 Tarragona, Felipe Roberto á costa de Hieronymo Martin; 1603 Milan, Jeronimo Bordon y Pedromartir Locarno, 8vo; 1603 Zaragoça, Angelo Tavanno; 1604 Brucellas, Iuan Mommarte, 8vo; 1605 Barcelona, Cormellas, 8vo, Aleman's 1st and 2d (as above); 1615 Milan, J. Baptista Bidelo, Aleman's 1st and 2d Pts.; 1619 Burgos, Aleman's 1st and 2d Pts.; 1641 Madrid, Pablo de Val, Aleman's 1st and 2d Pts., and so too 1661 Madrid; 1681 Amberes, Geronymo Verdussen, Aleman's 1st and 2d Pts., etc., etc., etc. Also notably 1723 Madrid, 1736 Amberes, 1750 Madrid, 1773 Valencia, 1787 Valencia, 1826 Paris (Lyon), 1829 Madrid, 1843 Barcelona, etc., etc. Even as a chapbook, Valladolid, 1850 Historia de las graciosas y divertidas aventuras del Picaro G. de A. (Br. Mus.)

FRENCH

1600. Gabriel Chappuy's Version of Part One

Guzman | d'Alfarache.| Diuisé en trois liures, par Mathieu | Aleman, Espagnol.| Faict François, par G. CHAPPVYS|Secretaire Interprete du Roy.| A PARIS,| *Par Nicolas & Pierre Bonfons,* | *au quatriesme pillier de la grand'|Salle du Palais.*| M.DC.| AVEC PRIVILEGE DV ROY.| 16 ff. + 237 ff. + 1 f.; then 1 f. + 100 ff.; then 100 ff. + 2 ff. 12mo. Dedication to "Pierre de Beringen, conseiller et premier valet de chambre du roy, gouverneur de la ville et chasteau d'Estapes." (Bibl. de l'Arsenal.)

1619. Chapelain's Version of Part One

LE | GVEVX, |OV | LA VIE DE GVZMAN | D'ALFARACHE, IMAGE | de la vie humaine.| *En laquelle toutes les fourbes & meschancetez|qui s' vsent dans le monde sont plaisamment | & vtilement descouuertes.*| Version nouuelle & fidelle d'Espagnol en François.| PREMIÈRE PARTIE.| *A PARIS,* | *chez PIERRE BILLAINE, au Palais, pres | la Chappelle Sainct Michel.* M.DCXIX.| AVEC PRIVILEGE DV ROY.| 16 ff. + 334 ff. + 1 f.; then 252 ff. + 19 ff. 8vo.

1620. Chapelain's Version of Aleman's Part Two

LE VOLEVR | OV | LA VIE DE GVZMAN | POVRTRAIT DV TEMPS | ET MIROIR DE LA VIE| humaine : | *Où toutes les fourbes & meschancetez qui se font dans le monde sont vtilement & plai|samment descouuertes.*| Pièce non encore veuë, & renduë fidelement de | l'original Espagnol de son premier & véritable|Autheur MATEO ALEMAN.| Seconde Partie | A PARIS, | chez TOVS-

SAINCT DV BRAY, rue Sainct Jacques, | aux Epicemeurs: Et en sa boutique au Palais, en la gallerie des Prisonniers.| M.DC.XX.| AVEC PRIVILEGE DV ROY.| 22 ff. + 1209 pp. + 5 ff. 8vo. Priv. for both is dated Feb. 26, 1619.

Other editions of Chapelain's version: 1632 Paris, 1st Pt. Henry le Gras, 2d Pt. Nicolas Gasse, 8vo; 1633 Rouen (both Pts.), J. de la Mare, 8vo; 1638 Paris (1st Pt.), Denys Houssaye, and 1639 (2d Pt.), 8vo; 1639 Lyon (both Pts.), Simon Regnaud, 8vo; 1645 Rouen (1st Pt.), David Ferrand, and (2d Pt.) 1646.

1695. Gabriel Bremond's Version

"Histoire de l'Admirable don Guzman d'Alfarache," Amsterdam, 1695, 3 vols. 12mo.

The same. Paris, veuve Mabre-Cramoisy 1695, 3 vols. 12mo.

La vie|de|Guzman|d'Alfarache.| Tome 1.| Contenant la I. et la II. Partie.| *A Paris,* | *Par Pierre Ferrand, Imprimeur* | *ordinaire du Roy, à Roüen.*| M.DC.XCVII.| Avec privilege du roy.| 3 vols. 2 ff. + 363 pp. + 207 pp.; then 336 pp. + 152 pp.; then 263 pp. + 157 pp. + 11 pp. 12mo. Also frontis. + 16 gravures.

Other edits.: Lyon, Laurent Langlois, 1705, 4 v. 12mo; Bruxelles, Geo. de Backer, 3 v. 8vo (priv. Dec. 31, 1700); Paris, Michel David, 1709; Paris, Jean Geofroy Nym, 1709; Amst. 1728; Paris 1728, 1733, 1734, etc., etc.

1732. Le Sage's Version

Histoire | de | Guzman | d'Alfarache, | nouvellement traduite,|et purgée des moralitéz superfluës.| Par Monsieur Le Sage|Tome premier (Tome seconde)|A Paris, | chez Etienne Ganeau, ruë S. Jacques, près | la ruë du Plâtre, aux Armes de Dombes.| 1732.| Avec privilege du roy.| 2 vols. 12mo.

Other edits.: Paris, 1734, 12mo; Amst. 1740, 12mo, and 1777; Maestricht, 1777, 1787; Lille, 1792; and n. d. (1794); Amst. (in Œuvres) 1783, etc., with a score of 19th century editions. For all of these, see Granges de Surgères, *Les traductions françaises de G. d'Alfarache*, Paris, 1886. Le Sage was abridged by Pons-Augustin Alletz in 1777, La Haye, 12mo, with after editions.

ITALIAN

1606. Barezzi's Version of Part One

VITA | DEL PICARO | GVSMANO D'ALFARACE. | DESCRITTA DA MATTEO ALEMANNO | DI SIVIGLIA,| et tradotta dalla Lingua Spagnuola nell' Italiana | da BAREZZO BAREZZI Cremonese. | . . . . CON LICENZA DE' SVPERIORI, ET PRIVILEGI.| IN VENETIA, Presso Barezzo Barezzi, M.DC.VI.| *Alla Libraria della Madonna* | 23 ff. (2 there by error) + 454 pp., 8vo (Br. Mus.), Dedication to Il sig. Alessandro Zancani, March 20, 1606; Davilas aprobacion in Span. reprinted. Faithful translation of 1st Part. Story of "Osmino E Darassa," however, divided into chapters.

Gallardo, *Ensayo*, Vol. I., p. 135, says, "*En italiano se tradujo, e imprimió en Venecia, año de 1615 y 1616;*" referring doubtless to the other parts; and in the *Ensayo histórico-apologetico de la literatura española* of Don Xavier Lampillas translated to Span. by Doña Josefa Amar y Borbon, Madrid, 1789, in Vol. V., p. 171, it is remarked "*El ya alabado Cremonés Barezzo Barezzi, le pusó en Italiano, y le publicó en Venecia en 1615.*" These editions I have been unable to see.

GERMAN

1615. Albertinus' Version

"Der Landstörtzer: Gusman von Alfarche, etc., Ægidius Albertinus, Munich, 1615. (As below, same publisher, etc.), 6 ff. + 723 pp. 8vo. (Br. Mus.)

Der Landtstortzer: | *Gusman* VON *Alfar-* | *che* (*sic*) oder *Picaro* genannt / | dessen wunderbarliches / abenthewr- | lichs vnnd possirlichs Leben / was gestallt er | schier alle Ort der Welt durchloffen / aller- | hand Stånd / Dienst vnd Aembter versucht / | viel Guts vnnd Böses begangen vnd auszge- | standen / jetzt Reich / bald Arm / vnd widerumb | Reich vnnd gar Elendig worden / doch | letzlichen sich bekehrt hat / | bescrieben wird. | Durch | *ÆGIDIVM* AL- BERTINVM, | Fürstl. Durchl. in Bayrn. Secretarium, | theils ausz dem Spanischen verteutscht / theils gemehrt vnnd ge- | bessert. | Erstlich | Gedruckt zu München / durch Ni- | colaum Henricum. | *ANNO M.DC.XVI.* | 5 ff. + 554 pp. + 8 pp. 8vo. (Br. Mus.)

Edits.: München, 1617, 8vo; München, 1618, 8vo; 1619, 8vo; 1631, 8vo; 1632, 8vo; Gusmanus reformatus das ist der Landstörzer G. v. A., etc. Cöln, 1658, 12mo; Franckfurt a. M., 1670, 8vo, etc.

1626. Frewdenhold's Sequel

Der Landstörtzer | GVSMAN, | Von *Alfarche*, oder *Picaro*, | genannt, | Dritter Theil / | Darinnen seine Reysz nach | Jerusalem in die Türckey / vnd Mor- | genlånder / auch wie Er von dem Türcken ge- | fangen / widerumb erledigt / die Indianischen Land- | schafften besuchet / vnd in Teutschlandt selbst alle Stätte | durchwandert / auch allerhand vnderschiedliche Dienste / | vnd Handwerck versuchet / vnd bald zu grossem Reich- | thumb auffgestiegen | bald widerumb in hőchste | Armuthgerahten | auszfůhrlichen | bescrieben wird. | . . . . Ausz dem Spanischen Original erstmals | an jetzo verteutscht | Durch | *MARTINUM* Frewdenhold.| Getruckt zu Franckfurt am Mayn | Im Jahr | M.DC.XXVI. | 8 ff. + 494 pp. 8vo. (Br. Mus.) Preface dated March 20, 1626. This is not a translation, but a sequel pure and simple, to be treated rather in an account of German rogue romances.

An ed. 1670, 12mo, and Lustige Lebensgeschichte Gussmans (von F. W. Beer), Leipzig, 1751, 8vo.

ENGLISH

1622. Mabbe's Version of Aleman's Two Parts

THE ROGVE: | OR, | THE LIFE | OF *GVZMAN* DE | ALFARACHE.| WRITTEN IN SPANISH | by MATEO ALEMAN.| *Seruant to his Catholike Maiestie, and borne in SEVILL.*| ∴ (Veritas. Filia. Temporis.)| *LONDON*,| Printed for *Edward Blount*. 1622.| 12 ff. + 267 pp., folio, then new title page for 2d Part, "*Printed by* G. E., *for* EDWARD BLOVNT.| 1622.| 8 ff. + 358 pp., folio. Dedicated by James Mabbe, the translator, to Sir John Strangewayes; fine edition, marginal notes, original prefaces translated, and commendatory verses by John Fletcher, Leonard Digges and Ben Jonson. (Bodleian.)

The same. OXFORD, | *Printed by* WILLIAM TVRNER, *for* ROBERT ALLOT,| *and are to be sold* in Pauls *Church-yard;* | Ann. Dom. 1630.| (Bound with Mabbe's *Celestina.*) Folio. (Bodleian.)

The same. To which is added the Tragi-Comedy of CALISTO | and MELIBEA, represented in *Celestina.*| The third edition corrected.| . . . . LONDON, *Printed by* R. B. *for* Robert Allot *and are to be sold* | *at his Shop in*

Pauls *Church-yard at the Signe of | the blacke Beare.* An. Dom. 1634.| Folio. The title page to second part, dated 1633. (Bodleian.)

The Rogue: Or The Excellence of History Displayed in the Notorious Life of that Incomparable Thief, Guzman de Alfarache, the Witty Spaniard. Written originally in Spanish by Matheo Aleman, Servant to his Catholike Majestie, and from the same Epitomiz'd into English by A. S. Gent., London. Printed by J. C. for the Author; and are to be sold by Tho. Johnson . . . . 1655. 8vo. B–R_4 in 8 s and the title. (Br. Mus.)

1656 etc.

The ROGUE:| OR,| THE LIFE | OF| *Guzman de Alfarache,* | The Witty Spaniard. | In TWO PARTS. | Written in SPANISH, | by *Matheo Aleman,*| Seruant to His Catholick Majesty | and born in *Sevil.* | *The Fifth and last Edition, Corrected.* | LONDON: |Printed by *J. C.* for *Philip Chetwind;* and are|to be sold by *Tho: Johnson,* at the Golden | KEY in S. *Pauls* Church-yard. | MDCLVI.| 2 ff. + 142 ff. + 1 f. + 100 pp.; new title thus: THE | ROGUE,|OR THE|SECOND PART..... *LONDON,* Printed by *Henry Hills,* in the | year MDCLV. 1 f. + 216 pp. 8vo.

THE SPANISH| ROGUE,|or, The Life of|GUZMAN de ALFARACHE.| Giving an exact account of all his| Witty and Unparalel'd | ROGUERIES. | *In two Parts.*|

> Guzman *shall live; he is become agen*
> *A new-born caveat to all living men;*
> *That some whose candles leading them amiss*
> *May mend their ways, by fetching light from his.*

Entered according to Order.| LONDON, | Printed for

Tho. Smith, in *Corn-hill* (n. d.; end of 17th cent. probably). 168 pp. 12mo. (Much abridged naturally.)

The Life of Guzman d'Alfarache: or, the Spanish Rogue: to which is added the Celebrated Tragi-Comedy, Celestina. Done into English from the New French Version, and compar'd with the original. By several Hands. London 1708. 8vo. 2 vols. with sculptures by Gaspar Boutets. (Lowndes.)

Other English editions: The Spanish Rogue, 1790(?); Pleasant adventures of G. of A. From the French of Le Sage, by A. O'Connor, 1812 and 1817; Life of G. de A. Translated by J. H. Brady, 1821 and 1823, and with Roscoe's Life of Lazarillo, 1881; Amusing adventures of G. of Alfaraque. Translated by E. Lowdell, 1883, etc., etc.

LATIN

1623. Part One

VITÆ | HVMANÆ | PROSCENIVM : | *IN QVO SVB PERSONA* GVSMANI | ALFARACII *virtutes & vitia; fraudes,* | *cautiones; simplicitas, nequitia; diuitiae, mendicitas;* | *bona, mala; omnia denique quæ hominibus cuius-* | *cunque ætatis aut ordinis euenire solent aut* | *possunt, graphice & ad viuum* | *repræsantantur.* | OMNI ÆTATIS ET CONDI- | tionis hominum tam instructioniquam | delectationi dicata. | *CASPARE ENS Editore* | COLONIÆ AGRIPPINÆ | Excudebat Petrus à Brachel: ANNO M.DC.XXIII. | 8 ff. + 400. 12mo. (Bodleian.) 21 chapters. Considerably altered and compressed. The chief feature is the introduction of Lazarillo de Tormes, who relates his story in place of the *Osmin y Daraxa*, in 63 pp., beginning, "*Lazaro de Tormes mihi nomen est, quamvis pleriq ; vt olim puerum, ita nunc etiam Lazarillum appellitent,* etc.

1624. Part Two

PROSCENII | VITÆ HVMANÆ.| *Pars Secunda.*| IN QVA SVB PERSONA | GVSMANI ALFARACII MI-|ræ fraudes, quibus tam ipse alios decepit|quam ab aliis deceptus est, tum varij|in vita hominum Euentus re-| præsentantur.| *Opera E Studio.* | GASPARIS ENS L.| COLONIÆ AGRIPPINÆ.| Excudebat PETRVS A BRACHEL. | ANNO M.DC.XXIV. | 8 ff. + 392 pp. 12mo. (Bodleian.) 22 chapters. Dedication 20th March 1624. Ens makes the promise: "*Quod si gratum hũc meum laborem Lectoribus fore intellexero; Deo vitam & valetudinem suppeditante, Tertiam partem addam, non minus iucundis & notatu dignis euentibus ac historiis insigne,*" etc.

A story replaces the Dorido y Clorinia labelled "Historiae verae sub fictis personis narratio." The Claudio y Dorotea story is omitted. This part ends with Part 2, Book 3, chap. 5, of the original.

1652. Three Parts

The same. 1st and 2d Parts. Same wording as above, different alignment: DANTISCI | Sumptibus GEORGII FORSTERI. 1652. 12mo. 1st, 8 ff.+269 pp.; 2d, 3 ff. + 266 pp. With this issued also the 3d part:

PROSCENII | VITÆ HUMANÆ | PARS TERTIA. | IN QVA | VELUT CATASTROPHE | Historiæ, seu mavis, Fabulae de vita | GUSMANI ALFARACII | imponitur.| Omne tulit punctum qui miscuit utile dulci.| Editore GASPARE ENS L. | ∴ DANTISCI |Sumptibus

GEORGII FORSTERI.| Frontis. + 2 ff. + 82 pp. + 2 ff. 12mo. (Br. Mus.)

It is noteworthy in the Latin Guzman that wherever a quotation direct from the original would occur, it is put in Italian, not in Spanish. Thus where occurs the proverb (Pt. 1, B. 2, ch. 8 of the original), *En Malagon, en cada casa un ladron ; y en lo del alcalde, hijo y padre*, the Latin does not translate it, but prints it in Italian, "*In Malagone in ogni casa un ladrone : & in quella dell Alcalde, il figlio e il padre*" (Latin. Book I., ch. 13), etc., etc. This shows indubitably Ens' dependence upon Barezzi's version. His borrowings from Albertinus' German redaction are obvious.

DUTCH

1655. Second Edition

Het Leven van | Gusman, d'Alfarache, | 't AFBEELDSEL | Van 't Menschlijck Leven : | *Onder de gedaente van een* | SPAENSCHEN | Landt-looper, en Bedelaer.| *Waer in de Aldergheslepenste Fielteryen ende* | *Schelm-stucken der Wereldt vermakelijck,* | *yder een ten nut werden ontdeckt.*| EERSTE DEEL.| Den tweeden Druck, vermeerdert | en verbetert. | TOT ROTTERDAM, | By *Abraham Pietersz*, Boeck-verkoo-| per. Anno 1655.| Frontis. + 5 ff. + 173 pp. + 3 gravures. The second part (Aleman's) has a separate title page, 1 + 140 pp. + 3 ff. 12mo. A compressed work retaining all essentials, but omitting tales. Preface 6 pp. with 2 Latin epigrams and 8 lines of Dutch verse. (Br. Mus.)

The same — de derde druk — 1658 te Rotterdam, Abraham Pietersz ; and Het Leven van Guzman d'Alfarache

. . . door een ongenoemde. Amsterdam, 1705, 12mo, 2 vols. (Jan Ten Brink.)

Den laatsten Druck merkelyk verbetert. Amsterdam, 1728, 12mo, 2 vols. (Br. Mus.)

1603. *Editio Princeps*

EL VIAGE | ENTRETENIDO | de Agustin de Rojas, natural de | la villa de Madrid. | CON VNA EXPOSICION | de los nombres Historicos y Poeticos, | que no van declarados. | A Don Martin Valero de Franqueza, | Cauallero del habito de Santiago, y | gentil hombre de la boca de | su Magestad. | Con Priuilegio de Castilla, y Aragon. | EN MADRID, | En la Emprenta Real. | M.DC.III. | Vendese en casa de Francisco de Robles. | 32 ff. + 749 pp. + 1 p. 8vo. Colophon: En Madrid, | Por Iuan Flamenco. | M.DC.III.

Church aprobacion by Gracian Dantisco, May 15, 1603; Royal, June 16, 1603. Laudatory sonnet by Salas Barbadillo. (Br. Mus.)

Nicolás Antonio gives 1583 erroneously, and Brunet after him 1583 Madrid, Alonso Gomez, 8vo.

The same. Lerida 1611, 8vo.

The same. EN MADRID, | en casa de la viuda de Alonso Martin. | Año 1614. | *A costa de Miguel Martinez.* | *Vẽdese en la calle mayor en las gradas de S. Felipe.* | 8vo, 16 ff. + 280 ff. Tassa, May 17, 1614, Fe de erratas May 12, and aprobacion May 15. (Ticknor Coll.)

The same. Año ⁘ 1615. | CON LICENCIA DEL ORDINARIO, | EN LERIDA. | *Por Luys Manescal, Mercader de Libros.* 4to. Aprobacion Jan. 4, 1611.

Other editions, 1624 Barcelona, 1640 Madrid, 12mo, 1793 Madrid, so-called Quinta edicion, corregida y emendada segun el expurgatorio del año de 1747, Benito Cano. 8vo.

1605. *Editio Princeps*

LIBRO DE | ENTRETENIMIENTO, DE | LA PICARA IVSTINA, EN EL | qual debaxo de graciosos discursos, se | encierran prouechosos auisos. | *Al fin de cada numero veras vn discurso, que te muestra | como te has de aprouechar desta lectura, para huyr los | enganos, que oy dia se vsan.* | Es juntamente ARTE POETICA, que contiene cincuenta | y vna diferencias de versos, hasta oy nunca recopilados, cuyos | nombres, y numeros estan en la pagina siguente. | DIRIGIDA A DON RODRIGO | Calderon Saudelin, de la Camara de su | Magestad. Señor de las Villas de la | Oliua y Plasençuela. &c. | *COMPVESTO POR EL LICENCIADO | Francisco de Vbeda, natural de Toledo.* | ∴ CON PRIVILEGIO. | Impresso en Medina del Campo, por Christoual | Lasso Vaca. Año, M.DC.V. | (Br. Mus.)

Front. + 8 ff. + 184 pp. + 232 pp. + 48 pp. Sm. 4to. Royal Privilege Aug. 22, 1604. Frontispiece is curious. On the stream of Forgetfulness is seen the ship of Picaresque Life with the Picaro Alfarache in the prow, his scrip labelled Poor and Content. On either side of the mast are Celestina and Justina; Bacchus is in the shrouds, and a pennant *El gusto me lleba* floating from the peak. Lazarillo in a row boat alongside has with him the Bull of Salamanca, and Death is at a neighboring port holding up the glass of *Disengaño.*

The same. "La PICARA Montañesa, llamada Justina," etc., Barcelona, Sebastian de Cormellas, 1605. 5 ff. + 282 ff. Sm. 8vo. (Brunet and Salvá.)

The same. DIRIGIDO | A DON ALONSO PIMEN-

TEL | Y ESTERLICQ . . . EN BRVCELLAS, | En casa de Oliuero Brunello, en la Fuente | de oro. Año M.D.C.VIII. | Front. + 9 ff. + 449 pp. + 3 pp. Sm. 8vo. Privilege, Nov. 7, 1607. Crude reproduction of former frontispiece.

LA PICARA | MONTAÑESA | LLAMADA IVSTINA, | etc. . . . Año 1640. | Impresso en Barcelona, en casa PEDRO | LACAVALLERIA. | *Vendese en la misma Imprenta.* | 5 ff. + 282 pp. + 1 p. 4to. Aprobacion Jan. 24, 1640.

Other edits.: 1640, Barcelona, Sebastian de Cormellas, 8vo; 1707 Barcelona, 8vo. La Picara Montañesa — 1735 — 4to, Madrid, Juan de Zuñiga, with notice on the work and its author.

ITALIAN. 1624

"Vita della Picara Giustina Diez." An edition (probably the 1st) with Barezzi in 1624. See below his privilege, October 8, 1624. Navarrete cites this; but Goedeke, *Grundriss*, I., p. 579, gives the following only:

1628

VITA DELLA | PICARA | GIVSTINA | DIEZ; | Regola de gli animi licentiosi: | *In cui con gratiosa maniera si mostrano gl' inganni,* | *che hoggidì frequentemente s' vsano; s'additano* | *le vie di superarli;* | *e si leggono* |

Sentenze graui — Precetti Politici
Documenti Morali — Auuertimenti curiosi.
E Fauole facete, e piaceuoli.

Composta in lingua Spagnuola dal Licentiato Francesco | *di Vbeda naturale della Città di Toledo:* | Et hora transportata nella fauella Italiana | da BAREZZO BAREZZI Cremonese. | *Dedicata al Molto Illustre, e generosissimo*

Sig. | IL SIG. GIOVANNI DA STETEN. | IN VENETIA, MDCXXVIII. | Appresso Barezzo Barezzi. | *Con Licenza de' Superiori, & Priuilegio.* | 12 ff. + 207 pp. 8vo. Dedication Oct. 8, 1624, with 2d Part as:

1629. Part Two

DELLA VITA | DELLA PICARA | GIVSTINA DIEZ | Volume Secondo, Intitolato | LA DAMA VAGANTE, | . . . DEDICATA AL MOLTO ILLVSTRE | SIG. CAVALIER ROVELLO. | IN VENETIA, Presso il Barezzi. MDCXXIX. | *Con Licenza de' Superiori, & Priuilegio.* | 17 ff. + 260 pp. + 1 f. 8vo. Dedication Apr. 4, 1629. (Bodleian.)

GERMAN

1627

Gräsze, *Lehrbuch einerallg. Literärgeschichte*, gives 1618 for the first German translation; but Goedeke, *Grundr.* II., p. 578, gives 1626–7 as below.

Der Landtstůrtzerin | JUSTINÆ DIETZIN PICARÆ | II. Theil / | Die frewdige *Dama* genannt: | In deren wunderbarlichem Le- | ben vnd Wandel alle List vnd betrůg so in | den jetzigen Zeiten hin vnd wider verůbet vnd getrie- | ben werden / vnnd wie man denselbigen zu | begegnen / sehr fein vnd artig be- | schrieben. | Beneben allerley schőnen vnd denckwűr- | digen Sprůchen / Politischen Regeln / arglistigen | vnnd verschlagenen Grieffen vnd Erfindungen / lehr- | hafften Erinnerungen / trewhertzigen Warnungen / | anmutigen vnd kurtzweiligen | Fabeln. | Erstlichen | Durch Herrn Licentiat *Franciscum di Ubeda* von | Toledo in Spannischer Sprach beschrieben / vnd in zwey | sonderbare Bűcher abgetheilt.| Nachmals von *Baretzo Baretzi* in Italianisch| *transferiert:* Vnd nun zum letzten auch in vnsere hoch Teut-|sche Sprach versetzt.| Franckfurt am Mayn:| Getruckt bey Caspar Rôteln : In Verlegung | Johannis Ammonii Burgers vnd | Buchhåndlers.| MDC.XXVII.| 8 ff. + 604 pp. 8vo. It follows Italian version exactly. (Br. Mus.)

Another edition, Franckfurt a. M., bey M. Kempffer, 1646. 8vo.

FRENCH. 1635

LA | NARQVOISE | IVSTINE. | *LECTVRE PLEINE DE RECREA-| tiues auentures, & de morales railleries,| contre plusieurs conditions humaines.*| ∴ | A PARIS, | chez PIERRE BILAINE, ruë sainct | Iacques, prés S. Yue à la bonne Foy. | M.DC.XXXVI. | *AVEC PRIVILEGE DV ROY.*| 7 ff. + 711 pp. + 1 p. (Bibl. Nat.)

Privilege, May 1, 1635, to Pierre Blaise, associating with him Pierre Bilaine and Anthoine de Sommaville. Brunet and others give 1635 for date, and so does Cat. of Bibl. Ste. Geneviève, where the copy identical with this lacks, however, the title page.

ENGLISH. 1707

(Translated in) THE | Spanish Libertines: | OR, THE | LIVES | OF | JUSTINA, The Country Jilt;| CELESTINA, The Bawd of Madrid, | AND | ESTE-VANILLO GONZALES, | The most Arch and Comical of | SCOUNDRELS. | To which is added, a PLAY, call'd, | An EVENINGS ADVENTURES. | *All* Four Written by Eminent SPANISH | Authors, *and now first made* English *by Captain* JOHN STEVENS. | LON-

DON | Printed, and Sold by *Samuel Bunchley*, at the *Pub- | lishing Office* in *Bearbinder-Lane*, 1707. | 4 ff. + 528 pp. 8vo. Justina occupies 65 pp. in 8 chaps. containing all incidents of the original compressed. (Br. Mus.)

1612. *Editio Princeps*

LA HYIA | DE CELES-|TINA.| Por Alonso Geronimo de Salas Bar- | badillo: impressa por la diligencia y | cuydado del Alferez Francisco | de Segura, entretenido | cerca de la persona del | Señor Virrey de | Aragon. | A Don Francisco Gassol, Caua-|llero del Orden de Santiago | del Consejo de su Magestad, y | su Pronotario en los Reynos | de la Corona de Aragon. | *Con Licencia.* | En Çarogoça, Por la Biuda de | Lucas Sanchez. Año de 1612. | A costa de Iuan de Bonilla, | mercader de libros.| 4 ff. + 91 ff. Sm. 12mo. Church permission, April 24, 1612. Royal permission, May 5, 1612. (Br. Mus.)

"La hija de Pierres y Celestina," Lerida, Luys Manescal, 1612, 16mo (a later edition than preceding), cited by Antonio, Barrera y Leirado, etc.

La Ingeniosa | Elena. | etc. . . . En Madrid. | Por Iuan de Herrera. | Año 1614.| Vendese en casa de Antonio Ro-| driguez, calle de Santiago.| 12 ff. + 154 ff. + 4. 12mo.

Saragossa edition copied in Milan, Juan Baptista Bidelli, 1616, 12mo; and La Ingeniosa Elena; Hija de Celestina. | . . . . Tercera Impresion | Año de 1737 | con Licencia: En Madrid: A costa de D. | Pedro Joseph Alonso y Padilla, etc. 8vo. (Both in Br. Mus.)

(The last, like 1614, edition adds 4 chapters of no value; the epitaph of Elena is 14 lines in the 1st edition, 8 lines and different in 1614, and these 8 joined with 8 others here.)

The novel is translated to French, as *Les Hypocrites, nouvelle de M. Scarron*, Paris. Ant. de Sommaville, 1655, small 8vo, reprinted with *L'Adultère innocent*, and *Plus d'effets que de paroles*, in *Les nouvelles tragi-comiques*, Paris, Ant. de Sommaville, 1661, sm. 8vo.

John Davies, of Kidwelly, translated to English the *Hypocrites*, the *Fruitless Precaution*, and the *Innocent Adultery* of Scarron in 1657, publishing them separately; the four *novelle* from Scarron's *Roman Comique* he issued in 1662; collecting the seven in 1667; and in 1670 bringing out the *Unexpected Choice*. Thus, by way of Scarron and Davies, the *Elena* was the first piece of Barbadillo to come into English.

1613. *Editio Princeps*

NOVELAS | EXEMPLARES | DE MIGVEL DE | Ceruantes Saauedra. | *DIRIGIDO A DON PEDRO FERNAN-|dez de Castro, Conde de Lemos, de Andrade, y Villalua, | Marques de Sarria, Gentilhombre de la Camara de su | Magestad, Virrey, Gouernador, y Capitan General | del Reyno de Napoles, comendador de la En-|comienda de la Zarça de la Orden | de Alcantara.* | Año ∴ 1613 | Cõ priuilegio de Castilla y de los Reynos de la Corona de Aragõ. | *EN MADRID*, Por Iuan de la Cuesta. | Vendese en casa de Frãcisco de Robles, librero del Reyrno Señor. | 12 ff. + 274 ff. 4to. Aprobaciones, July 2, and 9, 1612, and Aug. 8, 1612. (Bodleian.)

Other edits.: 1614 Madrid, Juan de la Cuesta, 8vo; 1614 Pamplona, Nic. Assiayn, 8vo; 1614 Bruselas, Roger Velpio y Huberto Antonio, 8vo; 1615 Pamplona, 8vo; 1615 Milan, J. B. Bidelo, 12mo; 1616 Venecia, 12mo; 1617 Madrid, J. de la Cuesta, 8vo; 1617 Lisboa, Antonio Alvarez, 8vo; 1617 Pamplona, Nic. Assiayn, 8vo; 1621 Barcelona, Esteban Liberós, 8vo; 1622 Pamplona, 8vo; 1622 Madrid, 8vo; 1624 Sevilla, Francisco Lira, 8vo; 1625 Bruselas, Huberto Antonio, 8vo; 1631 Barcelona, 8vo; 1648 Sevilla, P. Gómez de Pastrana, 8vo; 1664 Madrid, Julian de Paredes, 4to; 1664 Sevilla, Gómez de Blas, 4to; 1739 Haya, Neaulme, 8vo; 1769 Valencia, 8vo; 1783 Madrid, 8vo; In Col. de nov. escodidas 1791; 1797 Valencia, 8vo; 1799 Madrid, 12mo; 1805 Gotha, Stendel y Keil (t. 9 & 10 Bibl. Esp.); 1816 Madrid, 12mo; 1821 Madrid, 8vo; 1825 Lión, 18mo; 1818 Berlin; 1826 Paris, Obras escogidas, etc.; 1842–43 Madrid, 8vo; 1844 Barcelona, 18mo, etc. See *Ensayo Crítico sobre Las Novelas Ejemplares de Cervantes con la bibliografía de sus ediciones* por Luis Orellana y Rincón, Valencia, Ferrer de Cerza, 1890, for bibliography and account. For modern texts, see Rafael Luna in Revista Contemporanea, 1880; tomo 25 of coleccion de aut. esp., Leipzig, Brockhaus, 1883; and Novel. ejemp. Mit erklärenden Anmerkungen herausg. von Adolf Kressner, Leipzig, 1886, 16mo, etc.

FRENCH. 1618

"Les novvelles . . . oѷ sont contenvës plvsivers rares advantvres," etc., as below. F. de Rosset & le Sr. d'Avdigvier. Paris, 1618. 8vo.

1640

LES | NOVVELLES | DE MIGVEL | DE CERVANTES | SAAVEDRA. | OV SONT CONTENVËS PLV- | SIEVRS RARES ADVANTVRES, ET | memorables exemples d'Amour de Fideli- | té, de Force de Sang, de Ialousie, de mau- | vaise habitude, de charmes, & d'autres acci- | dens, non moins étranges que veritables. |

Traduites d'Espagnol en François: les six premiers par F. DE | ROSSET, *& les autres six par le S.* D'AVDI-GVIER. | Avec l'Histoire de Ruis Dias, & de Quixaire Prin- | cesse des Moluques, composée par le | Sieur DE BELLAN. | *Reueuë & corrigée en ceste derniere Edition.* | ∴ A PARIS, | Chez IEREMIE BOVILLEROT, Imprimeur, | demeurant en la Court du Palais, vis à vis | de la Conciergerie. | M.DC.XXXX. | 8vo. 4 ff. + 696 pp. (Ticknor Coll.)

Pierre Hessein published at Amsterdam in 1700 a translation reprinted there in 1709 and 1713, and in Paris in 1713 and 1723. In 1768 a French edition of the *Quixote* and the *Novelas* appeared at Amsterdam in 12mo; and the *Novelas* there that year alone in 8vo. Among other editions were those of Amsterdam, 1705, 8vo; Rouen, 1723; Paris, 1775, by Coste d'Arnobat; Paris, 1787, by Claris de Florian; Paris, 1788, 2 v., 8vo; Paris, 1809, 4 v., 12mo; and Louis Viardot's version, Paris, 1858, 2 v., 8vo., etc., etc.

ITALIAN. 1616–26

According to Lampillas (*Ensayo histórico-apologetico de la literatura Española*, Madrid, 1789, Vol. 5, p. 187), Il novelliere castigliano di Michiel di Cervantes Saavedra "En 1616 salieron de las prensas de Venecia traducidas en Italiano." In 1626 there was an edition similar to that noted below, and in 1629, according to Lampillas, Donato Fontana undertook a Milanese redaction.

1629

IL | NOVELLIERE | CASTIGLIANO | DI MICHIEL DI CERVANTES | SAAVEDRA; | *Nel quale, mescolandosi lo stile graue co'l faceto, si' narrano | aueni-*

menti curiosi, casi strani, e successi degni | d' ammiratione | e si dà ad ogni sorte di persona occasione d'apprendere | e precetti Politici, e documenti Morali, e concetti | Scientifichi, e fruttuosi : | *Tradotto dalla lingua Spagnuola nell' Italiana* | Dal Sig. GVGLIELMO ALESSANDRO | de Nouilieri, Clauelli : | *E da lui fattiui gli Argomenti, e dichiarate nelli margini | le cose più difficili.* | ⁖ IN VENETIA, Presso il Barezzi, MDCXXIX. | *Con Licenza de' Superiori, & Priuilegio.* | 8vo, 8 ff. + 720 pp. (Ticknor Coll.)

El Coloquio de los Perros was published separately as late as 1819 by Jovenal Vegezzi.

ENGLISH. 1640. 1st

EXEMPLARIE | NOVELLS : | IN SIXE BOOKS. | . . . FVLL | OF VARIOVS ACCIDENTS | BOTH DELIGHTFVLL | AND PROFITABLE. | By MIGVEL De CERVANTES | SAAVEDRA; | One of the prime Wits of *Spaine,* | for his rare Fancies, and | wittie Inventions. | Turned into English by DON DIEGO | PVEDESER. | LONDON, | Printed by *John Dawson,* for *R. M.* and are to be sold | by *Laurence Blaicklocke :* at his Shop at the Sugar-loafe | next Temple-Barre in Fleet street, 1640 | 3 ff. + 324 pp. Folio. (The Two Damosels, the Ladie Cornelia, the Liberall Lover, the Force of Bloud, the Spanish Ladie, and the Jealous Husband.) (Bodleian.) Republished with new title-page, "Delight in Several Shapes," in 1654. Folio. William Godwin calls this version of James Mabbe, "Perhaps the most perfect specimen of prose translation in our language." — Lives of Edward and John Philips, London, 1815, p. 246. Later editions based on this professed falsely to be by Shelton.

Select novels. The first six written by Miguel Cervantes . . . the other by Francis Petrarch. . . . Englished by William Pope, London, 1694.

El Zeloso Estremeno; The Zealous Estramaduran; a Novel, with the Fair Maid of the Inn; the History of the Captive; the Curious Impertinent; the Prevalence of Blood; the Liberall Lover; and the Rival Ladies. From the Spanish. Translated by J. Ozell. London, 1709. 12mo.

A Collection of Select Novels, written originally in Castillian . . . made English by Harry Bridges, Esq., Bristol, 1728. 8vo.

See also in Samuel Croxall's A Select Collection of Novels and Histories, London, 1729, in 6 volumes.

A Dialogue between Scipio and Berganza, two Dogs, belonging to the city of Toledo, giving an Account of their Lives and Adventures, with their Reflections on the Lives, Humours, and Employments of the Masters they lived with. To which is annexed the Comical History of Rincon and Cortado. Both now first translated from the Spanish original. London, 1767. 8vo. Etc., etc.

GERMAN, Etc.

Rinconete y Cortadillo translated by Niclas Vlenhart with Lazarillo de Tormes, q. v. Augsburg, durch Andream Aperger, In Verlegung Niclas Hainrichs, 1617, as "Historien von Isaac Winkelfelder und Jobst von der Schneid, wie es disen beyden Gesellen in der weltberümten Stadt Prag ergangen, was sie daselbst für ein wunderseltzame Bruderschafft angetroffen, vnd sich in dieselbe einverleiben lassen." Editions: Leipzig, 1624, Michel Wachsmann; 1656, 1724, etc. The latter called, "Ceremoniel der Gav-Dieb, Banditen und Spitz-Buben, Sonderlich-Curieuse Historia Von Isaac Winckelfelder, und Jobst von der Schneidt: . . . Aller Welt, Zur Lehr und Warnung, Vor Beutelschneider-Meuchelmörder-Banditen-Spitzbuben u. Diebe-Rott, sich wohl Vorzusehen und zu Hüten, . . . etc.

Some of the novels appeared in Georg. Ph. Harsdörffer's "Der grosse Schauplatz jämmerlicher Mord-geschichte." 2 Theile. 12mo. Frankfurt, 1650–51; and an enlarged edition 1652. Of the picaresque tales there was here the Gegenbetrug (Casamiento Engañoso) and the Edle Dienstmagd (Ilustre fregona), both of which reappear in "Der alten und neuen Spitzbuben und Betrieger böshaffte und gewissenlose Practiquen und andere viele List, und lustige Welt-Händel," 1700.

In 1752 at Frankfurt and Leipzig appeared "Satyrische und lehrreiche Erzählungen von Cervantes nebst dem Leben dieses berühmten Schriftsteller . . . in das Teutsche übersetzt" (by Conradi); and in 1779, at Leipzig, Julius von Soden had his "Moralische Novellen des Cervantes . . . zum erstenmal aus dem Original übersetzt." At Königsberg, in 1801, was issued the "Lehrreiche Erzählungen," etc., etc., etc., other translations of the novelas appearing in 1802, 1810, 1825, 1826, 1839, 1840, both at Pforzheim and Stuttgart, 1868, etc. In Dutch the novelas came out as Vermakelyke Minneyren, Amsterdam, 1731; and in Danish as Laererige Fortaellinger, Copenhagen, 1780.

To deal more than sketchily with the *Novelas exemplares* would lead too far afield. For further details as to translations and lists of their imitations see Lowndes, Hazlitt, Goedeke, Koerting, Salvá, Gallardo, etc., etc., and Kelley's *Caspar Ens*, etc., Paris, 1897; Bahlsen's *Eine Komödie Fletcher's, ihre Spanische Quelle und die Schicksale jenes Cervanteschen Novellen-Stoffes in der Welt-litt.,"*

Berlin, 1894; and *Cervantes und seine Werk nach deutschen Urtheilen, mit einem Anhange: Die Cervantes-Bibliographie.* Ed. by E. Dorer, Leipzig, 1881; and the same author's earlier *Cervantes-Literatur in Deutschland, Bibliographische Uebersicht*, Zürich, 1877.

1615. *Editio Princeps*

ENGAÑOS | DESTE SIGLO. | Y HISTORIA SVCEDIDA | EN NVESTROS TIEMPOS, | diuidida en seys partes. | *DIRIGIDA A DON* | *HENRIQVE DE GONDY*, | *Duque de Retz.* | Compuesta por FRANCISCO LOVBAYSSIN DE | LAMARCA Gentilhombre Gascon. | ∴ EN PARIS, | en casa de IVAN ORRY, Librero, en | la calle de Santiago. | ɔIc. Iɔc. XV. | CON PRIVILEGIO DE SV MAGESTAD. | 12mo. 10 ff. + 280 pp. In 6 *partes*. A sonnet in French signed DAVDIGVIER, addressed Au Sieur de Lamarque. (Ticknor Coll.)

In French the *Engaños* had its chief success. It was first translated by François de Rosset as Les Abus du monde, Paris, Du Bray, 1618, 12mo; then by the Sieur De Ganes de Languedoc as Les tromperies de ce siècle, . . . avec des annotations, Paris, Mathurin Hénault, 1639. Sm. 8vo. (Several subsequent editions, among them Rouen, de la Haye, 1645, sm. 8vo; and Rouen, 1654, 8vo.) A compressed translation in Histoire des Cocus, La Haye, Au Croissant, 1746, reprinted at San Remo, by J. Gay et Fils, 1875. (50 copies.)

1617. *Editio Princeps*

DISCVRSOS | MORALES. | POR IVAN CORTES de TO- | losa criado del Rey nuestro Señor, natural, y vezino de Madrid. | Dirigido a Martin Frances hijo mayor de Mertin Frãces, | Teniente de la Tesoreria general de Aragon, y Ad-|ministrador de las Generalidades del dicho Reyno. | En Çaragoça, con Priuilegio, por Iuan de la Naja y Quarta- | ner Impressor del Reyno de Aragon, y de la Vniuersi-|dad, y a su costa, Año 1617.| 12 ff. + 203 ff. + 3 ff. 8vo. Church permission, May 1, 1617; Royal, May 23, 1617. (Br. Mus.)

The third book here is the *Libro de las novelas*, containing *Novela del Licenciado Periquin*, *Novela de la comadre*, *Novela del nacimiento de la verdad*, and *Novela de vn hombre muy miserable.*

1617. *Editio Princeps*

EL | PASSAGERO. | ADVERTENCIAS | VTILISSIMAS A LA | VIDA HVMANA. | *POR EL DOCTOR CHRIS- | toual Suarez de Figueroa.* | A LA EXCELENTISSIMA | Republica de Luca. | ∴ | CON PRIVILEGIO,|En Madrid, *Por Luys Sanchez*, Año 1617.| Vendese en la torre de Santa Cruz. | 4 ff. + 492 ff. 8vo. Tassa, Nov. 16, 1617. See especially ff. 286–388. (Bibl. Nat.)

2d edition of El Passagero, 1618, Barcelona, Geronimo Margarit. 8vo. 6 ff. + 370 ff.

1618. *Editio Princeps*

RELACIONES | DE LA VIDA DEL | ESCVDERO MARCOS DE | OBREGON. | AL ILLVSTRISSIMO SE-|*ñor Cardenal Arçobispo de Toledo, don Ber-|nardo de Sandoual, y Rojas amparo de la vir-|tud, y padre de los pobres.* | POR EL MAESTRO VICEN-|te Espinel, Capellan del Rey nuestro señor | en el Hospital Real de la ciudad | de Ronda. | Año ∴ 1618. | CON PRIVILEGIO.|

En Madrid, Por Iuan de la Cuesta. | *A costa de Miguel Martinez.* | Vendese en la calle mayor, a las gradas de S. Felipe. | 8 ff. + 187 ff. + 1 f. 4to. Tassa, Dec. 12, 1617; Fé de Erratas, Dec. 9, 1617; and auto del Conseio Real, Oct. 19, 1617. (Br. Mus.)

The same. 1618. Con licencia, en Barcelona. | Por Sebastian de Cormellas, al Call, y a su costa. | 8 ff. + 232 ff. 4to. Barcelona Aprobacion, Jan. 12, 1618. (Br. Mus.)

The same. 1618. Barcelona. Geronimo Margarit. 4to.

Other edits.: Sevilla, 1641, Pedro Gomez de Pastrana; Madrid, 1657, 8vo. Gregorio Rodriguez (1660? Madrid, 8vo); Madrid, 1744, 4to; and Madrid, 1804, Mateo Repullés; in *Bibl. de aut. esp.*, 1851; Barcelona, 1863, Narciso Ramirez; 1868, in *Tesoro de aut. esp.*; 1881, Barcelona, in Bibl. "Arte y Letras," with an essay "Vicente Espinel y su obra," by J. Perez de Guzman.

FRENCH. 1618

Les | RELATIONS | DE MARC | D'OBREGON. | *TRADVITES PAR LE SIEVR* | *D'AVDIGVIER.* | A Monsieur de CADENET | ∴ | A PARIS, | chez PIERRE DE FORGE ruë Sainct | Iacques, aux Colomnes. | M.DC.XVIII. | *AVEC PRIVILEGE DV ROY.* 24 ff. + 400 pp. (Br. Mus.)

Privilège, May 22, 1618, for 6 years. The Advertissement is interesting. The translator says he had gained too high an opinion of the work from the praises of its Spanish approbations, adding "*il ne se faict pas bon engager sur la parolle des Espagnols. Ils sont si liberaux à promettre, & si magnifiques à se vanter, qu'ils se rendent admirables à ceux qui ne les cognoissent,*" etc. Only the *Premiere Partie*, in 24 *Relations*, appears here.

ENGLISH. 1816

THE HISTORY OF THE *LIFE OF THE SQUIRE* MARCOS DE OBREGON, . . . etc. TRANSLATED INTO ENGLISH, | FROM THE | MADRID EDITION OF 1618, By MAJOR ALGERNON LANGTON, 61st REGIMENT. VOL. I. (II) LONDON: PRINTED FOR JOHN BOOTH, DUKE STREET, PORTLAND PLACE, 1816. 2 vols. 42 ff. + 358 pp. and 5 ff. + 494 pp. 8vo. Interesting biographical sketch of Espinel with a consideration of the indebtedness of *Gil Blas* to *Marcos*.

GERMAN. 1827

Leben und Begebenheiten des Escudero Marcos Obregon. Oder Autobiographie des Spanischen Dichters Vicente Espinel, aus dem Spanischen zum erstenmale in das Deutsche übertragen, und mit Anmerkungen und einer Vorrede begleitet von Ludwig Tieck. Breslau, im Verlage bei Josef Max und Komp. 1827. 8vo. Notes are not extensive (24 pp.). Preface has v–lxii pp.

1619. *Editio Princeps*

LA | DESORDENADA | CODICIA DE LOS | BIENES AGENOS. | *Obra apazible y curiosa, en la qual* | *se descubren los enrredos y ma-|rañas de los que no se con-|tentan con su parte.* | Dirigida al Illustrissimo y Ex-|cellentissimo Señor, Don | LUYS DE ROHAN, | Conde de Rochafort. | EN PARIS, | En casa de ADRIAN TIFFENO, | á la | enseña de la Samaritana. | MDCXIX.| 5 ff. + 347 pp. 12mo. Reprinted with *Antipatía de los Franceses y Españoles* of same author, Dr. Carlos García, in Tomo VII. of Libros de Antaño, Madrid, 1877; and also in 100 copies privately printed, Sevilla, 1886. 8vo.

FRENCH. 1621

L'Antiquité | DES | LARRONS. | Ouvrage non moins curieux que delectable; | Composé en Espagnol par | DON GARCIA: | et traduit en François, par le Sr. | DAVDIGVIER. | A PARIS, | chez Tovssainct DV BRAY, ruë S. | Iacques, aux Epics meurs. | M.DC.XXI. | Auec Priuilege du Roy. | 5 ff. + 245 pp. + 3 pp. 8vo. Privilege, June 29, 1621. (Br. Mus.) Other editions, Paris, 1623, and Rouen, 1632.

ENGLISH. 1638

The | SONNE OF | THE ROGUE, | or | The POLITICK | THEEFE. | WITH THE AN- | TIQUITIE OF | THEEVES. | A work no lesse Curious then delectable; first written | in Spanish by Don Garcia. | Afterwards translated into | Dutch, and then into French by S. D. | Now Englished by W. M. | LONDON, | Printed by I. D. and are to be sold by | Bernard Langford at the Bybell | on Holborn-Bridge, 1638. | 7 ff. + 254 pp. 12mo. Colophon: Imprimatur Thomas Weekes, Februarie 5, 1637. (Br. Mus.)

1650. Reprint with different title and woodcut, as:

LAVERNÆ, | OR THE | SPANISH GIPSY: | The Excellency of | THEEVES and THEEVING: | With their Statutes, Laws, Customes, | Practises, Varieties, and whole Art, Mystery, Antiquity, | Company, Noblenesse, and Differences: | Also their Originall, Rise, and | Beginning, of what Parents, Education, | and Breeding the Author was: | With a pleasant DISCOURSE hee had | in Prison with a most famous | THEEFE. | And also his last disgrace: being a work | no lesse Curious then Delectable. | First written in Spanish | by Don. Garcia: |

Now in English by W. M. | London, Printed not in Newgate, | 1650. | 7 ff. + 254 pp. 12mo. (Br. Mus.)

1620. *Editio Princeps*

LAZARILLO | DE MANZANA-| RES, CON OTRAS | cinco Nouelas | *COMPVESTO POR IVAN COR-| tes de Tolosa natural de la villa de | Madrid.* DIRIGIDO A DON IVAN YBA-| ñez de Segouia, cauallero del Orden de Calatraua, y Tesorero general de | su Magestad. | Año 1620. | CON PRIVILEGIO. | *En Madrid.* Por la viuda de Alonso Martin | *A costa de Alonso Perez mercader de libros.* | 6 ff. + 257 ff. Sm. 8vo. Aprobacion, Maestro Vicente Espinel, May 9, 1619, etc.: Fé de Erratas, Dec. 7, 1619. (Bibl. Nat.) Rare.

The *Lazarillo* occupies 99 ff., others in turn are: *Novela de la comadre, Novela del Licenciado Periquin, Novela del desgraciado, Novela del nacimiento de verdad,* and *Novela del miserable.*

1620. *Editio Princeps*

EL SVBTIL | CORDOVES PEDRO | DE VRDEMALAS. | *A DON FERNANDO PIMEN- | tel, y Requesenes.* | AVTOR ALONSO GERONIMO | de Salas Barbadillo. | *CON VN TRATADO DEL Cauallero Perfecto.* | Año ⁘ 1620. | *CON PRIVILEGIO.* | En Madrid. Por Iuan de la Cuesta. | 4 ff. + 268 ff. Sm. 8vo. Fé de Erratas, Jan. 6, 1620. Author's dedication same day. (Bibl. Nat.)

1620–21

"Guia y Avisos de forasteros," Madrid, 1620. 4to. (Noted by Ticknor as 1st edition.)

Nicolás Antonio speaks of an edition 1621, Madrid, 4to, viuda de Alonso Martin, which Ticknor holds to be an error. The book, however, exists, the title reading:

"Avisos de los peligros que hay en la vida de Corte: Novelas morales y ejemplares escarmientos; por el Licenciado Don Antonio Liñan y Verdugo, A D.Francisco de Tapia y Silva Conde de Bartamerli. *Omne tulit punctum qui miscuit utile dulci.* Año 1621. Con privilegio en Madrid por la Viuda de Alonso Martin, A costa de Miguel de Siles, mercader de libros. Vendese en su casa, en la Calle Real de las Descalzas. 4to. 8 ff. + 148 ff. Tassa, Oct. 3, 1620. Privilegio, Aug. 15, 1620, Erratas Oct. 22, 1620, and Aprobacion signed by Vicente Espinel July 19, 1620 (Gallardo, etc., vol. 3).

"Gvia y avisos de forasteros, adonde se les enseña a hvir de los peligros que ay en la vida de Corte;" (as below) Por el licenciado Don Antonio Liñan y Verdugo. Valencia, Siluestre Esparsa, 1635. 8vo. 8 ff. + 148 ff. (Salvá.)

GUIA, | Y AVISOS DE FORASTEROS, | QUE VIENEN A LA CORTE: | HISTORIA DE MUCHA DIVERSION, | gusto, y apacible entretenimiento, donde veràn | lo que les sucediò à unos recien-|venidos: | SE LES ENSEÑA A HUIR DE LOS PELIGROS | que hay en la Corte; y debaxo de Novelas morales, | y exemplares Escarmientos, se les avisa, y ad- | vierte de còmo acudiràn à sus negocios | cuerdamente. | *SV AVTOR | El Licenciado Don Antonio Liñan y Verdugo.* | ∴ CON LICENCIA. | En Madrid: En la Imprenta de Francisco Xavier Garcia, | calle de la Salud. Año de 1753. | *Se hallarà en la Librerìa, y nueva Lonja de Comedias de Joseph | Garcia Lanza, en la Plazuela del Angel.* 8 ff. + 222 pp. 4to. (Bibl. Nat. and Ticknor Coll.)

1620. *Editio Princeps*

NOVELAS MORALES | VTILES POR SVS | DOCVMENTOS. | *COMPVESTAS POR DON DIEGO* | *Agreda, y Vargas.* | A Bartholome de Añaya, y Villanueua, señor de las | Nobilissimas casas de Villanueva, . . . | EN VALENCIA | Con licencia, por Iuan Chrysostomo Garriz. | Año M.DC.XX. | *A costa de Felipe Pincinali mercader de libros.* | 4 ff. + 600 pp. 8vo. (Bibl. Nat.)

The same. En Barcelona, Sebastian de Cormellas, 1620. 8vo. 8 ff. + 576 pp. (Salvá.) Copies of same edition too with 1621 title-page. An edition Madrid, 1620, por Tomas Junti, 12mo, is cited in Bibl. Grenvilliana; and an edition of 1724, 8vo, appeared at Madrid.

FRENCH. 1621

NOVVELLES | MORALES, EN SVITE | DE CELLES DE CERVANTES; | . . . Tirées de l'Espagnol de DON DIEGO AGREDA, | & mises en nostre langue.| Par I. BAVDOIN. | ⁘ A PARIS, | chez

{ TOVSSAINCT DV BRAY, & IEAN LEVESQVE } ruë S. Iacques. | M.DC.XXI. |

Auec Priuilege du Roy. | 4 ff. + 427 ff. 8vo. Oct. 11, 1620; achevé d'imprimer, June 30, 1621. (Bibl. Nat.)

1621. *Editio Princeps*

LA | SABIA FLORA | MALSABIDILLA. | *A DON IVAN ANDRES* | *Hurtado de Mendoça Marques de Cañete, Señor* | *de las villas de Arjete y su partido, Montero ma-* | *yor del Rey nuestro señor, Guarda mayor* | *de la Ciudad de Cuenca.* | AVTOR ALONSO GERO- | nimo de Salas Barbadillo. | Año ⁘ (*VIRGA FVI TEMPORE*)

1621. | CON PRIVILEGIO, | *En Madrid*, Por Luis Sanchez. | *A costa de Andres de Carrasquilla merca-| der de libros.* | 7 ff. + 167 ff. 8vo. Aprobacion, Oct. 31, and Nov. 2 and 8, 1620. Barbadillo's dedication, Feb. 10, 1621. (Bibl. de l'Arsenal.)

1621. *Editio Princeps*

EL NECIO | BIEN AFORTVNADO. | A DON FRANCISCO | y don Andres Fiesco, Caualleros | de la Nobilissima Republica | de Genoua. | AVTOR ALONSO| Geronimo de Salas Barbadillo, | vezino y natural desta villa | de Madrid. | Con Privilegio. | En Madrid, por la viuda de Cos- | me Delgado. Año 1621. | A costa de Andres de Carrasquilla | Mercader de Libros. | 12 ff. + 154 ff. 12mo. Church aprobacion, Oct. 31, 1620; Royal, Nov. 8, 1620. (Br. Mus.)

ENGLISH

1670. Ayres' Translation

The | FORTUNATE FOOL. | Written in Spanish | BY | Don Alonso Geronimo de SALAS | BARBADILLO of Madrid. | Translated into English | BY | PHILIP AYRES, Gent. | London, | Printed and are to be Sold by Moses Pitt at | the White Hart in Little Britain,| 1670. | 8 ff. + 382 pp. 8vo. Licensed Oct. 21, 1669, by Roger l'Estrange. (Br. Mus.) And again as:

THE | LUCKY IDIOT: | OR, | FOOLS HAVE FORTUNE. | Verified in the LIFE of | D. Pedro de Cenudo, | Whose Follies had generally a prosperous | Event: But when he pretended to be | Wise was usually Unfortunate. | Improv'd with Variety of Moral Remarks, | and diverting amusements. | Written in *Span-*

ish, by Don *Quevedo de Alcala.* | Now Rendred into Modern English by a | Person of Quality. | *Omne tulit Punctum, qui miscuit utile dulci:* | *Ridentem dicere verum, Quis vetat.* | *LONDON:* Printed for H. HITCH and L. HAWES, at the *Red-* | *Lyon*, in *Pater noster Row;* S. CROWDER and Co. | facing St. *Magnus* Church, *London-Bridge.* 1760. | 12mo. 168 pp. (Ticknor Coll.) Thirteen chapters, abridged, but the alterations slight. The Introduction signed J. L.

1624. Part One

"Alonso moço de muchos amos," etc., precisely as below. Con privilegio en Madrid por Bernardino de Guzman. A Costa de J. de Vicuña Carrasquilla. 8vo. 8 ff. + 166 ff. Suma del Priv. October 24, 1623; Tassa October 25, 1624; Fé de erratas October 28, 1624. (Noted in Gallardo, *Ensayo*, I., col. 66.) Rare.

1625. Second Edition of Part One

ALONSO | MOÇO DE | MVCHOS | Amos. | *DIRIGIDO A DON LVYS FAXARDO* | *Marques de los Velez, y de Molina, Adelantado, y* | *Capitan General del Reyno de Murcia, y Mar-* | *quesado de Villena, reduzido a la* | *Corona Real.* | Compuesto por el Doctor Geronymo | de Alcala Yañez, Medico y cirujano, | vezino, y natural de la Ciudad | de Segouia | ∴ | CON LICENCIA. | En Barcelona, por Esteuã Liberòs, 1625. | *A Costa de Miguel Menescal.* | 8 ff. + 160 ff. Sm. 8vo.

Aprobacion, April 21, 1625. Tassa refers to October 25, 1624. (Br. Mus.)

1626. *Editio Princeps* of Part Two

SEGVNDA | PARTE DE | ALONSO MOZO | DE MVCHOS | AMOS. | COMPVESTO POR EL DOC-

TOR | Geronimo de Alcalá Yanez y Ribera, | Medico, vezino de la ciudad | de Segouia. | *DIRIGIDA AL DOCTOR DON* | *Agustin Daza, Dean y Canonigo de la santa y Ca- | tedral Iglesia de Segouia, y Refrendario de su | Santidad en las Signaturas de Gra- | cia, y de Iusticia.* | CON PRIVILEGIO. | En Valladolid, por Geronymo Morillo | Impressor de la Vniversidad. | Año M.DC.XXVI. | 16 ff. + 322 pp. + 1 f. 8vo.

Royal permission, December 16, 1625; Tassa, November 14, 1626, etc. (Br. Mus.)

Other eds.: 1788 Madrid, Benito Cano; El donado hablador, vida y adventura de Alonso.... 1804 Madrid, Ruiz. 8vo. 2 vol., with a few notes; and again 1847, Paris, Baudry. 8vo. In Tomo II.; Tesoro de novelistas españoles.

1626. *Editio Princeps*

VARIA | FORTVNA | DEL SOLDADO | PINDARO. | *Por don Gonçalo de Cespedes y Meneses vezino y na- | tural de Madrid.* | Al Excelentissimo señor don Manuel Alonso Perez de | Guzman El Bueno Duque de Medina Sidonia. | ⁖ (VIAS. TVAS. DOMINE. DEMONSTRATA. MIHI.) *Con todas las licencias necessarias,* | LISBOA. Por Geraldo de la Viña. 626. (*sic*) | 4 ff. + 188 ff. 4to. (Misprints chapter captions.) (Br. Mus.)

Licenses in Portuguese, January 8, 1625, and February 4 and 6, 1625, might indicate an earlier, 1625, edition.

Other eds.: 1661 Madrid, Melchoir Sanchez, 8vo; 1696 Zaragoça, Pasqual Bueno, 12mo; 1733 Madrid, 4to; 1845 Madrid, Vicente Castelló undertook an edition in 8vo, not completed.

1626. *Editio Princeps*

HISTORIA | DE LA VIDA | DEL BUSCON, LLAMADO | DON PABLOS; EXEMPLO | de Vagamundos, y espejo | de Tacaños. | *Por don Francisco de Quevedo Villegas, Cavallero | de la Orden de Santiago, y señor de | Iuan Abad.* | ∴ | CON LICENCIA. | En çoragoça. Por Pedro Verges, a los Seña- | les, Año 1626. | 3 ff. + 85 ff. 8vo. Aprobacion, April 29, 1626; Licencia del Ordenario, May 2, 1626, to Roberto Duport Librero. (Br. Mus.)

In Estevan de Peralta's aprobacion the story is referred to as "notable por la enseñança de las costumbres, sin ofensa alguna de la Religion."

Other eds.: Valencia 1627, Chrysostomo Garriz, 8vo. 4 ff. + 104 ff.; and Barcelona, 1627 Lorenço Deu, dedicated by Roberto Duport, "A Don Fray Juan Agustin de Funes, Caualler o | de la Sagrada Religion de San Iuan Bautista de | Ierusalen, en la Castellania de Amposta, | del Reyno de Aragon." | (Ticknor Coll.) 5 ff. + 83 ff. Lisboa, 1630, 8vo, (Salvá); Pamplona, 1631, 8vo, Carlos de Labàyen; Lisboa, 1632, 8vo, Mathias Rodrigues. Also an edition:

EN RUAN, | A costa de CARLOS OSMONT, | en calle del Palacio. | M.DC.XXIX. | ("Añadieronse en essa vltima Impression otros tratados del mismo Autor" viz. Visions and Cavallero de la Tenaza. 8vo. This edition led Puibusque to assert gravely the existence of a second picaresque tale by Quevedo, entitled *Historia de la vida del buscon llamado Ruan*, confusing the place with the rogue's name. (See Hist. comparée des lit. esp. et franç., Paris, 1843.)

The *Buscon* appeared also in collections of Quevedo's works, e.g., the *Enseñanza entretenida i donairosa morali-*

dad, 1648, Madrid, Diego de la Carrera, 4to; and again, 1657, Lisboa, Pablos Craesbeeck, 4to; in the *Obras*, 1650, Madrid, Diego de la Carrera y viuda de Juan Sanchez, 2 vols., 4to; in the *Obras en prosa*, 1664, Madrid, M. Sanchez, 2 vols., 4to; in the *Obras*, 1660–1671, Bruselas, F. Foppens, 3 vols. in 4, 4to; in the *Obras*, 1699, Amberes, H. y C. Verdussen, 3 vols., 4to; in the *Obras*, 1790–1794, Madrid, A. de Sancha, 12 vols. in 11, 8vo; and the various editions of the *Obras festivas* down to that of 1886, Paris, Garnier hermanos, 18mo.

A fuller bibliography of the *Buscon* would here be superfluous after the exhaustive work on the subject contained in the *Obras Completas de Don Francisco de Quevedo Villegas. Edición crítica, ordenada e ilustrada por D. Aureliano Fernández-Guerra y Orbe de la Real Academia Española. Con notas y adiciones de D. Marcelino Menéndez y Pelayo . . . Tomo Primero, Aparato Biográfico y Bibliográfico* published by the Sociedad de bibliófilos Andaluces in Sevilla, 1897, E. Rasco. 8vo. There, Dutch, French, German, and English redactions of this, and Quevedo's other works, are noticed at length.

FRENCH

1633. La Geneste's Version

L'AVANTVRIER | BVSCON, | HISTOIRE | FACECIEVSE, | *Composée en Espagnol, par Dom Francisco | de Quevédo, Caualier Espagnol.* | Ensemble les lettres du Cheualier de l'Espargne. | ∴ A PARIS, | Chez PIERRE BILLAINE ruë | S. Iacques, à la bonne Foy, deuãt S Yues. | M.DC.XXX.III. | *Auec Priuilege du Roy* | 2 ff.+ 397 pp. + (Chevalier de L'Espargne) 2 ff. + 44 pp. Privilege, June 7, 1633. La Geneste has a new ending, Buscon falling in love with a merchant's daughter, becoming a servant in her house, and finally marrying her. (Bibl. Nat.)

Other edits.: 1639, 1641?, and 1644 of Paris; 1644 Lyon; 1641, 1645, and 1647 Rouen; 1653? Paris; 1655 Rouen; 1662 Lyon; 1668 Paris; 1668 Bruxelles; 1671 Francfort, etc., etc.

1699. Raclots' Version

Les Œuvres de Don Francisco de Quevedo Villegas, chevalier Espagnol. . . . Nouvelle traduction de l'Espagnol en Français, par le Sieur Raclots, parisien, . . . Brusselles chez Josse de Grieck, Imprimeur et marchand Libraire, proche La Steen-Porte, à Saint-Hubert, 1699, avec privilège du Roy. 12mo. (Bibl. Nat.)

Really a reworking of La Geneste with slight changes, and the French conclusion retained; although some attempt is made to render the Spanish more exactly.

1776. Restif de la Bretonnes' Continuation

ŒUVRES | CHOISIES | DE DON FRANÇOIS | DE | QUÉVÉDO. | Traduites de l'Espagnol; | En Trois Parties. | CONTENANT | LE FIN-MATOIS, | LES LETTRES | DU CHEVALIER DE L'EPARGNE, | LA LETTRE | sur les Qualités d'un Mariage. | Castigat ridendo mores. | Imprimé A LA HAIE. | etc., etc. (1776). 3 vols. 12mo. 3d part here added by Restif de la Bretonne to Vaquette d'Hermilly's translation has 80 pp., and the title. (See my text for account of it.) Le Fin Matois ou Histoire du Grand Taquin traduite de l'Espagnol de Quevedo, avec des notes historiques et politiques, nécessaire pour la parfaite intelligence de cet auteur.

"La Vida del Buscon, nueva edicion, ou la Vie du

Chercheur, suivie d'un traité sur la nature de l'homme, traduite de l'Espagnol avec des notes historiques par ch. F. M. Mersan, Lyon, 1793, 8vo, 2 vols.

In 1843, 1868, 1872, 1877, and 1882, appeared editions of Germond de Lavigne's *Histoire de Don Pablo de Ségovie*, modified one after another and with surprising errors in early prefaces.

ITALIAN, 1634

HISTORIA | Della vita | Dell' Astutissimo e Sagacissimo | Buscone | CHIAMATO DON PAOLO, | Scritta da D. Francesco de Queuedo, | Tradotta dalla lingua Spagnuola | DA GIO: PIETRO FRANCO, | al clarissimo Signor Giulio Mafetti. | *Con Tauola de' Capitoli, Licentia de'* | *Superiori, e Priuilegio* | ∴ (Sole quid Lucidius. ecc. 17) IN VENETIA, | MDCXXXIV. | Presso Giacomo Scaglia | 7 ff. + 137 ff. Dedication dated Feb. 21, 1634. (Br. Mus.)

ENGLISH

1657. First Version of Buscon

THE | LIFE | AND | ADVENTURES | OF | BUSCON | the Witty *Spaniard.* | Put into English by a Person of Honour. | To which is added, The | PROVIDENT KNIGHT. | By *Don Francisco* de *Quevedo,* A Spanish | Cavalier. | *London,* Printed by J. M. for Henry Herringman, and | are to be solde at his Shop at the *Anchor* in New- | Exchange in the Lower-Walk, 1657. 4 ff. + 288 pp. 8vo. (Br. Mus.)

The same. 'The Second Edition.' Printed for Henry Herringman, at the *Blew* | *Anchor* in the Lower Walk of the *New-Exchange.* | MDCLXX. | 247 pp. 8vo. (Br. Mus.)

1683. Abridged Version

The Famous | HISTORY | OF | Auristella, | Originally Written | By *Don Gonsalo de Cepedes.* | TOGETHER | With the Pleasant STORY | OF | PAUL of *Segovia,* | BY | *Don Francisco de Quevedo.* | *Translated from the* Spanish | LONDON, | Printed for *Joseph Hindmarsh,* Book- | seller to his Royal Highness, at the | *Black Bull* in Cornhil, 1683. | 3 ff. + 3—140 pp. 12mo. Pablos begins p. 66, much compressed, omits Alcalá experiences and ends with letter to hangman at p. 122. "On the Qualities of a Marriage," etc., follows.

John Stevens' Translation. 1707

THE | Comical Works | OF | *Don Francisco de Quevedo,* | AUTHOR | OF THE | VISIONS: | CONTAINING, | . . . The Life of *Paul* the *Spanish Sharper.* . . . etc. | Translated from the Spanish. | LONDON, Printed and are to be sold by | *John Morphew* near *Stationers-Hall,* 1707. | Front. + 6 ff. + 564 pp. Pablos occupies pp. 159–347 inclusive. The first piece in book is "The Night-Adventurer, or the Day-Hater," not by Quevedo, but simply Salas Barbadillo's *Don Diego de Noche* of Madrid, 1623, and included here in imitation of its inclusion in French redactions of the Visions after that of 1645 at Rouen. Dedication of all to Joseph Hodges, son to Sir Wm. Hodges, Bart., whose family is said to have just returned from Spain. (Br. Mus.)

Reprinted also in 1709, J. Woodward; and 1742, 12mo.

Pedro Pineda, 1743, based on this his translation in the *Quevedo's Works* in 3 vols., 8vo, London; as did the Edinburgh, Mundell & Son, 1798 edition in 3 vols.; the version in Thomas Roscoe's Spanish Novelists, 1832;

that in the "Romancist and Novelist's Library," Vol. II., 1841, and H. E. Watts' *Pablo de Segovia, the Spanish Sharper*, of 1892.

GERMAN

"Der abenteuerliche Buscon, eine kurzweilige Geschichte (French and German) mit angehängten Schreiben des Ritters der Sparsamkeit." Frankfort, 1671. 12mo. (Gräsze.)

In 1781 by Fred. Just. Bertuch in Bd. II. of Magazin der Spanischen und Portug. Litteratur, Dessau; and anonymously Hamburg, 1789, 8vo (Gräsze); and in Bd. II., Sammlung Spanischer Original-Romane, Urschrift und übersetzt von J. G. Keil, 8vo, Gotha, 1810–1812, as *Leben des Erzschelms genannt don Paul, von Franc. de Quevedo Villegas;* and in 1842 in Vol. I. of Bibl. der vorzügl. Belletristiker des Auslandes, etc., etc.

DUTCH

Vermakelyke historie van den koddigen Buscon. In 't Spaansch beschreven door Don Francisco de Quevedo Villegas . . . In 't Nederduytsch vertaalt. Amsterdam, by Jan ten Hoorn, Boekverkoper, woonende tegenover het Heeren Logement in den Historyschrijver, 1699. 173 pp. 8vo.

In De vol-geestige werken van Don Franciso de Quevedo Villegas, Spaansch Ridder. Amsterdam, Joh. Sluyter en Son., n. d., 2 vols., 12mo. (ten Brink.)

"Hollebollige Buscon," Amsterdam, 12mo. (n. d.) (Gräsze.)

1627

"Sueños y Discursos de verdades descubridoras de Abusos, Vicios, y Engaños en todos los Oficios, y Estados del Mundo . . . Valencia, 1627." Aprobacion, May 10, 1627, Licencias of May 14 and June 3.

Editions of Barcelona, 1627; Çaragoça, 1627, Pedro Cabarte; Barcelona, 1628, Pedro Lacavallería; then:

1629

DESVELOS | SOÑOLIENTOS | Y DISCVRSOS | DE VERDADES | SOÑADAS: | Descubri doras de abusos, vicios, y engaños, | en todos los oficios, y estados | del mundo. | *EN DOZE DISCVRSOS.* | PRIMERA, Y SEGVNDA PARTE. | *Por don Francisco de Queuedo Villegas.* | . . . Año ∴ 1629. | Con Licencia y Priuilegio: En Barcelona, Por PE-|DRO LA CAVALLERIA, en la calle den | Arlet, *Junto la* Libreria. | 8 ff. + 168 ff. 8vo. (Br. Mus.)

Ruan, a costa de Carlos Osmont, 1629 (together with the *Buscon*).

Lisboa, por Luis de Souza, 1629. 8vo.

Altered as *Ivgvetes de la niñez, y travessuras de el ingenio,* Madrid, 1629.

Pamplona, Carlos de Labáyen, 1631.

Ivgvetes, etc., Madrid, 1631; Sevilla, Andres Grande, 1634; Barcelona, Lorenço Deu, 1635; Barcelona, P. Lacavalleria, 1635; Sevilla, Francisco de Lira, 1641.

Sueños in *Enseñanza entretenida,* Madrid, Carrera, 1648; in *Primera parte de las obras en prosa,* Madrid, Pedro Coello, 1649; in *Enseñanza,* Lisboa, Craesbeeck, 1657; in *Obras,* Madrid, Carrera, 1650; Perpiñan, 1679, etc., etc. *Ivgvetes,* Barcelona, 1695, etc.

FRENCH

"Les visions de don Francisco de Quevedo Villegas,

traduites de l'espagnol par le sieur de la Geneste." Paris, chez Pierre Billaine, 1633. 12mo.

Other edits: Paris, 1634; Blois, 1637; Lyon, 1639; Paris, 1640 and 1641; Rouen, 1645 and 1647; Paris, 1647; Rotterdam, 1653; Rouen, 1655; Cahors, 1655; Paris and Brussels, 1667; Rouen, 1683; Lyon, 1686; Brusselles, in *Œuvres* chez Josse de Grieck, 1699; as Les Nuits Sévillanes, Bruxelles, 1700; Cologne, 1711; 1718, Bruxelles, etc., etc.

DUTCH

Seven Wonderlijcke Gesichten van don. F. de Q. V. Ridder van S. Jaques Ordre . . . In 't Nederlands gebracht, door Capiteyn Haring van Harinxma. Leeuwarden, Fonteyne, 1641. 24mo. (Gräsze.) With editions of Amsterdam, 1645; Haarlem, 1662; Dordrecht, 1668; Amsterdam, 1669; the 1645 and 1662 editions entitled *Spaensche droomen.*

ENGLISH

The visions of Dom Francisco de Quevedo Villegas, made English by Sir Roger L'Estrange — London, 1667. 8vo. (Guerra y Orbe.) Editions of 1668, 1671, 1673, 1678 (6th edition), 1682 with an apocryphal 2d part, 1688, 1689, 1696, 1702, 1708 (10th edition), 1715, 1745, 1795, etc., etc.; 1823, 1832 by Wm. Elliot, etc. Visions . . . burlesqued (in verse) by a person of quality, Lond., 1702, 12mo; and the New Quevedo, or Visions of Charon's Passengers. London, 1702. 12mo.

GERMAN

Visiones de Don Quevedo, dasist Wunderliche Satyrische und Warhafftige Gesichte Philanders von Sittewalt — 1639 — (by Johann Michael Moscherosch).

The same. Straszburg — Johan-Philipp Mülben, 1642, 8vo. 7 visions — an edition Franckfurt, Anthonio Hummen, 1644, 8vo. Jetzo auffs Newe verbessert, in zwey Theil abgetheilet, mit schönen kupffer Stucklein und warhaffter Abbildung der Visionen zum Erstenmal in Truck verfertiget. Moscherosch's own additions are included here. Other editions: 1645, 1646–7, 1648, 1649, 1650, etc., etc.

In Italian — Scelte delle Visioni, trasportate dall' Idioma Spagnuolo, da G. A. Pazzaglia — 1704, 8vo, and in Latin — (Gräsze) Argentorati, 1642, 8vo.

The bibliography of Quevedo's *Sueños* need be given here at no greater length, not only because of its detailed consideration in the first volume of the *Obras Completas de Don F. de Q. Villegas* — edited by Fernández-Guerra y Orbe and Menéndez y Pelayo, Sevilla, 1897; but because the visions themselves are not properly picaresque, though allied to the genre.

1631. *Editio Princeps*

LAS HARPIAS | EN MADRID, Y CO- | che de las Estafas. | *POR DON ALONSO* | *de Castillo Solorçano.* | A DON FRANCISCO MAZA, | de Rocamora, Conde de la Granxa, Señor de las villas de Moxente, Agos- | to, y Nouelda, &c. | Año, ⁖ 1631. | *CON LICENCIA*, | En Barcelona, Por Sebastian de Corme- | llas, al Call. *Y à su costa.* | Sm. 8vo, 3 ff. + 116 ff. Aprobacion dated August 8, 1631; and the church aprobacion, April 8, 1631.

(Ticknor Coll.) Very rare — lacking in the Br. Mus. and the Parisian libraries. The second edition was issued at Barcelona, Cormellas, 1633, 8vo. 116 ff. Aprobaciones dated August 8 and April 8, 1632.

1632. *Editio Princeps*

LA NIÑA DE | LOS EMBVSTES | TERESA DE MAN- | ÇANARES, NATVRAL | de MADRID. | POR DON ALONSO DE | Castillo Solorzano. | *A Ioan Alonso Martinez de Vera, cauallero de | la Orden de Santiago, Tersorero, y Teniente de | Bayle de la ciudad de Alicante.* | Año ∴ 1632. | EN BARCELONA. | POR GERONYMO MARGARIT. | *A costa de Juan Sapero Librero.* | 4 ff. + 131 ff. Sm. 8vo. (Bibl. de l'Arsenal.)

Aprobacion, April 19, 1632, and another, Aug. 21, 1632.

1634 (?)

"Aventuras del Bachiller Trapaza," etc. — noted by Barrera y Leirado as published at Valencia 1634. In the following edition, the aprobacion dated Zaragoça might indicate a 1635 edition. As the *Garduña* was its avowed sequel, it must have preceded that, and if Antonio's statement of 1634 for the *Garduña* be correct, this must have appeared early that year or before.

1637

AVENTVRAS | DEL BACHILLER | TRAPAZA, QVINTA ESSENCIA | de Embusteros y Maestro de | Embelecadores. | Al illustrissimo señor Don IVAN | Sanz de Latràs, Conde de Atares, Señor de las | Baronias y Castillos de Latràs, y Xamerregay | y de los Lugares de Ançanego, Sieso, | Arto, Belarra, y Escalete, y | Cauallero de la Orden | de Santiago. | POR DON ALONSO DE CASTILLO | SOLORZANO, | CON LICENCIA | En Çaragoça: Por Pedro Verges, Año 1637. | A costa de Pedro Alfay mercader de libros. | 4 ff. + 157 ff. 8vo.

Church approval July 22, 1635; and Royal, October 18 and 26, 1635. (Br. Mus.)

In his dedication Solórzano says: "*Obras de este genio se han ofrecido a grandes Principes y Senores, y no las han desestimado por esso, antes admitidolas, y honradolas, que si por la corteza manifestan donayre, su fondo es dar aduertimientos, y doctrina para reformar vicios, como lo vsaron los antiguos, escriviendo Fabulas.*"

An edition 1733 Madrid, P. J. Alonso y Padilla, 8vo, called Tercera Impression; and 1844, Madrid, A. Yenes, 8vo.

1634 (?)

"La Garduña de Sevilla" according to Nicolás Antonio — Lucronii, 1634, 8vo, and according to Barrera y Leirado (*Catálogo bibliográfico y biográfico del teatro antiguo español*, Madrid, 1860, p. 76), Valencia, 1634, 8vo; he adds, "*Se reimprimió en Logroño, en el mismo año.*"

1642

LA | GARDVÑA DE | SEVILLA, Y ANZVELO | DE LAS BOLSAS. | AL ILVSTRISSIMO SEÑOR | don Martin de Torrellas, y Bardaxi, Here- | dia, Luna, y Mendoça, Andrada, y | Rocaberti, Conde | De Castel Florido, Señor de las Baronias de | Antillon, y de Noballas, villa de la Almol- | da, Naual, y Alacon, &c. | POR DON ALONSO DE | Castillo, Solorçano | Año ∴ 1642. | En Madrid. En la Imprenta del Reyno. | *A costa de Domingo Sanz de Herran, Mer- | cader de libros.* | 8 ff. + 192 ff. 8vo.

Aprobacion, March 29 and May 13, 1642 — Tassa, July 23, 1642. (Bibl. Nat.)

The same. 1644. EN BARCELONA. | En la Emprenta administrada por Sebastian | de Cormellas Mercader. *Y a su costa.* | 192 ff. 8vo. (Bibl. de l'Arsenal.)

Aprobacion y Licencia, July 24, 1644; and a permission in Latin of August 5, 1644.

Other eds.: Quarta impres. 1733, Madrid, P. J. Alonso y Padilla, 8vo. Nueva edicion — 1844, Madrid, Viuda de Jordan é hijos, 8vo, etc.

FRENCH

1661. D'Ouville's translation

LA | FOVYNE | DE | SEVILLE, | OV **L'HAME-**ÇON | DES BOVRSES. | *Traduit de l'Espagnol de D. Alonço | de Castillo Souorçano.* (*sic*) | A PARIS, | chez LOVYS BILAINE, au second pilier de la grande | Salle du Palais, au Grand Cesar, | M.DC.LXI. | *AVEC PRIVILEGE DV ROI.* | 2 ff. + 592 pp. + 1 f. 8vo. (Bibl. Nat.)

Privilege Feb. 26, 1661, registry "sur le Liure de la Communauté," April 8, 1653. Preface explains that after Le Metel Sieur d'Ouville's death, this was found among his papers and is now edited by "un des plus delicats esprits du siècle," viz., Boisrobert, d'Ouville's brother-in-law. The promise of the second part is made, provided it be discovered and the reader approve this first installment. The conclusion of the story is modified also to admit a continuation, for where the Spanish declares that Rufina and Jaime spend the rest of their lives in the silk shop at Saragossa in acts of virtue, the French says, "*Nous les y laisserons, & remettrons à la seconde partie de ce Liure à vous faire sçavoir comme ils en sortirent,*" etc., promising new deceits more agreeable than the preceding. The Spanish chapters are run together, the French work being arranged in 4 Livres. Reprinted as *Histoire et avanture de Dona Rufine, courtesane de Séville, traduite par d'Ouville.* Paris, 1731, 2 vol. 12mo.

ENGLISH

1665. Davies' Translation

LA PICARA, | OR THE | TRIUMPHS | OF | Female Subtilty, | Display'd in the *Artifices* and *Impostures* of a | Beautiful *Woman*, who Trappan'd the most | experienc'd *Rogues*, and made all *those* un- | happy who thought *her* handsome; | Originally, | A Spanish Relation, | Enriched with three Pleasant | NOVELS. | Render'd into English, with some *Alte-* | *rations* and *Additions*, | By JOHN DAVIES of *Kidwelly*. | LONDON, | Printed by *W. W.* for *John Starkey*, at the *Mitre* | within *Temple-Bar*, 1665. | 4 ff. + 304 pp. 8vo. (Br. Mus.)

"Imprimatur, Roger l'Estrange, September 30, 1664," inside title leaf. Dedicated to Sir John Berkenhead, confessing it to be taken from the French version. Of Guzman it is said here, "The humour took so well in this Nation, that He and his Rogueries were several times committed to the Press . . . he not only trapan'd all he dealt with, but also became a Precedent and Pattern to all those, who, out of necessity, or inclination have been forc'd to live by their shifts, or, as some would have it, by their wits," etc.

THE | LIFE | OF | Donna *Rosina*, | A | NOVEL, | Being, | A Pleasant Account of the Artifices | and *Impostures* of a Beautiful Woman, | etc. . . . *Originally a* Spanish *Relation. In* Three Parts. | *Done into* English, *by the Ingenious Mr.* E. W. | *a known celebrated* AUTHOR. | LONDON, Printed and Sold by *B. Harris*, | at the Golden *Boar's Head* in *Grace Church-* | Street. Price One Shilling | (n. d., circa 1700.) 2 ff. + 158 pp. + 2 ff. 12mo. (Br. Mus.) A compression of 1665 edition, novels omitted, and Rosina and Jaimo hanged at close.

1717. Version of L'Estrange and Ozell

THE | *Spanish* Pole-Cat: | OR, THE | ADVENTURES | OF | Seniora *Rufina;* | In Four BOOKS, | etc. . . . . *Begun to be Translated* | By Sir *Roger* L' Estrange; And Finish'd, | By Mr. OZELL. | LONDON, Printed for *E. Curll* in | Fleet Street; and *W. Taylor* in *Pater-* | *Noster-Row.* 1717. Price 4*s.* | (Br. Mus.)

Frontispiece + 1 f. + 394 pp. + 2 pp. 12mo. No preface. A new translation. Frontispiece, a Roman scene not pertinent. Reprinted as:

Spanish *Amusements:* | OR, THE | ADVENTURES | Of that Celebrated *Courtezan* | Seniora RUFINA | CALL'D, The | Pole-Cat of *Seville.* | etc. . . . . In Six *NOVELS.* | . . . The SECOND EDITION. | LONDON: | Printed for H. CURLL in the *Strand,* 1727. | (Price 4*s.*) | Frontis. + 2 pp. + 394 pp. + 2 pp. 12mo. Same as above.

Novels of *Garduña* published separately as:

Three Ingenious *Spanish* | NOVELS: | NAMELY, | I. The Loving REVENGE: | Or, Wit in a WOMAN. | II. The Lucky ESCAPE: Or, The | JILT Detected. | III. The Witty EXTRAVAGANT: Or, The Fortunate LOVER. | . . . . . Translated with Advantage. | By a Person of Quality. | The Second Edition. | LONDON: | Printed for *E. Tracy* at the *Three Bibles* | on *London Bridge,* 1712. | (Br. Mus.)

Front. + 2 ff. + 162 pp. 12mo. First story here is third of Garduña; second story here is first of Garduña; third story here is second of Garduña.

This is John Davies' Translation, although his titles for the stories were closer to the original — and in the Spanish order — *All Covet, All Lose; The Knight of the Marigold; the Trepanner Trepanned.*

DUTCH

1725

HET | LEVEN | VAN | RUFFINE, | OF HET | WESELTJE | VAN | SIVILIEN. | Behelzende veele Wonderbaare | listige Bedriegeryen, en Dief- | stallen; vermengt met verscheide Seltsame Trouw- | gevallen. *In het Spaans Beschreven*, door | ALONCO DE CASTILLO SOARCANO. | TE AMSTERDAM, | By GERRIT BOS, Boekverkoper, in | de Kalverstraat, by de Kapel, 1725. | 7 ff. + 440 pp. 8vo. (Br. Mus.)

1641. *Editio Princeps*

EL DIABLO | COIVELO. | NOVELA DE LA | OTRA VIDA. | TRADVZIDA A ESTA | por Luis Velez de Gue-|uara. | A LA SOMBRA DEL | Excelentissimo Señor Don Rodrigo de Sandoual, de Silua, de Mendoça, y de la | Cerda, Principe de Melito, Duque de Pastrana, de Estremera, y Francauila, Marques | de Algecilla, Señor de las Villas de Val-|daracete, y de la casa de Silua | en Portugal, &c. | *En Madrid, en la Imprenta del Reyno.* 1641. | A costa de Alonso Perez Librero del | Rey nuestro señor. | 8 ff. + 135 ff. Sm. 8vo. Latest Privilege, Dec. 17, 1640. (Bodleian.)

Other eds.: 1646, Madrid, Imprenta del Reyno, 8vo; Barrera y Leirado and Brunet speak of Barcelona edit. of 1646, 8vo; an edition Barcelona, Antonio de la Cavalleria, with Aprobacion 1680, 8vo; Tercera Impression 1733, Madrid, P. J. Alonso y Padilla; 1779, Barcelona, Carlos Gibert y Tutó, 8vo; 1812, Madrid, 8vo; 1817, Burdeos, 16mo; 1828, Paris, 32mo, etc., etc.

FRENCH, Etc.

Le diable boiteux of Alain René Le Sage, 1707, Paris,

Barbin, 12mo; 2d edit. 1707, Barbin, 12mo; 3d, 1707, Lyon, A. Briasson; 1707, Amsterdam, Desbordes. Enlarged 1726, Paris, Veuve Ribou; 1727 Paris, as well as 1736, 1737, 1755, 1765, 1779, and 1786; 1739 and 1747 Amsterdam, 1797 Dijon, etc.; and thirty editions in 19th century. The Devil upon Crutches, 1748, London, J. Osborn; The Devil upon Two Sticks, 1783, Edinburg, etc. Into Spanish as El observador nocturno ó el Diablo Cojuelo, etc. 1812, Madrid, Benito Cano; and Paris and Perpignan, 1824. But all of these are a far remove from the Spanish original, thus effectually displaced in popular favor abroad by Le Sage's *rifacimento.*

1644. *Editio Princeps*

EL SIGLO | PITAGORICO, | Y vida de D. Gregorio | Guadaña. | *Dedicado a Monseñor* | *FRANÇOIS BASSOMPIERRE,* | *Marques de Harouel, Caballero de las Hordenes* | *de su Magestad Cristianissima, Mariscal* | *de Francia, y Coronel general* | *de los Suisses.* | POR | Antonio Henrriquez Gomez. | EN ROAN, | En la emprenta de LAVRENS MAVRRY. | Año de 1644. | *CON LICENCIA.* | 8 ff. + 268 pp. 4to. (Br. Mus.)

5th transmigration, pp. 45–151 inclusive, is the picaresque *Vida de D. Gregorio Guadaña.*

The same. Segunda Edicion, purgada de las Erratas Ortographicas | ⁘ | Segun el Exemplar | EN ROHAN, | De la Emprenta de LAVRENTIO MAVRRY. | M.DC.LXXXII. | 4 ff. + 284 pp. 4to. Dedicated to D. Gaspar Marques Barbaran. (Br. Mus.)

The same. EN BRUSELAS, | En Casa de FRANCISCO FOPPENS, MDCCXXVII. Front. + 3 ff. + 284 pp. 4to. (Bodleian.) Also an edition 1788 Madrid. 8vo.

1646. *Editio Princeps*

LA | VIDA I HECHOS | DE | ESTEVANILLO GONZALEZ, | Hombre de buen humor. | *Compuesto por el mesmo.* | Dedicada à el Excelentissimo Señor OCTAVIO PICOLOMINI DE ARAGON, Duque | de Amalfi, Conde del Sacro Romano Impe-| rio, Señor de Nachot, Cavallero de la Orden | del Tuson de Oro, del Consejo de Estado i | guerra, Gentilhombre de la Camara, Capi-|tan de la guardia de los archeros, Mariscal de | Campo General, i Coronel de Cavalleria i In-|fanteria de la Magestad Cesarea, i Governador | general de las armas i exercitos de su Magestad | Catholica en los Estados de Flandes. | EN AMBERES, | En casa de la Viuda de Iuan Cnobbart. 1646. | 8 ff. + 382 pp. + 4 pp. 4to. Suma del Privilegio, June 28, 1646. (Bodleian.)

Other edits.: 1652, Madrid, Gregorio Rodriguez, sm. 8vo; 1720, Madrid, Juan Sanz, 8vo; 1729, Madrid, P. J. Alonso y Padilla, 8vo; 1795, Madrid, Ramon Ruiz, sm. 8vo.

ENGLISH

In The Spanish Libertines: etc. Captain John Stevens, London, Samuel Bunchley, 1707. (See ante, p. 431.) Estevanillo occupies 273 pages, and is translated in full and with great spirit, divided into 15 chapters, the Spanish arrangement retained up to the eleventh. All the verses of the original are suppressed except in two places. The piece is the last of the novels in the collection, and only followed by the comedy, An Evening's Adventures. Stevens speaks of Estevanillo in terms of high praise.

FRENCH

1734. Le Sage

Histoire d'Estevanille Gonzalès, surnommé le garçon de bonne humeur, tirée de l'Espagnol par Monsieur Le Sage, Paris, chez Prault, 1734, 2 v., 12mo, and reprinted 1754, 12mo; not even an imitation of the above, borrowing but slightly from it, in spite of the appropriation of the title. See my text.

1652

"La Vida del Conde de Matisio." Juan de Zavaleta. 1st edition, 1652 (inaccessible).

Then reprinted in 1667 with:

OBRAS | EN PROSA, | DE | DON IVAN | DE ZAVALETA. | CORONISTA | *DEL REY NVESTRO SEÑOR.* | POR EL MISMO AÑADIDAS. | Y POR EL DEDICADAS | AL | ILVSTRISSIMO SEÑOR | CONDE | DE VILLAVMBROSA. | DEL CONSEIO SVPREMO DE CASTILLA, | en su Real Camara. | Y PRESIDENTE DEL REAL CONSEIO DE HAZIENDA, | y sus Tribunales. | CON PRIVILEGIO, *En* Madrid. *Por Andres Garcia de la Iglesia.* | Año de 1667. | A costa de Iuan Martin Merinero, Mercader de Libros. Vendese en su | casa en la Puerta del Sol. | 4 ff. + 490 pp. (double columns.) 4to. Censura, Oct. 4, 1666; Privilegio, Nov. 16, 1666. (Bibl. Nationale.)

1st piece here is *Teatro del hombre, el hombre,* with subtitle (after a Gongoristic introduction), *Vida del Conde de Matisio.* 55 pp.

Other editions of *Obras* are, 2d, 1672, Madrid, 4to, and 4th, 1692, of Madrid, 4to; and 5th, 1704, Barcelona, 4to; the so-called 7th, issued at Madrid 1754–58, in 4 vols. 8vo, etc.

1657. *Editio Princeps*

LA FLEMA | DE PEDRO | HERNANDEZ.| *Discurso Moral y Politico.* | Añadido, y enmendado por su Autor, el Li-|cenciado Marcos Garcia, Cirujano que fue | de su Magestad, y Lector de Cirugia en el | Hospital General desta Corte. | DEDICATORIA | *A Agustin Ximinez, Tesorero de la Capilla | Real, y de gastos de Iusticia del Consejo | Supremo de Castilla.* | ∴ (DE FORTI DVL-CEDO) Con privilegio en Madrid. *Por Gregorio | Rodriguez.* Año de 1657. | *A costa de Gabriel de Leon, mercader de libros.* | 8 ff. + 120 pp. 8vo. Aprobacion, May 28, 1656; Privilegio, June 19, 1656, etc. (Br. Mus.)

1663. *Editio Princeps*

DIA, Y NOCHE | DE MADRID, | DISCVRSOS DE LO MAS | notable que en èl passa. | DEDICADOS | *A Iuan Martin Vicente, Familiar de el Santo | Oficio de la Suprema, y General Inquisicion, y | de la Real Guardia de a cauallo de su | Magestad.* | SV AVTOR, | *FRANCISCO SANTOS.* | *Criado del Rey nuestro señor*, | CON PRIVILEGIO. | En Madrid. *Por Pablo de Val. Año* 1663. | *A costa de Iuan de Valdes, Mercader de libros.* | *Vendese en su casa, en la calle de Atocha,* | *en frente de Santo Tomas.*| 16 ff. + 356 pp. + 6 ff. 8vo. (Br. Mus.)

Licencia del Ordinario April 16, 1663; Fé de Erratas Oct. 2, 1663. Other editions 1674, Madrid, Ioseph Fernandez de Buendia, 8vo; 1718, Madrid, Angel Pasqual, 8vo; 1766, Madrid, 8vo.

1663

"Meriendas del Ingenio y Entretenimientos del Gusto" por Andres de Prado, Zaragoza, 1663, 8vo. Six Tales, and among them the *Ardid de la pobreza, y astucias de*

Vireno. I have been unable to see an edition of the *Meriendas*, but the six novelas are printed in the "Coleccion de novelas escogidas, compuestas por los mejores ingenios españoles." Madrid, en la Imprenta real, 1787–94. 8 vols. in 4, 8vo; and the *Ardid de la pobreza* in the *Bibl. de aut. esp.*, Vol. 33.

1667

"Periquillo el de las Gallineras," etc. Francisco Santos (1667 says Alvarez y Baena, Hijos de Madrid, Vol. 2, p. 217).

1668

PERIQVILLO EL DE LAS | GALLINERAS. | *ESCRITO POR FRANCISCO SANTOS.* | Dedicado al Exmo Señor D. Bernardo Fernãdez | Manrique, Marquès de Aguilar, &c. | ∴ Con licencia. *EN MADRID.* Por Bernardo | de Villa-Diego, año de 1668. | *A Costa de Gabriel de Leon, Mercader de libros.* | *Vendese en su casa, en la Puerta del Sol.* 12 ff. + 256 pp. (Ticknor Coll.)

Aprobacion of el maestro fray Tomàs de Auellaneda, dated 8 Sept. 1667, Licencia de el Ordinario 13th Sept., 1667; Aprobacion of Fray Antonio de Figueroa 30th Sept. 1667; and Fè de Erratas, 30th August, 1668. Even the dedication, in accordance with Santos' style, was in dream form.

PERIQUILLO | EL DE LAS | GALLINERAS. | ESCRITO | POR FRANCISCO SANTOS, | Criado de su Magestad. | Con licencia: En Valencia, Año 1704. | A costa de los Herederos de Gabriel de Leon, Mercader | de Libros. Vendese en su casa en la | Puerta del Sol. | 8vo. Old privilege of Sept. 8, 1667. In 17 Discursos. (Br. Mus.)

Also in 3d volume of Santos' Obras en prosa y verso, Madrid, Francisco Martinez de Abad, 1723. 4 vols. Sm. 4to.

AUTHORITIES

OTHER THAN GENERAL HISTORIES OF LITERATURE CHIEFLY CONSULTED IN THE PREPARATION OF THIS WORK

Alvarez y Baena, Joseph Antonio, *Hijos de Madrid . . . diccionario histórico*, etc., 4 vols., Madrid, 1790.

Antonio, Nicolás, *Bibliotheca hispana vetus et nova*, 4 vols., Madrid, 1783–88.

Bahlsen, Ludwig, *Spanische Quellen der Englischen Litteratur, besonders Englands zu Shakespeares Zeit* (*Zeitschr. für vergl. Lit. Gesch.* N. F. VI.), 1893.

——, *Eine Komödie Fletchers, ihre Spanische Quelle und die Schicksale jenes Cervanteschen Novellen-Stoffes in der Weltlitteratur*, Berlin, 1894.

Baumstark, Reinhold, *Don Francisco de Quevedo, ein Spanisches Lebensbild*, etc., Freiburg im Breisgau, 1871.

Barine, Arvède, *Les gueux d'Espagne* (*Rev. d. deux mondes*, vol. 86, p. 871 *et seq.*).

Barrera y Leirado, Cayetano Alberto de la, *Catálogo bibliográfico y biográfico del teatro antiguo español*, etc., Madrid, 1860.

Brink, Jan ten, *Dr. Nicolaas Heinsius, Junior, eene studie over den Hollandschen schelmen roman der zeventiende eeuw*, Rotterdam, 1885.

Brunetière, Ferdinand, *L'influence de l'Espagne dans la littérature française* (*Revue d. deux mondes*, March, 1891, p. 215 *et seq.*).

Chasles, Emile, *Michel de Cervantes, sa vie, son temps, son œuvre politique et littéraire*, Paris, 1866. Especially here *L'Espagne picaresque*, p. 254 *et seq.*

Chasles, Philarète, *Études sur l'Espagne et sur les influences de la littérature Espagnol en France et en Italie*, Paris, 1847.

Claretie, Léo, *Le Sage romancier, d'après de nouveaux documents*, Paris, 1890.

Cornhill Magazine (vol. 31, p. 670 *et seq.*), *The Spanish Comic Novel: Lazarillo de Tormes.*

Deutsche Jahrb. für Polit. und Litt. (III., p. 411 *et seq.*), *Mendoza's Lazarillo de Tormes und die Bettler- und Schelmen-Romane der Spanier*, Berlin, 1862.

Dumaine, C. B., *Essai sur la vie et les œuvres de Cervantes, d'après un travail inédit de Luis Carreras*, Paris, 1896.

Dunlop, John Colin, *History of Prose Fiction*, ed. H. Wilson, 1888.

Farinelli, Arturo, *Die Beziehungen zwischen Spanien und Deutschland in der Litteratur*, Berlin, 1892.

Fernandez de Navarrete, Eustaquio, *Bosquejo histórico sobre la novela española* (*Bibl. de aut. españoles*, vol. 33).

——, Martin, *Vida de Miguel de Cervantes Saavedra*, Madrid, 1819.

Fournel, Victor, *Préface* to *Le Roman Comique*, ed. P. Jannet, Paris, 1857.

Gallardo, Bartolomé José, *Ensayo de una biblioteca española de libros raros y curiosos*, 4 vols., Madrid, 1862, 1866–87.

Garriga, Francisco Javier, *Estudio de la novela picaresca*, Madrid, 1891.

Gräsze, J. G. T., *Lehrbuch einer allgemeiner Literärgeschichte*, Dresden, 1837–59.

Haack, Gustav, *Untersuchungen zur Quellenkunde von Lesages Gil Blas de Santillane*, Kiel, 1896.

Hazañas y la Rua, Joaquin, *Mateo Aleman*, Sevilla, 1892.

Kelley, James Fitzmaurice, *Phantasio-Cratuminos sive Homo Vitreus*. In *Revue Hispanique*, vol. IV., p. 45 *et seq*. Paris, 1897.

Koerting, Heinrich, *Geschichte des französischen Romans im 17ten Jahrhundert*, Oppeln u. Leipzig, 1891.

Llorente, Juan Antonio, *Observaciones críticas sobre el romance de Gil Blas de Santillana*, Madrid, 1822.

Marchena, Josef, *Lecciones de filosofía moral y elocuencia*, Burdeos, 1820.

Menéndez y Pelayo, Marcelino, *Notas y adiciones* to the *Obras completas de Don Francisco de Quevedo* (*Tomo Primero*), edited by Guerra y Orbe. Sevilla, 1897.

Merimée, Ernest, *Essai sur la vie et les œuvres de Francisco de Quevedo*, Paris, 1886.

Morel-Fatio, Alfred, *Études sur l'Espagne*, Paris, 1888. Especially here, *Recherches sur Lazarille de Tormes*, and *L'auteur du premier Lazarille de Tormes*, I., p. 115 *et seq.*

——, *Préface* to *Lazarille de Tormes*, Paris, 1886.

——, *L'Espagne au XVI et au XVII siècle*, Bonn, 1878.

Morillot, Paul, *Scarron et le genre burlesque*, Paris, 1888.

Payer, Rudolf von, *Eine Quelle des Simplicissimus* (*Zeitschr. für deutsche Phil.*, XXII., p. 93 *et seq.*).

——, *Der Schelmen Roman unter besonderer Berücksichtigung seiner Verbreitung in Oesterreich-Ungarn* (*Oesterr. Ungar. Rev.*, VII., p. 285 *et seq.*), 1889.

Peters, R., *Paul Scarron und seine Spanischen Quellen*, Erlangen, 1893.

Puibusque, Adolf, *L'histoire comparée des littératures espagnole et française*, Paris, 1844.

Quaritch, Bernard, *Bibliotheca hispana*, London, 1895.

Rennert, Hugo A., *The Spanish Pastoral Romances*, Baltimore, 1892.

Salvá y Mallen, Pedro, *Catálogo de la biblioteca de Salvá*, etc., Valencia, 2 vols., 1872.

Schneider, Adam, *Spaniens Anteil an der deutschen Litteratur des 16. und 17. Jahrhunderts*, Strassburg, 1898.

Surgères, Granges de, *Les traductions françaises du Guzman d'Alfarache*, Paris, 1886.

Warren, F. M., *History of the Novel Previous to the Seventeenth Century*, New York, 1895. Especially here, *The Picaresco Novel in Spain*, p. 284 *et seq.*

Watts, H. E., *Quevedo and his Works: with an Essay on the Picaresque Novel* (In *Pablo de Segovia, the Spanish Sharper*, London, 1892, p. xv *et seq.*).

Winkel, J. te, *De invloed der Spaansche letterkunde op de Nederlandsche in de zeventiende eeuw.* (In *Tijdschrift voor Nederlandsche taal- en letterkunde*, vol. I., p. 59 *et seq.*), Leiden, 1881.

INDEX

[For the sake of brevity titles of translations are omitted here, such books being treated with their originals. A few significant references to the Bibliography, however, are included.]

www.ingramcontent.com/pod-product-compliance
Lightning Source LLC
Chambersburg PA
CBHW031348290326
41932CB00044B/364
* 9 7 8 3 7 4 4 7 7 6 2 3 3 *